TYBURN

LONDON'S FATAL TREE

ALAN BROOKE & DAVID BRANDON

SUTTON PUBLISHING

First published in 2004 by
Sutton Publishing Limited · Phoenix Mill
Thrupp · Stroud · Gloucestershire · GL5 2BU

Reprinted in 2004 (twice)

British Library Cataloguing in Publication Data
A catalogue record for this book is available from the British Library.

ISBN 0-7509-2971-5

Typeset in 11/14.5 pt Sabon.
Typesetting and origination by
Sutton Publishing Limited.
Printed and bound in England by
J.H. Haynes & Co. Ltd, Sparkford.

Contents

Acknowledgements

A book that covers some six centuries of history is inevitably indebted to the research of other historians, especially those working in the history of crime and the history of London. Of the many libraries and archives the authors have used, particular thanks go to the staff of the Guildhall Library in London for their courtesy and helpfulness.

We record our gratitude to Christopher Feeney of Sutton Publishing for his constructive advice as well as his diligent and scrupulous reading of the draft.

Friends and relations have given moral support and encouragement throughout and our heartfelt thanks goes to them.

Alan Brooke and David Brandon
Peterborough, 2003

Introduction

The name 'Tyburn' is synonymous with the idea of public execution. It was one of London's major places of execution from the twelfth century until 1783. A review of those who died there and of the crimes they committed as well as an examination of Tyburn's place in popular culture provides valuable and entertaining insights into the economic, social and political changes that took place in London and elsewhere in Britain during this period.

Among those who met their Maker at Tyburn were possibly William Wallace, the Scottish patriot; Perkin Warbeck, pretender to the throne who claimed to be one of the princes supposedly murdered in the Tower; Claude Duval, almost the prototype for the myth of the handsome, dashing and courteous highwayman; Jack Sheppard who kept escaping from the dreaded Newgate Prison and the hated Jonathan Wild, perhaps London's first master criminal. Most of those who died at Tyburn had been hauled through the streets from Newgate in the City and the road from there to Tyburn brought the two locations together in a grisly symbiosis.

Many martyrs for their religious beliefs died at Tyburn, and memorials to some of them can still be seen nearby. In 1661 the corpses of Cromwell, Ireton and Bradshaw, execrated as regicides, were exhumed, transported to Tyburn, hanged and then beheaded, whereupon the bodies were thrown into a pit adjacent to the gallows. The outcome of this extraordinary event has provided one of history's perennial teasers – the question of what has happened to Cromwell's head.

Over the centuries, dozens of executioners practised their art at Tyburn. One of the best known, although by no means the most competent, Jack Ketch, went on to provide a generic name for all public executioners. Who were these men? What skills did they require? How did the technology of hanging change over the years?

The journey of the condemned felons from Newgate to Tyburn provided free and popular entertainment for London's masses and it became highly ritualised, particularly in the sixteenth, seventeenth and eighteenth centuries. Prisoners stopped off at wayside inns as they passed through cheering crowds or, if their offences and their demeanour angered the spectators, they had to run the gauntlet of a hail of verbal and physical abuse. They were expected to show fortitude and the watching crowds warmed to the felon who made a valedictory speech in which he cursed the fates or, even better, those who had brought him to this sorry pass.

The hangman expected his perks from selling the rope and the clothes of the deceased while the physically afflicted in the crowd pressed forward to touch these because it was widely believed that they had curative properties. In later years, fights occasionally broke out as the relatives of the deceased fought those who wanted to take the body away for dissection. The vendors of the felon's so-called 'dying confessions' hawked their wares among the crowd, as did a multitude of prostitutes. Pickpockets enjoyed rich takings. The wealthy hired expensive grandstand seats to obtain the best views at Tyburn Fair. All this etched itself deeply into the popular culture of London.

Before the 1960s, crime and the culture of the masses were subjects largely ignored by historians. Sensationalised, anecdotal writing about crime and punishment, the activities of individual criminals and the underworld of criminality had long been popular and had created popular preconceptions and prejudices. Dashing highwaymen carried out audacious robberies on Hounslow Heath, Jonathan Wild featured as the first 'Napoleon of Crime' and the escapades of Jack Sheppard appeared in innumerable 'penny dreadfuls'. Vast crowds gleefully watched the death agonies of notorious miscreants at Tyburn, Execution Dock and other hanging places. Children were transported for stealing worthless trifles. This kind of writing, although entertaining, provided little real understanding of the nature of crime. From the 1960s, however, historians have turned their attention to popular culture, the behaviour of crowds, the causes and nature of criminal activity and the evolution of the country's judicial and penal systems. The result is a far greater understanding of the dynamic relationship and interaction between crime and wider social, economic and political factors.

Many historians have concentrated their efforts on the seventeenth, eighteenth and nineteenth centuries. They have related changing levels and types of crime to the severe tensions evident in a society going through the uneasy transformation from a rural and predominantly agricultural base to a largely industrial and urban one. The authors wish to contribute to this ongoing process of historiography by focusing on one particular locality famous in the popular culture of London. There is little recently published material on Tyburn and its associations and this book, aimed at the general reader, is intended to make a modest addition to the social and cultural history of crime and punishment, the history of London and the history of Tyburn in particular.

The use of Tyburn as a place of execution goes back to at least the last decade of the twelfth century. Tyburn was located well to the west of the City of London and hence the phrase 'go west' emerged in Elizabethan times, ironic reference to the direction most often taken by those condemned prisoners despatched for execution from the Tower, Newgate or elsewhere. On execution days, bells rang in City churches and large crowds turned out to witness the processions to Tyburn. A sense of holiday, of carnival, developed around the procession to Tyburn and the events at the gallows.

The sight of the felon publicly expiring, convulsed with terror and agony, was intended to be a frightful lesson to those who watched. Contemporary accounts leave little doubt that large numbers of people thoroughly enjoyed the spectacle of a public execution. They could be extremely angry when a last-minute reprieve deprived them of their anticipated pleasure. Few hangmen attempted to despatch their victims as quickly and humanely as possible and indeed some were shamefully inept. The sight of a felon dying on the gallows was not an edifying one but it provided a popular form of public entertainment, the appeal of which transcended social class. There is little evidence that the crowds who gathered at Tyburn saw what was enacted there as a deterrent to the carrying out of serious crime.

Hangings took place eight times a year at Tyburn until 1783 and eight times a year after that outside Newgate gaol. Those who died at Tyburn had mostly committed their offences in Middlesex and the City of London. While many felons who died at Tyburn had trades and were printers, whip-makers or drapers, for example, and some were from the ranks of the well-to-do, large numbers were from the poorest and most debased sections of society, trapped in a hopeless cycle of poverty and despair. The majority had committed property crimes. Many who made up Tyburn's gory harvest were adopted Londoners, often young, who had migrated to the capital in search of wealth and fame, only to find neither.

Hanging played a key role in the maintenance of authority in England from the Middle Ages to the nineteenth century and yet it became central to popular culture. It was made the subject of innumerable jokes, ballads and satires. The heroic progress of some felons to Tyburn was nothing less than a parody. It was a ritual mocking of an occasion intended by the authorities to display the awful omnipotence of the law. It therefore undermined the authorities themselves. Ridicule, gallows humour, nonchalance, abuse of the hangman or the Ordinary, the priest who accompanied the condemned felons – all these had the effect of making the event the very opposite of what the authorities intended.

Most condemned felons wanted to die well, given the very public forum in which they would do so. Many used the occasion to make speeches. Sometimes they were cringing confessions or hopeless protestations of contrition or innocence. These cut little ice with the crowd, whereas those felons who used the occasion to denounce and defy the authorities or to spin a salacious yarn or quip with the crowd usually aroused an enthusiastic response. Legend has little to say of the felons – and they were probably the majority – who went to their deaths publicly evacuating their bladders and bowels through abject terror. For all those who underwent the ordeal with their chins up, the majority had to be physically supported into the cart at Newgate or from it to the scaffold at Tyburn. As V.A.C.

Gatrell says, 'most of those hanged were far from the swashbucklers of legend and could not behave like heroes if they tried. They were of such obscurity, their crimes so common, their deaths so humdrum, that their executions failed to earn a broadside, a ballad, or a notice in the newspapers' (Gatrell 1994: 40).

It is impossible to give a definitive figure for the numbers of those who were executed at Tyburn. Alfred Marks states that the gallows received the condemned from the courts of Westminster and the Guildhall but its main suppliers were the Middlesex and the Old Bailey Sessions. Marks bases his estimate for executions at Tyburn on the figures supplied by the work of John Cordy Jeaffreson from the Middlesex County Records (four volumes; 1897–1902). Between 1609 and 1618 there were 714 people executed in Middlesex. Marks assumes that felonies committed in the City must have been greater in number and therefore proffers a combined figure for the same period of approximately 1,408. From this he goes on to give an estimate for the number of deaths at Tyburn during the reign of Elizabeth I and comes up with a figure of over 9,000. Clearly there is a great deal of guesswork involved but Marks is bold enough to suggest that over the 600 hundred years of Tyburn's history as a place of execution, at least 50,000 died there. This makes a yearly average of around eighty. Others have put the figure much higher but with even less hard evidence.

Any discussion of Tyburn taps into a rich and fascinating diversity of history. This book will outline some of the associations of the Tyburn area from medieval times to 1783 when hangings ceased at this location. It also traces related themes such as the way in which the penal system changed over time and the role played by the crowd in the rituals of execution. It briefly surveys other hanging places in London and gives descriptions of some of the hangmen who officiated at Tyburn. There are examples of Tyburn featuring in literature and an attempt is made to reconstruct what a condemned prisoner travelling from Newgate to Tyburn would have seen and sensed at about the middle of the eighteenth century. To encourage a feeling for history in the field, the route to Tyburn is described as it may be followed at the present time with aspects of its topography, buildings and rich, varied historical connections.

ONE

Tyburn: River, Resort of Bawds and Place of Death

London is clustered in the valley and along the flood plain of the River Thames as it approaches the sea. Both to the north and south of London there is high land where sands and gravels are superimposed on the clays which underlie the metropolis. To the north, flowing off these heights, which are very evident in the Highgate and Hampstead areas, are a number of streams which form tributaries of the Thames. Probably the best known of these are the Westbourne, the Fleet and the Tyburn.

'Tyburn' is a word of Saxon origins and its first mention is probably in the forged Charter of King Edgar (951) where it is written as 'Teo-burna'. 'Burna' and its derivations are frequently found in English place names and they mean stream, bourne or brook. It is possible that the 'ty' part of the name indicates the union of two streams or a division into two branches enclosing an area of dry land. Another explanation is that the Tyburn was associated with the Saxons and the Germanic god Tiw who gave his name to Tuesday. If this latter explanation has any validity then this is ironic because Tiw was the god of law. Another explanation is that the name was originally 'Teoburna' meaning 'boundary stream'.

The Tyburn is a small stream, the main source of which is a spring in the Lyndhurst Road area of Hampstead, once known as 'Shepherdswell'. The water was appreciated for its clarity and was collected and sold by the bucket. The Tyburn runs almost due south close to Fitzjohns Avenue, behind the Hampstead Theatre, under Adelaide Road and past Swiss Cottage, after which it is joined at Woronzow Road by a small tributary. Woronzow Road owes its

1

strange name to Count Simon Woronzow who came to Britain as Russian Ambassador in the eighteenth century and liked it so much that he settled in Marylebone and never went back home.

The tributary rises close to Hampstead Town Hall, flows through the Belsize Park district and skirts the western side of Primrose Hill. The combined stream crosses the Regent's Canal branch of the Grand Union Canal in a cast-iron pipe aqueduct. It skirts Regents Park where it picks up a very small tributary rising under London Zoo and it then runs under Gloucester Place. The various components of the Tyburn once flowed through meadowland, at least as far as Swiss Cottage. From the middle of the nineteenth century, however, they had largely disappeared under bricks and mortar. South of Swiss Cottage it is likely that the stream was conduited and in use as a sewer as early as the 1670s.

The Tyburn is shown in a map by William Faden, dated 1785, sweeping first west and then eastwards to the stables of the Horse Guards near the Baker Street Bazaar. It flows under Marylebone Road and just west of Marylebone High Street, the bends of the northern end of which still provide evidence of the course of the invisible stream. Aybrook Street nearby takes its name from the Aye Brook which was an alternative medieval name for the Tyburn. It crossed Marylebone Lane twice. As it approaches Oxford Street the small valley the Tyburn has created is still visible. It runs under Oxford Street near what is now Stratford Place, close to Bond Street Underground station. Maps by Morden and Lea, dated respectively 1690 and 1700, show what is now Oxford Street crossing a nameless stream on a bridge at this point. Later editions show this stream named the 'Aye Brook 'or 'Tybourne'. This bridge, which became part of the turnpike from St Giles to Kilburn in the 1720s, was a constant source of acrimony between various local government bodies and the turnpike trustees.

The presence of the Tyburn proved a nuisance to the engineers building the Central Line or 'Twopenny Tube' in 1900 because water from it kept flooding into the workings. Further north, St Cyprian's church in Glentworth Street, Marylebone, needed especially deep foundations because of the presence of the Tyburn close by. In 1875 workmen building a sewer in Stratford Place chanced on a structure made of stone which historians believe was erected in the first half of the thirteenth century and is possibly London's earliest reservoir. It was built around 1240 to store water from the Tyburn which was then despatched through elm or lead pipes via the Great Conduit to Cheapside to provide a water supply for the City of London. The existence of this water supply enhanced the importance of the area and in the reign of Elizabeth I a Banqueting House was built over the great cisterns associated with the conduit. The New River took over the provision of the main water supplies for the City in 1609 but the Banqueting House continued to be used for the junketings of the City fathers until it was pulled down in the 1730s. Stratford House was later built on its site. North Audley Street is no great distance away and here workmen once unearthed a Roman bath which it is thought took its water supply from the Tyburn.

The Tyburn now makes its surreptitious way through Mayfair by Lower Brook Street, the name again recalling the presence of the stream, to the foot of Hay Hill, through Lansdowne Gardens, down Half Moon Street and under Piccadilly at what used to be called the Kingsbridge. Mayfair takes its name from the erstwhile fair that was held on what was once called Brook Fields. This fair had become so disorderly, attracting belligerent, drunken crowds, mountebanks and confidence tricksters of all sorts and whores and pickpockets galore, that it was finally abolished in the latter half of the eighteenth century. The Tyburn then dips quite sharply through Green Park, heading in the direction of Buckingham Palace. The Tyburn's subterranean presence may have been responsible for the mist that was once a feature on damp autumnal nights in the Green Park area.

From this point the rest of the Tyburn's course is disputed. Three main possibilities have been identified. One is that it approached Buckingham Palace from whence it went underground and pursued a course down what are now St James Street, Orchard Street and College Street and then alongside the walls of Westminster Abbey and into the Thames. The second variation claims that the Tyburn divided when it got to the Westminster area and its two courses created Thornea Island on which the Abbey stands. The third is that from the present site of Buckingham Palace, the Tyburn turned west and forming the ancient boundary of the City of Westminster, flowed close to Tachbrook Street, across what are now Vauxhall Bridge Road and Grosvenor Road, and into the Thames in the Pimlico area. To add to the confusion surrounding the Tyburn, there is also a Tyburn Brook, a very small stream rising near Marble Arch and flowing into the Westbourne which forms part of the Serpentine at that point.

There is a story that Queen Anne (r. 1702–14) was rowed up the Tyburn in the Royal Barge as far as Brook Street and indeed traces of a mooring place were found in the vicinity during building works in the middle of the nineteenth century. It is recorded that the Tyburn once provided excellent sport for anglers.

Tyburn or 'Tybourne' is mentioned in Domesday Book and was the name originally given to the area now known as Marylebone. Only in later times did the usage of the name Tyburn evolve so that it applied just to the vicinity of the gallows. The original Tyburn district possessed a small church dedicated to St John the Baptist near the present Oxford Street and was built in 1200. It was in a lonely, low-lying and watery spot not far from where hangings were already taking place. By 1400 this church had become ruinous and the neighbourhood notorious for robberies. It was replaced but a further church was built around 1740 and this was known as St Mary's-of-the-Bourne or by-the-Bourne which is probably how 'Marylebone' evolved. St Mary's church became inadequate as the population of the area grew rapidly. After some delay a new church was opened in 1817 close to the present Oldbury Place and Marylebone Road. The Tyburn flows nearby and the bend at the north end of Marylebone High Street indicates its approximate course. The earlier St Mary's was demoted to the status of 'Parish Chapel' and demolished in 1949. As late as 1720, the area north-east of the gallows remained well wooded and largely rural. Several monarchs, including Henry VIII, Elizabeth I and James I, are said to have enjoyed the thrill of the hunt in the area. What is now

Marylebone High Street contained scattered rural hovels, some of them thatched and picturesquely decorated with climbing roses. This rustic idyll was about to change for ever.

In 1710 the manor of Marylebone was bought by the Duke of Newcastle whose only daughter married Edward Harley. In 1711 Harley was created Earl of Oxford, from whom the names of Harley Street and Oxford Street are derived. He embarked on large-scale quality housing development which meant that the old manor of Marylebone had 577 houses in 1739 and 2,600 in 1795.

After the revocation of the Edict of Nantes in 1685, many Huguenot refugees settled in the area around Marylebone and they opened a 'French Chapel' close to Marylebone Lane. This is depicted in Hogarth's engraving 'Noon', the second of his engravings in the series *The Four Times of the Day*, published in 1738 and caricaturing French manners and customs. A pleasure ground known as the French Garden opened up in an area now covered by Devonshire Place, Beaumont Place and Devonshire Street. At first used largely for the playing of bowls, by the 1740s these grounds had become known as Marylebone Gardens, providing firework displays, fashionable social events and an assembly hall doubling as a theatre. The music in these gardens was at one time under the direction of Dr Thomas Augustine Arne (1710–78) who composed 'Rule, Britannia'. New works produced by Handel in his later days often had their first British performance at Marylebone. The criminal fraternity is always attracted to places where the rich assemble. Pickpockets, footpads and highwaymen flocked to the area. Many of the drunken revellers were easy game as they left the gardens and wandered home befuddled. So common were the attacks on its patrons that the manager of the gardens was forced to provide mounted guards to escort patrons to their homes. The history of pleasure gardens in London is one of decline from the initially smart and ultra-fashionable through the raffish to the simply tawdry and disreputable. So it was with Marylebone Gardens. Its owner gave up the unequal struggle in 1778 and closed the gardens down. By this time Marylebone was largely built over and the presence of the gardens had helped to give the area a notoriously bawdy and boisterous character. It became renowned for cock-fighting, bear-baiting and prize-fighting. A number of pubs such as the Queen's Head and Artichoke, the Yorkshire Stingo and the Farthing Pie House were all located close to the Tyburn and helped to give the area a reputation for drunkenness, violence and general debauchery.

'Tyburn' or Marylebone is rich in historical associations. Lord Byron was baptised in the parish church and Horatia Nelson's name can be found in the parish register. Interestingly, her entry is the only one which does not show the parents' occupations. Dr Johnson at one time resided at 38 Castle Street and Mrs Thrale, later Mrs Piozzi, with whom he was well acquainted, lived at 33 Welbeck Street. His biographer, James Boswell, lived not far away at 122 Great Portland Street and doubtless found much to please him in the raffish character of the place. Charles Dickens resided at 1 Devonshire Place. Many great artists lived in the district, including J.M.W. Turner, George Romney, John Flaxman and Sir Edwin Landseer. Captain Edward Marryat, author of *Mr Midshipman Easy*, was a resident as was Charles Wesley, the poet, Methodist and father of hymnology. He once preached an open-air sermon at York Gate, near the north end of Marylebone High Street and next to the Tyburn. He is buried in the yard of the old St Marylebone Church where his illustrious neighbours include George Stubbs, well known for his paintings of horses and other livestock.

What of the area around the notorious 'fatal tree' where so many wretches met their deaths over the centuries? There is considerable doubt about the exact site or sites of the gallows at Tyburn. It is possible that Tyburn was first used as a place of execution in 1196. In 1222, Henry III ordered the erection of two gibbets for the purpose of hanging thieves and malefactors in the place where the gallows were formerly situated – 'The Elms'. 'The King ordered two permanent gallows to be built on the basis that there were no more suitable trees' (Barker 1970: 45). In 1393 a 'Tyburn Gallows' in the parish of Paddington is mentioned. In 1478 the site of the gallows is given as being in the Manor of Hide. Two fields are mentioned with the names of 'Galowmede' and 'Galowfield'. These were close to where Marble Arch now stands and suggest a place of execution.

The earliest identification in graphic form of Tyburn as a site for executions seems to be the map which appears in the first edition of Camden's *Britannia* dating from 1607. This shows the gallows situated at the junction of the present Edgware Road, Oxford Street and Bayswater Road. One suggestion is that in much earlier times there was a gallows close to Stratford Place and adjacent to where the Tyburn crossed Tyburn Road, later Oxford Street. The Tyburn River formed the west boundary of the old 'Tyburn' or 'Marylebone' district. It may be that the gallows moved from here some time late in the fourteenth century but that when it was re-erected somewhat to the west, the old name Tyburn stuck. The issue is made more confusing by the fact that there was a district sometimes called Tyburnia which approximates with Bayswater and from which a small stream called the Tyburn Brook emerged to flow south to join the Westbourne and thence to make its way through to the Thames.

The gallows are depicted in a number of illustrations from the seventeenth century and these allow a picture to be built up of the site and its immediate surroundings while making due allowance for artistic licence. An illustration of 1680 shows preparations being made for an execution. A pair of ladders is propped against the gallows, on the top of which are three men who have been getting the rope ready. The condemned man stands in a horse-drawn cart beneath the gallows with the rope around his neck. The prison Ordinary or chaplain, also standing in the cart, reads prayers to the prisoner. A man stands by the head of the horse ready for the command to pull the horse away and leave the prisoner suspended. There is another horse and cart waiting in the foreground which contains a coffin ready to receive the body. In the distance stands a large crowd.

Despite the expansion of London, particularly to the west of the City, Tyburn's rural location can still be seen depicted, as it appeared at the time of the last execution in 1783, by the Norwich-born artist William Capon. The scene looks towards Hyde Park from the last house in Upper Seymour Place. In the forefront on the right-hand side is a wooden viewing gallery from which spectators could get a grandstand view of the executions. Over twenty years later Capon reworked this sketch into a watercolour which emphasised Tyburn's earlier rural nature. It gives a very strong sense of a location well beyond the urban sprawl. Interestingly, Capon's painting does not show the gallery but there is a shadow cast in the right foreground where the gallery had been on his original drawing.

Even if the exact spot where the first executions took place cannot be identified, there remains the question of why the Tyburn district was chosen in the first place. The answer probably lies with its rural location. Tyburn had gibbets as well as the gallows. It was the practice to display the remains of certain criminals in gibbets or open cages after they had been executed and removed from the gallows. They were intended to act as a mute warning to the living of the wages of sin. At times there would have been an accumulation of dead bodies poisoning the air and while viewing the bodies may have been a popular diversion, no one wanted to live too close to the stench that would have been created (Marks 1908: 62). At Tyburn, at least until the eighteenth century, the sight and smell of these corpses were some distance from major human habitation. However, London was no stranger to smells or the poisoning of the air. Noxious aromas emanated from breweries, slaughterhouses, dung-heaps, vinegar works and other commercial premises and from waste and refuse piled in the streets or thrown unceremoniously into open watercourses.

Other explanations of the origin of Tyburn's location suggest that the prominent group of elms growing in the area would have been used regularly for executions before the later invention of the gallows (Baker, 1989: 190). It may also have been significant that they were located at, or close to, a crossroads. In many cultures, crossroads have been seen as a place of supernatural significance symbolising a portal, gate or door providing a transition from this life to the next. Additionally, crossroads have often been thought of as the meeting places of witches or demons. It is probably no coincidence that in Christian countries, crosses and statues of saints or other objects of reverence were often established at crossroads.

For the ancient Greeks the elm was a symbol of death and for the Normans it was the tree of justice. An early name given to Tyburn was 'The Elms' but this is not particularly illuminating because there were other locations known by the same name including Smithfield, the precincts of Westminster (Dean's Yard) and the abbey lands at Covent Garden. Was 'The Elms' a generic name for places of execution? Particular confusion surrounds Tyburn and Smithfield, which were both places where executions took place from early times. For example, different accounts claim Tyburn and Smithfield as the places which witnessed the deaths of both FitzOsbert in 1196 and William Wallace in 1305.

An iron plaque is set in the pavement opposite the end of Edgware Road about 50 yards west of Marble Arch, claiming to mark the spot where the gallows stood. Exactitude, however, is probably unachievable, because the claims of 49 Connaught Square are advanced as also are those of the junction of Edgware Road and Bryanston Street, both sites being a little to the north of Marble Arch. It may well be that the site changed from time to time. In 1759 a movable gallows was erected as and when needed, the site of the old triangular gallows being required for the toll house built to serve the new turnpike. Although the toll house was demolished in 1829, its site is shown on old maps and should provide a pretty exact location for the 'Triangular Tree'.

When the turnpike was removed the site of the gate was recorded in a monument on the south side of the road, somewhat to the east of Marble Arch. It consisted of a slab of cast iron with a gable top bearing on both sides the legend 'Here stood Tyburn Gate 1829', this being the year in which Tyburn Turnpike was abolished. This monument made no pretence at showing the position of the gallows and itself succumbed to road improvement works early in the twentieth century.

Today, standing among the fumes and the constant roar of the traffic around Marble Arch, it takes a considerable effort of the imagination to bring to the mind's eye the vast crowds, many of them drunken revellers, for whom Tyburn Fair provided a free, regular and welcome diversion from the everyday tedium of life in the metropolis.

TWO

The King's Gallows: Death at Tyburn
in the Middle Ages

It is difficult to establish whether any executions took place at Tyburn before 1196. Capital punishment is said to have been abolished by William I but reinstated under Henry I (r. 1100–35) so it is possibly during that time that the first executions were staged at Tyburn. Records of criminal activity and punishment are sparse but certainly in 1177 in the reign of Henry II a large gang of rich and well-connected young men carried out a series of attacks and robberies on private houses. One of the gang was John Senex, a Londoner who was caught and possibly executed at Tyburn.

William FitzOsbert, also known as 'Longbeard', is frequently identified as the first person to be hanged at Tyburn, the year being 1196 and his crime sedition, but Smithfield is also claimed as his place of execution (Richardson 2000: 23; Ackroyd 2000: 57). FitzOsbert led a revolt of merchants and artisans against taxes resulting from the ransom paid for the retrieval of Richard I. On his return from the Crusades in 1193, Richard had been captured on his way through Austria by Duke Leopold who, clearly a shrewd businessman, sold him to the Emperor, Henry VI. Ransom was set at 150,000 marks and the burden of paying this fell largely on better-off Londoners. They got poor value for money for Richard only briefly touched English shores before hastening off abroad once more in an attempt to consolidate his continental possessions. He never returned. FitzOsbert's insurrection was quickly and ruthlessly put down and William was seized in the church of St Mary-le-Bow in Cheapside where he and some of his supporters had taken refuge. The accounts of FitzOsbert differ according to the prejudices of the chronicler. Matthew Paris views him with some sympathy calling him the 'defender of the poor against the royal extortioners'. William of Newburgh, however, claims that FitzOsbert's motives were base.

The dean of St Paul's, Ralph of Diceto, and Gervase of Canterbury both offer contemporary accounts of FitzOsbert's execution. Gervase states that FitzOsbert was suspended by his feet from the neck of a horse, where he 'was drawn from the aforesaid Tower through the City to the Elms . . . bound by a chain . . . he was hanged in company with his associates and perished'. Gervase does not mention Tyburn but refers to the Elms which might have been Smithfield and this clearly confuses the issue of the location of this execution. However, Ralph of Diceto comments that FitzOsbert, 'his hands bound behind him, his feet tied with long cords, [was] drawn by means of a horse through the midst of the City to the gallows near Tyburn [where] he was hanged' (Gomme 1909: 5): a clear reference to Tyburn by a contemporary writer.

Another source of confusion between the Elms at Tyburn and those at Smithfield concerns an execution that took place in 1222. Two different accounts record a civil disturbance in London. One states that it resulted from a wrestling match that got out of hand and led to an armed confrontation between the citizens of Westminster and those of the City. The other suggests that there were strong disagreements over the succession to the throne of Henry III. At that time, London and much of south-east England was in the hands of the French Dauphin, Louis, while much of the north was controlled by rebellious barons. One of the Dauphin's supporters, Constantine FitzAthulf, who had been a sheriff of London in 1197, caused a riot at a tournament when he proclaimed his allegiance to Louis. FitzAthulf was subsequently executed at the Elms. It is not clear whether this refers to Smithfield or Tyburn. We know that FitzAthulf was sent by water to his place of execution, which was not an uncommon practice when there was a fear of popular intervention. A condemned person could be taken to Tyburn by water from Westminster or the Horseferry, or to the vicinity of Smithfield via the Fleet River. Knowing that Henry III ordered the sheriff of Middlesex to build two good gibbets at Tyburn, the royal gallows, it could be that Tyburn has a strong claim to be the place of FitzAthulf's death. These were to replace older and presumably decaying ones, which suggests that punishment and execution were well established at Tyburn by that time.

The punishment of drawing the condemned on a hurdle pulled by horses to the place of execution, hanging the prisoner and taking him down before death, disembowelling, beheading and then cutting into quarters, appears first to have been recorded for an execution in 1241. A later case in 1242 concerning William de Marisco, or William Marsh, highlights the brutality of this particular form of punishment which featured so largely in the history of Tyburn. Marsh, who was the son of Geoffrey, Justiciar of Ireland, was accused of murdering Henry Clement, a messenger sent by the Irish peers to the King. He was also accused of attempting to assassinate Henry III. Having protested his innocence, Marsh fled to Lundy Island off Bideford Bay where he resorted with other fugitives to robbery and piracy. Marsh and sixteen of his men were eventually captured and thrown into the Tower. Gregory's Chronicle (Camden Society 1876: 65) records that 'William Marche was drawe and hangyd at Tyburne.' Marsh is depicted in a contemporary illustration being drawn by a horse from the Tower to Tyburn to suffer his punishment. He was hanged, disembowelled and then his bowels were burnt. His body was quartered and the parts were despatched for display in four provincial cities. Prior to his death, Marsh confessed his sins to a friar, John of St Giles, who told him to suffer his punishment with patience as a means of penance (Luard 1890: iv 193–6). It is not known whether Marsh found this advice helpful under such trying circumstances. The confessing of sins by the condemned was to take on a much more public, ritual and ideological significance during the period from the sixteenth century.

After the death of William Marsh, executions continued at Tyburn during the rest of the thirteenth century although records are not specific. It was towards the end of this century that the persecution and eventual expulsion of the Jews from England reached its height. The Jews had been subjected to the systematic seizure of their assets from the reign of Henry III and although they were by now largely impoverished, their presence was still resented by many. Almost three hundred Jews in London were sentenced to be hanged and drawn in the late thirteenth century and it is possible that some of these executions took place at Tyburn.

Punishments varied in the type and severity of the pain and humiliation they inflicted. In October 1295, Sir Thomas de Turberville, who may have been executed at Tyburn, was condemned to death for entering into treasonable communication with France as well as suggesting a French invasion in support of William Wallace, the Scottish patriot and hero. Before he was hanged, he was drawn to the gallows on a bull's hide and attended by hangmen dressed as devils who taunted him all the way and hit him with cudgels.

The beginning of the fourteenth century witnessed the execution of William Wallace for his stand against the English. In August 1305 Wallace was brought to London after his capture and accused of treason. However, as he had never sworn allegiance to the English king he could not be justly accused of this particular offence. From the point of view of the English prosecutors this was a mere technicality. Nothing very definite is known about Wallace's birth or early life and the same seems to be the case with regard to the place of his death. Many accounts state that he was executed at Smithfield but some suggest Tyburn. He was taken from the Tower through the City to 'the Elms' where he was hanged, beheaded and his various bodily parts burnt. In the case of Wallace's execution it appears that the ritual included 'abscisis genitalibus' – cutting off the privy parts of the condemned (Marks 1908: 32). The execution of Wallace also established the gruesome precedent of displaying the heads of executed felons on the Drawbridge Gate of London Bridge, a practice that was to continue for at least 350 years. There is a memorial outside St Bartholomew's Hospital which claims that Wallace was executed near that spot in Smithfield in 1305.

The year after Wallace's execution two other Scottish leaders were brought to London. One of them was Simon Fraser. According to the chronicles, Fraser was drawn from the Tower through the streets to the gallows as a traitor, hanged as a thief and beheaded as a murderer (Luard iii: 134–5). His head was fixed on a pole alongside that of Wallace on London Bridge. Although there is no specific reference to Tyburn, it was claimed in a ballad that Fraser was taken from Cheapside to Tyburn wearing a garland on his head and fetters on his legs.

Although evidence for the period from the mid-fourteenth to the sixteenth century is somewhat patchy, Tyburn is known to have played its part in connection with some of the notable people and events of the time. Roger Mortimer, the exceptionally ambitious Earl of March, had become the lover of Queen Isabella and conspired with her to depose the weak Edward II. Although the King was indeed deposed and later horribly murdered, their efforts rebounded on them because they resulted in the accession to the throne of the young Edward III, a man of very different kidney from his father. He initiated a covert raid on Nottingham Castle in which Mortimer was seized and dragged off to London. He was placed in the Tower and then, according to John Stow, he was 'drawne to the Elmes and there hanged on the common gallows' (Stow 1605: 229–30). Other chronicles have stated that Mortimer was drawn from the Tower to the Elms about a league outside the City of London. The Grey Friars Chronicle, however, is more specific, stating that he was 'Hangyd and drawne at Tyburn for tresoun'. Mortimer was left to hang for two days and two nights before being buried in Greyfriars Church.

Among the thousands executed at Tyburn throughout its long history there was a steady flow of those who had taken part in rebellions. An early threat to London came during the reign of Richard II. In 1377, at the age of ten, he succeeded Edward III. Within four years he was faced with a serious rebellion when peasants led by Wat Tyler took up arms in protest over the new poll tax, marched from Kent and Essex to storm the City and demanded to see the King. The revolt was suppressed but provided an excuse for taking reprisals against perceived dissenters. One such group were the Lollards, the name given to the followers of John Wycliffe. The Lollards were heretics active in England in the latter part of the fourteenth and the first half of the fifteenth centuries. Believed to be

England's only native medieval heretical body, they originated in Oxford in the 1370s.

Tyburn as a place of execution came very much to be associated with the Lollards in the popular mind and somehow even the origins of its name were described by some as due to this association: 'Tieburne, some will have it so called from Tie and Burne, because the poor Lollards for whom this instrument was first set up, had their necks tied to the beame, and their lower parts burnt in the fire' (Clinch 1890: 67).

The troubled times of the reign of Richard II at the close of the fourteenth century had helped the spread of Lollard ideas. With the accession of the House of Lancaster in 1399 an attempt was made to reform and restore constitutional authority in Church and state. In 1401 the Act 'De Haeretico Comburendo' – on the burning of heretics – was introduced. This Act was directed against the Lollards, 'who thought damnably of the sacraments and usurped the office of preaching'. Evidence shows that many Lollards were executed in London, particularly at Smithfield and places such as St Giles but few are definitely known to have died at Tyburn despite the claim mentioned above that Tyburn was erected precisely for the purpose of executing them.

There are many cases of people being drawn, hanged and quartered in London after Mortimer's execution in 1330. Among these was Alderman Nicholas Brembre in 1388. He was an immensely ambitious man who had been a close adviser to Richard II, but, being prepared to stop at nothing to elevate his own position, found that he had made powerful enemies who were only too happy to bring him down and had few friends to support him. Detailed information on executions around this time is scanty but one definite case is that of a man who was murdered in his own home by an intruder who broke in for the purposes of theft. John Stow suggests that there was a miscarriage of justice as the murdered man's wife was accused and burnt and three servants were executed for the crime at Tyburn. Only later, in 1391, was the actual intruder brought to justice and hanged.

Famine hit the City in 1391 and ill-feeling was exacerbated when rumours circulated about the King's extravagant lifestyle. In 1399, in a climate of intense social unrest resulting from high taxes, John Hall was executed at Tyburn for being an accomplice to the murder of the Duke of Gloucester, the seventh and youngest son of Edward III, and one of a group of nobles who had opposed Richard II for some years. From 1397 these men were arrested, Gloucester himself being imprisoned in Calais. However, he died within weeks amid suspicion that he had been murdered. Now more rumours circulated to the effect that Richard had ordered four knights to kill Gloucester. Two years later Hall was arrested and charged as an accomplice to the murder of Gloucester, it being alleged that he had kept the door of Gloucester's room open which allowed the knights to enter with ease and smother him. On 17 October 1399 Hall was drawn from the Tower to Tyburn where he was hanged, had his bowels burnt and was then quartered. His head was brought to the place where Gloucester had been murdered. Following Richard's abdication in favour of Henry IV, the four knights were later arrested and executed at Cheapside. Ironically, Richard II was himself murdered shortly afterwards at Pontefract Castle on 14 February 1400.

After Richard's death there were plots to overthrow his successor Henry IV. Seditious material attacking Henry was published and distributed, but in 1402 the King moved against the perpetrators, some of whom were arrested and eventually executed at Tyburn. Roger Clarendon, a knight and eight friars were 'strangled at Tiborne and their [*sic*] put into execution' (Halle 1809: 26). In addition, Walter de Baldocke, the prior of Launde in Leicestershire, and another friar were executed although it is unclear whether this happened at Tyburn.

Those who recorded executions during these times did not always make it clear exactly where these happened. Some records state no more than 'executed in London'. For example, William Serle who had been a servant of Richard II spread the idea after 1400 that the King was still alive and additionally forged a seal in his name. Serle was recorded as having been 'drawn from Pontefract through the chiefest Citties of England and put to death at London'. Gregory's Chronicle, however, actually states that Serle was executed at Tyburn.

Despite the sparseness of sources relating to Tyburn during these centuries, those that are available give the impression that it is mostly men of rank who died there – women get scarcely a mention. In 1416, for example, there is a record that Benedict Wolman, custodian of the Marshalsea Prison, was executed at Tyburn, while in the 1420s Sir John Mortimer met a similar fate. He had been lodged in the Tower on a charge of treason and then attempted to escape, a crime deemed to be petty treason. He received a beating and was then hanged, drawn and quartered at Tyburn. If poor people were indeed executed at Tyburn, then the chroniclers clearly thought their deaths were not usually worth mentioning. A few who appear in the records are the thief Will Wawe hanged at Tyburn in 1427; William Goodgroom, a horse dealer in 1437; John David, an apprentice, executed in 1446; and John Scott, John Heath and John Kenington who went to their deaths for slandering the King and some of his council. Others of the commonalty who died at Tyburn are not even named. They included a locksmith executed in 1467 for robbery and four yeomen of the Crown hanged in 1483.

Tyburn witnessed the culmination of a remarkable case in the 1440s. Roger Bolingbroke, an astrologer and magician, along with Canon Thomas Southwell of St Stephen's Chapel at Westminster, were charged with treason for attempting to kill Henry VI by sorcery. The purpose of the plot, in which Eleanor Cobham, Duchess of Gloucester, was also implicated, was to replace Henry as King with his uncle the Duke of Gloucester. It was alleged that on 25 July 1441, Bolingbroke 'with all his instruments of necromancy' worked his malevolent spell although it had clearly not achieved its aim. All the plotters were arrested and when undergoing questioning Bolingbroke blamed Eleanor for causing him to 'labour in the sayd art' of witchcraft and sorcery. Bolingbroke, Southwell and Eleanor were indicted for treason. Margery Gourdemaine was also accused of involvement. Margery, often known as the 'Witch of Eye', had been charged eleven years previously on suspicion of practising witchcraft and Eleanor was said to have used Margery's services against the King. Margery was burnt as a witch at Smithfield in October 1441. Southwell perished in the Tower after prophesying that he would never die at the hand of the law. Eleanor, after performing a penance by walking barefoot through the streets of London carrying a lighted candle and dressed in a white sheet, was imprisoned for life. Bolingbroke was drawn from the Tower to Tyburn where he was hanged and quartered. (This strange case is reflected in Shakespeare's *Henry VI*; see Appendix, p. 227.)

Events on the gallows were sometimes accompanied by elements of black humour and never more so than in the case in 1447 of five condemned men who had been brought to Tyburn and were being made ready for execution and subsequent dismemberment. They had just been stripped when, at the eleventh hour, a reprieve arrived. Now, the law stated that the hangman was entitled to the clothing of any prisoner. This practice, although bizarre to modern eyes, was a useful perk for the hangman because these items, often believed to have supernatural properties, could be sold for considerable sums. The reprieve notwithstanding, the hangman was utterly determined not to forego his perks and he refused to hand the clothes back to the prisoners who must have started feeling very chilly. What entertainment there must have been for the crowd that day as the hangman and the shivering, naked but reprieved prisoners stood on the gallows arguing vehemently about the clothes. While derisive shouts and ribald catcalls doubtless rang in the air as the men trudged home naked, they must have been only too glad of the reprieve and eager to put a distance between themselves and the Tyburn gallows.

In 1455 racial violence erupted in the City aimed at the Lombards who were successful Italian merchants. Three men attacked a Lombard who responded by complaining to the mayor, as a result of which one of the attackers was arrested. This prompted action by fellow apprentice mercers and supporters of the arrested man, who having managed to get him released, proceeded to seek out and attack other Lombards. The situation threatened to get out of hand until the master of the Mercers' Company intervened. Although order was restored, some of the rioters were arrested for robbing the Lombards and they were eventually hanged at Tyburn. The sighting of Halley's Comet a few months later was widely seen as an unhappy portent of unrest and certainly the following year further outbreaks of violence took place against those regarded as rapacious foreign merchants, unduly favoured by the powers that be.

Outbreaks of plague and other epidemic disease were a feature of fifteenth-century London. In 1485 what became known as the 'English sweating sickness' made its first appearance. Unusually, this took most of its victims from the ranks of the upper classes. Since these contained many literate people who were therefore those most able to leave a lasting testimony, it seems that the disease carved a swathe of fear through English society. However, probably much more terrifying for the populace as a whole was the plague, known to have taken around 20,000 lives in just one visitation, in this case that of 1499. Such traumatic events must have destabilised society and helped create the conditions which kept a constant flow of wretches, many of so humble a status that their names were never recorded, 'going west' to receive the hangman's attentions at Tyburn.

In 1485 Henry Tudor had established his dynasty when he became King Henry VII after defeating Richard III at the battle of Bosworth. However, he soon found his claim to the throne threatened by a number of pretenders. One such was Perkin Warbeck. He adopted the identity of Richard of York, the younger of the two 'Princes in the Tower', and rested the strength of his claim on his assertion that he had been allowed to escape when his brother was murdered. The story gained enough plausibility for his claim to be accepted by Charles VIII of France and Margaret of Burgundy, who acknowledged him as her nephew. The rebellion in Cornwall mentioned below, gave Warbeck great hope and he travelled to Bodmin where he declared himself King Richard IV. But his career in this character was short-lived and although he attracted some support, he was captured. At first his life was spared but when he attempted to escape, he was sent to the Tower and on 23 November 1499 he was drawn on a hurdle to Tyburn and hanged.

In 1497 Henry VII, regarded by many at the time and since as a usurper, faced the most challenging rebellion of his reign. The news that taxes would have to be raised in order to finance a military invasion of Scotland was met with widespread outrage. Nowhere was this more so than in Cornwall where an army of 15,000 rebels was assembled which then proceeded to march on London. A pitched battle was fought on Blackheath in June 1497 at which more than a thousand Cornishmen died and the rebellion was effectively suppressed. The leaders, Lord Audley, Thomas Flamank, a lawyer and Michael Joseph, a blacksmith, were captured and tried and found guilty of treason. Audley was executed at the Tower but Flamank and Joseph, being of lower social status, hanged, drawn and quartered at Tyburn. All three enjoyed a certain social equality later on however, when their heads were set upon poles on London Bridge. Joseph is said to have declared on his way to Tyburn, that he should 'have a name perpetual and a fame permanent and immortal' (Marks 1908: 123).

THREE

Tyburn in Tudor Times: Victims of Religious Persecution and Others

The Tyburn gallows received many victims during the sixteenth century, a very large number of them falling foul of the religious turmoil of the period. Henry VIII's break with the Roman Catholic Church in the 1530s and the Act of Supremacy declaring him the head of the English Church began a process of religious change that was to lead over the next six decades to the execution of large numbers of Catholics and Protestants for their beliefs and practices. Following the Act of Supremacy, a Treason Act was passed in February 1535 which bound all ecclesiastical and lay officials to renounce papal law and uphold the supremacy of the King.

Soon after the passage of this Act, three Carthusian monks, Robert Lawrence, Augustus Webster and John Houghton were executed at Tyburn. Their ordeal was described by another Carthusian monk, Maurice Chauncy. He said that they were roughly fastened on a hurdle and then dragged by horses all the way to Tyburn over roads that were rough and hard in places and wet and muddy in others. When they arrived at the gallows, where a large and expectant crowd had gathered, the executioner bent his knee before the condemned men and craved their forgiveness. The monks then ascended the ladder but were asked if they would submit to the King's command in order to obtain a pardon. They refused. The first to be executed was Houghton. When the rope was cut, his body fell to the ground where it apparently began to 'throb and breathe'. He was moved away from the gallows and placed naked on a hurdle whereupon he was eviscerated by the executioner, his entrails and other organs being thrown into a fire. The others were subjected to the same horrors and 'all of their remains were thrown into cauldrons and parboiled, and afterwards put up in different places in the city' (Marks 1908: 136).

On 25 May 1535 Sebastian Newdigate, the King's Sergeant, was arrested for unwisely denying the King's supremacy. He was imprisoned in the Marshalsea where he was kept for fourteen days bound to a pillar, standing upright with iron rings around his neck, hands and feet. He was said to have been visited by the King himself and to have been offered riches and honours galore if he would only recant. He refused to do so, an act that Henry was hardly going to overlook, and Newdigate went to the Tower briefly before being executed at Tyburn on 19 June 1535.

Henry's religious changes and the process of dissolving the monasteries that was embarked upon at the same time were unpopular in some parts of the country. Moreover, they occurred when there were many other issues on which discontent could easily focus. This general disenchantment led to a series of uprisings in 1536, starting in Lincolnshire and developing particularly in the northern counties, that came to be known collectively as the Pilgrimage of Grace. Henry VIII for all his braggadocio, was insecure about his kingdom but every bit as ruthless in suppressing subversive activity as his father had been and he moved quickly to arrest and execute the ringleaders and crush the rebellion. In May 1537, Lord Darcy, Sir Henry Percy and the Abbots of Fountains, Jervaulx and Sawley died at Tyburn for their involvement.

Henry VIII married Anne of Cleves in 1540, but within months the marriage was annulled and he swiftly married Catherine Howard who was much younger and fitter and already well-versed in sexual matters. It is likely that by this time Henry was either impotent or was certainly unable to be the kind of sexual partner craved by Catherine, a healthy young woman of considerable spirit. On 13 February 1542 Catherine was executed at Tower Hill for adultery. Earlier, in December 1541, Thomas Culpepper and Francis Dereham had been executed at Tyburn. It was alleged that Dereham and Catherine had been lovers before her marriage while Culpepper had been her lover while she was married to the King.

Dereham was hanged, drawn and quartered while Culpepper, by virtue of being Gentleman to the King's Privy Chamber, was accorded the privilege of death by beheading. It is to be hoped he appreciated the honour.

Reflecting on the late 1530s in a sermon he gave in May 1549, Hugh Latimer mentioned the large number of executions that had taken place in London at that time. He stated that there were 'three weekes sessions at Newgate and fourthnyghte sessions at the Marshalsea'. Among the gory harvest produced by these sessions were, for example, in 1538, Sir John Allen and an 'Irish Gentleman' who were hanged and quartered at Tyburn as were Henry Harford, Thomas Hever and Henry Pole. In 1540 it was the turn of Thomas Empson, Laurence Cooke, William Horne, Giles Horne, Clement Philip, Darby Gening and Robert Bird. All these men had been found guilty of treason for denying the King's supremacy. Many others, some of whom remain anonymous, died for the same offence. German Gardiner was the last martyr to die at Tyburn during the reign of Henry VIII. He was executed at the same time as John Larke and John Ireland. The latter had once been Thomas More's chaplain. All three had their heads and quarters buried under the gallows, but a fourth condemned prisoner despatched with them, Thomas Heywood, was pardoned for recanting his opinions as he was on the hurdle being taken to Tyburn.

Henry was succeeded by his nine-year-old son, Edward VI, in 1547. There were many sources of grievance at this time. Unwontedly rapid population growth, price inflation, poor harvests, rent increases, food shortages, currency debasements, plague and the weak regimes of Protector Somerset and the Duke of Northumberland, led to considerable social and political instability. The religious factor, too, was never far away, especially under Edward's successor, Mary. Both reigns were highly turbulent with rebellions in the provinces, unpopular wars abroad and unsuccessful fiscal policies.

In 1553, at the age of thirty-seven, Mary became Queen. She attempted to reverse the reforms of her father and return England to the Catholic faith. Although a full restoration of Catholicism was intended, it never became possible. Her marriage to Philip of Spain and the threat to Protestantism sparked off rebellion in Kent led by supporters of the former Protectors Somerset and Northumberland. In 1554, 3,000 Kentish rebels led by Sir Thomas Wyatt were prevented from entering the City at Ludgate and the rising collapsed, Wyatt himself being executed at Tower Hill. Many other rebels were also executed: gallows were set up specially in Fleet Street, Cheapside, Holborn, Leadenhall, London Bridge, Bermondsey, Charing Cross and at Hay Hill near Hyde Park where three people were hanged in chains. In this case Tyburn saw little use, its one victim being William Thomas, Clerk to the Council. He had tried unsuccessfully to commit suicide but was drawn from the Tower to Tyburn in May 1554 where he was hanged, beheaded and quartered. His head was set upon London Bridge and his quarters were placed over Cripplegate.

The Catholic Church was formally restored under Mary in January 1555 and the execution of Protestants followed quickly – starting at Smithfield in February. The unhappy but fortunately short reign of Mary ended in 1558 and saw the death of many other martyrs at the same location. However, Tyburn came into its own as the place of execution for Catholics during Elizabeth's reign. Religion continued to be a potent factor in political affairs after Elizabeth's accession in 1558 and fuelled many of the plots and conspiracies that were a feature of her rule. The very existence of Mary, Queen of Scots (1542–87), as a pretender to the English throne created a focus for Catholic dissension as well as being a source of considerable anti-Catholic hostility. Her presence in Scotland and later imprisonment in various locations in England was a destabilising factor, given her avowed religion and close relationships with threatening Catholic countries such as France and Spain. For many Catholics, Mary was the rightful claimant to the English throne. She therefore, sometimes unwittingly, became the focus for a number of plots which were intended to remove Elizabeth. The threat presented by Mary, Queen of Scots, was finally expunged when she was executed at Fotheringhay Castle in Northamptonshire on 8 February 1587.

In 1569 a rebel army was raised by the Earls of Westmoreland and Northumberland in the northern counties in defence of the Catholic faith. The rebels who supported Mary, Queen of Scots, were suppressed by Lord Sussex. Two adherents of the rebellion, Thomas Norton and his nephew Christopher, were condemned for high treason and sentenced to be 'hanged, headed and quartered' at Tyburn. Christopher was forced to watch, aghast, as his uncle was hanged, cut down while still alive and then disembowelled. His misery did not last long because he was soon despatched in a similar fashion. The heads of the two men were taken away to be displayed on London Bridge.

In Elizabeth's reign, the need to stabilise the Protestant Church was important not only for religious but also for political reasons. Several factors were significant. Elizabeth was excommunicated by the Pope in 1570. Long-standing traditional beliefs meant that this was still widely seen as an appalling fate for the Queen and her subjects and evidence of the papacy's determination to use terror in order to re-establish its hegemony in religious matters. Additionally, the illegal arrival in England of Catholic priests bent on supporting those recusants absolutely determined to continue practising their religion, meant that Catholicism was officially seen as insidious and subversive. The Elizabethan regime insisted that Catholics were executed for treason and not for heresy. This meant that Catholics were hanged and quartered but the state was able to boast that it tolerated religious differences and only executed Catholics because they treasonably refused to swear an oath accepting the Queen as Supreme Governor of the Church in England.

The famous 'Triple Tree', the triangular gallows at Tyburn, was erected during Elizabeth's reign. At a height of 18 feet it looked imposing and forbidding and prompted the poet John Taylor to declare that in all his travels around the country, he had never seen the like. The triangular frame of the gallows was capable of hanging eight people from each beam and therefore twenty-four in all, which it did indeed do on a number of occasions. The Triple Tree loomed large in the popular imagination and on Tyburn Fair days vast crowds would gather in its vicinity, eager for the entertainment that went with the rituals of punishment and execution enacted there. The first mention of the Triple Tree in actual use dates from 1 June 1571 when it was recorded: 'The saide [John] Story was drawn upon a herdell from the Tower of London unto Tiborn, where was prepared for him a newe payre of gallows made in the triangular maner' (Harleian Misc. iii. 1809: 100–8). The fact that the Triple Tree came into use at a time of the harshening of the penal code and the relentless pursuit, prosecution and execution of Catholic dissenters is no coincidence.

Story, who was the first Regius Professor of Civil Law at Oxford, had been imprisoned in 1563 for his persecution of Protestants during the reign of Mary. He eventually escaped and fled to Flanders but seven years later he was captured and brought back to England. He was a man of sixty when he found himself charged with high treason for allegedly conspiring with a noted magician against the Queen's life and also for providing the Spanish with information useful for a possible invasion of England. The Tyburn crowd was extremely hostile to Story. A pamphlet was circulating which set out to discredit him by describing how, while at Oxford, Story had been a womaniser and bawdy reveller. Whatever the truth of this, Story made his mark on the gallows because it is said that while he was being disembowelled, he managed to summon enough strength to strike a blow at the executioner. However, his agonised screams at the butchery inflicted on him suggest that the executioner had the last laugh (Pollen 1920: 154). Tyburn saw the death of many more Catholic martyrs after Story including Thomas Woodhouse, John Nelson, Thomas Sherwood and Everard Hanse.

In many instances, the executioner had some degree of discretion on how he might inflict the decreed punishment. For example, he could choose whether or not to strangle the condemned prisoner before going on to disembowel him. The great eighteenth-century jurist Sir William Blackstone commented that in most cases a degree of humanity was employed which ensured that the prisoner was dead before being eviscerated.

The gallows were considered to be a place of great spiritual and magical power, particularly but not exclusively where the death of martyrs was concerned. For example, the hands of those who had been executed were believed to possess curative powers and it was common for people with various maladies to stroke themselves with the hands of a felon who had just died. The hangman, too, was believed to be endowed with special powers because of his unique relationship with his victims. However, those who were employed in erecting the gallows undertook a ritual to protect themselves from the taint that went with touching the scaffold (Sawday 1995: 82).

When a victim had been executed and the ritual of dismembering and displaying the body had been completed, the state on some occasions sought to make political capital by advertising the consequences of treason on handbills and other public notices. Catholics tried to counter this by making the bodies of their martyrs, or even the various component parts of them, into relics. For example, after the death of Everard Hanse his bodily remains and even the bloodstained earth beneath the gallows were gathered up and eventually became either revered relics or commodities bought and sold for profit on the open market. In 1583 William Hart, a Catholic priest, was executed at York. No sooner was he cut down than there was a rush to pillage his clothes and in the mêlée parts of his body were actually torn off and carried away either as relics for devotional purposes or as objects that could be offered for sale. When order was eventually restored, the executioner was left gloomily to quarter what was by now a very incomplete corpse.

On 28 May 1582, three Catholic priests, Thomas Ford, John Shert and Robert Johnson, were condemned for high treason. They were taken from the Tower and then hanged, disembowelled and quartered at Tyburn. Shert provided good value for the watching crowd when he not only admonished them with a wagging finger but also declared that he would have the last laugh because they, as Protestants outside the Catholic Church, would die in a state of damnation. He then provided even better entertainment when, about to be hanged, he made a despairing grab at the rope and this allowed the sheriff to proclaim that, 'notwithstanding his obstinacy, see how willing he is to live'. In 1608 George Gervase used his valedictory speech to inform the assembled multitude at Tyburn that he wanted not 'the prayers of heretics'.

Many Catholics attempted to affirm their status as martyrs against the efforts of the authorities who wanted them to be seen simply as traitors. Their speeches and actions were intended to impress the spectators at the execution site with the steadfastness of their beliefs. So it was that at Tyburn and elsewhere, before and even during the most brutal punishments, some of the martyrs responded with acts of defiance and even with expressions of joy at the end to which their faith had brought them. In acting in this way, they also managed to cock a snook at the state which had sent them to their deaths as traitors.

In December 1581 the martyrs Edmund Campion, Alexander Briant and Ralph Sherwin died at Tyburn, all found guilty of treason. Perhaps because of his fame, Campion had a hurdle to himself while the others had to share one between them as they were dragged westwards from the Tower to their deaths. Educated at Oxford before becoming a Catholic priest, Campion joined the Jesuits in 1571 and then returned illegally to England to support and develop Catholic practices there. These efforts ended when he was arrested at Abingdon and later he had to run the gauntlet of scoffing crowds when he was paraded through London to the Tower tied to a horse and with a sign stuck to his hat which read, 'Campion the seditious Jesuit'. Although tortured, he refused to recant. When the three prisoners arrived at Tyburn, the crowd was markedly hostile, probably because of the perceived threat of invasion from Spain and the fact that Catholic priests were widely believed to be spies. Campion made a point of kissing the halters, ladders, gibbets and the executioner and his assistants. He died defiantly. Briant infuriated the crowd when he embarked on his last speech by talking of his days at Oxford. He was interrupted by someone in the crowd who shouted, 'What have we to do with Oxford? Come to the purpose and confess thy treason.' Briant again denied the charge and began reciting Psalm 51 in Latin when, to the crowd's delight, the cart on which he was standing was pulled away and he was left hanging. The spectators were then treated to the agonies he suffered because the rope was not fixed firmly around his neck. It slid up his chin and he was still alive when he was cut down. He then attempted to stagger to his feet but the executioner threw him to the ground and began to disembowel him.

Other martyrs also used the occasion of their hanging to emphasise the strength they obtained from their religious convictions. One such was Mark Barkworth. He had spent time in what was called 'Limbo', the horrible underground dungeon at Newgate, then sang all the way from there to Tyburn; even when he was cut down from the rope he stood upright and, much to the delight of the crowd, shouted 'Lord! Lord! Lord!' while struggling with the executioners. No amount of propaganda on the part of the authorities could disguise the defiance of Barkworth and many other Catholics who died for their beliefs at Tyburn. Even some of those who stood mocking them in the crowd must privately have admired their fortitude and religious conviction.

One who watched the heroism of Campion on the scaffold was so impressed that he went on to become a Jesuit priest. His name was Henry Walpole and he became a chaplain to the Spanish army in Flanders between 1589 and 1591. Later on in Spain he met Edward Squire, an ex-mariner who had once worked in the royal stables but had been captured at sea and placed in prison. Walpole was influential in Squire's decision to convert to Catholicism. Together they concocted a plan to kill Queen Elizabeth by the unusual method of applying a powerful poison to the saddle of her horse. Squire's knowledge of the royal stables was crucial to this plan which he hoped would provide him with generous financial rewards. On the strength of this plot, Walpole persuaded the Spanish authorities to release Squire. Both men returned to England in 1593 and an unsuccessful attempt was made by Squire on the Queen's life. Walpole meanwhile had been arrested for Jesuit activities and under torture admitted to complicity in Squire's assassination plan. Walpole was executed at York and Squire was hanged and quartered at Tyburn for high treason in November 1598.

Elizabeth was the target of plots, conspiracies and attempts on her life throughout her reign and events between 1583 and 1587 brought her government under severe pressure. These plots included John Somerville's plan to kill Elizabeth by pistol fire and the Babington plot of 1586 which effectively sealed the fate of Mary, Queen of Scots. Earlier than this the Throckmorton plot of 1583 had involved an attempt to free Mary and place her on the English throne. Francis Throckmorton, the son of Sir John Throckmorton, Chief Justice of Chester, was a Catholic who acted as a go-between for Mary and the Spanish Ambassador in London, Bernadino Mendoza. Throckmorton was arrested with a letter to Mary in his hand and confessed under torture that he was engaged in a grand 'Enterprise' to assassinate Elizabeth. After his confession he was alleged to have said that Mary was the dearest thing in the world to him. The so-called 'Casket Letters' that were found in Throckmorton's home listed Catholic noblemen who supported Mary and details of potential invasion ports where a Catholic army could land. He was charged with treason at the Guildhall and condemned to death. In July 1584 he was hanged, disembowelled and quartered at Newgate. The Ambassador, Mendoza, was expelled and left the country threatening darkly that he would be back – and next time he would have an army to support him.

Another conspiracy in which Tyburn received the plotters was hatched in 1584 and involved George Haydock, John Nutter, Thomas Hemerford, James Fenn and John Munden. They met their Maker at Tyburn on 12 February 1584. All had said Mass before setting out on their journey to Tyburn. The first to be dealt with was Haydock, the youngest and the weakest in health. An eye-witness described him as 'a man of complexion fayre, of countenance milde and in professing of his faith passing stoute'. He recited prayers all the way to Tyburn and acknowledged Elizabeth as his rightful queen but confessed that he had called her a heretic and then expressed the wish that all Catholics would pray for him and his country. To this, one bystander retorted by crying, 'Here be noe Catholicks'. The cart was then driven away and the attendant is said to have pulled the rope several times before Haydock fell. He was then disembowelled while alive. A similar fate awaited the others. Insult was added to injury in the case of Fenn who was stripped of all his clothes except his shirt. After the cart was driven away even his shirt was pulled off his back, so that he hung stark naked, 'whereat the people muttered greatly', as well they might.

Between 1581 and 1603, no fewer than 180 Catholics were executed for treason, the vast majority of them at Tyburn. In 1604 Thomas Alfield would have had every reason to feel aggrieved. He was executed at Tyburn after receiving a reprieve which for some unknown reason arrived too late to save him. On occasion, punishment on the scaffold might be modified. For example, Polydore Plasden, also known as Oliver Palmer, at his execution stoutly declared that Elizabeth was his lawful queen whom he would defend to the best of his power against all her enemies and continued by saying that he would pray for her and her whole realm. On the orders of Sir Walter Raleigh, he was allowed the privilege of hanging until he was dead, rather than being cut down and disembowelled while still alive. However, Eustace White who went to the scaffold at the same time as Plasden was not so fortunate. He was cut down alive and managed to rise to his feet only to be tripped up, whereupon two men stood on his arms while the executioner butchered him.

The authorities responded to the displays of Catholic martyrdom from the 1580s by executing priests along with other felons in order to blur the religious significance of martyrdom by associating those who died for their beliefs with others who were hanged for serious criminal activity. This action tended to rebound somewhat because Catholics then likened their deaths to that of Christ, who was flanked on the cross by common thieves. Another similarity with Christ was the attempt made by several priests to convert condemned felons during imprisonment or on the way to execution. The night before he was executed, the priest William Pattenson converted six out of seven of his fellow occupants of the condemned cell. Not all those indicted for treason were Catholic priests, however. For writing seditious books, Henry Barrow, John Greenwood and Robert Bowley were executed at Tyburn in March 1593.

On 7 June 1594 Roderigo Lopez was hanged and quartered at Tyburn. He was a Spanish Jew who had settled in England in 1559 and become a house physician at St Bartholomew's Hospital. He attended Sir Francis Walsingham and the Earl of Essex and in 1586 Elizabeth had appointed him as her chief physician. Because of his knowledge Lopez proved to be useful to both the English Crown and to Spain. Lord Burghley, Elizabeth's chief minister, used Lopez as an interpreter but also as a source of intelligence about Spain and Portugal. His fall from favour began when a group of Spaniards tried to use him in a plot to poison Elizabeth. Lopez was offered a gold ring and a substantial financial bribe to carry the assassination out. However, the conspirators' correspondence, which was written in code, was seized by Walsingham's spies and Lopez and some of the conspirators were arrested and charged with treason. Under torture Lopez was confirmed as being involved. He confessed but then recanted. It did him no good. He was carried in the customary fashion on a hurdle from Westminster to Tyburn. While on the gallows, Lopez, according to William Camden, affirmed that he loved the Queen as he loved Jesus Christ, 'which from a man of the Jewish profession was heard not without laughter'. Lopez and the two others with him were hanged, disembowelled and quartered. It seems that the Queen had some sympathy for Lopez and may have doubted his conviction. For the rest of her life she wore at her waist the ring Lopez had received from Philip of Spain (Hyamson 1908: 136–9).

In 1595 the poet Robert Southwell was hanged at Tyburn. He had received his theological training at Douai and had secretly returned to Britain to officiate at clandestine services. Among the families in whose houses he had ministered were the Bellamys of Uxenden Hall near Harrow-on-the-Hill. In 1592 the entire family was arrested. One who was closely questioned by the Queen's notorious agent Richard Topcliffe, was Anne Bellamy. He abused his position because he eventually seduced her and made her pregnant. She confessed that her family had indeed used Uxenden Hall to hear Mass and that the priest involved was Southwell. Topcliffe had Southwell arrested, a move he regarded as a really significant blow against the Catholic heretics. The unfortunate Southwell was subjected to torture and three years' confinement in a dungeon until he was despatched to be hanged and quartered. When he arrived at Tyburn, he stood in the cart and before preaching from Romans 14, asked forgiveness for his sins. He acknowledged that he was a Catholic priest and declared that he never intended any harm or evil against the Queen. The hangman slowly strangled Southwell and when an attendant began to cut the rope of the still breathing priest, Lord Mountjoy and a number of other eminent spectators interrupted and told him to let Southwell alone to die before he was disembowelled. Many others among the crowd repeated the demand. Southwell's writings, both in prose and verse, had been popular. His verse was widely admired and it is probable that Shakespeare had read Southwell and may even have imitated his literary methods.

Topcliffe (1532–1604) was notorious for the brutal relish with which he hunted out and questioned recusants and Jesuits over a period of twenty-five years which saw him become in effect the man in charge of enforcing anti-Catholic measures. He made extensive use of torture and he even racked prisoners in his own home. His proud boast was that he had invented a rack of his own which inflicted far worse pain than ordinary common racks. Southwell suffered on one of Topcliffe's racks. He was hung from a wall by his hands, with a sharp circle of iron round his wrist pressing on an artery, his legs bent backwards and his heels tied to his thighs. For a little light relief, when not engaged in hounding Catholics, Topcliffe turned his hand to torturing gypsies.

In the 1580s, one of the leaders of resistance to religious change in Ireland was the rebel Sir Brian-na-Murtha O'Rourke who was active in Connaught. The O'Rourkes were among the most celebrated clans in Irish history and it was claimed that he had 'made a wooden image for the Queen, and caused the same to be trailed at a horse's tail . . . and horseboys to hurl stones at it, every day' (Montrose 1999: 108). It was also said that he gave shelter to three hundred sailors of the Spanish Armada when their ship was wrecked off the coast of Sligo. O'Rourke was indicted for high treason because he had acted contrary to the laws of the Church of England and Ireland and because he celebrated 'Popish' ways. He fled to Scotland but was delivered up to the English by King James VI. In October 1591, O' Rourke was held in the Tower where an interpreter acted for him as he knew no English. O'Rourke insisted that he would only answer to the Queen and not the court before which he stood. His wish was not granted. Found guilty of high treason, he was hanged at Tyburn in November 1591. On the scaffold it was reported that he refused to acknowledge the authority of the Queen and, when taunted that he had bowed to idols, he retorted in his own language that there was a great deal of difference between the Queen and the images of saints.

Shortly after O'Rourke's execution, Thomas Lee, an English officer fighting in Ireland, was appointed Provost-Marshal of Connaught. By August 1598, Tyrone was in open rebellion and Lee found himself being held in Dublin Castle under suspicion of treasonable communication with the rebels. Lee was in fear of his life but the case was not prosecuted and he returned, somewhat shaken, to England in February 1601 just at the time of the Earl of Essex's ill-considered and disastrous attempt to remove Elizabeth's councillors and install himself in their place. However, Lee seemed to have a nose for trouble and, although not a part of this particular conspiracy, he later participated in a plot to seize the Queen and compel her to release Essex, for which he was arrested and convicted in February 1601. On the gallows at Tyburn, Lee spoke up in defence of Essex but he himself seems to have been a spent force as a result of all the excitement he had endured over the last few years. With an air of weariness and resignation, he said of himself that 'he had lived in misery and cared not to live, his enemies were so great and so many'.

The 1590s were a volatile period, characterised by high prices, food shortages, plague, heavy taxation and the wars against Spain and Ireland. In 1592 over 14 per cent of London's population died from plague, a total of 10,675 recorded deaths. The decade also witnessed possibly the worst price inflation of early modern times culminating in 1597 in the lowest real wages ever recorded in

English history. The polarisation between the wealthy and the destitute majority became ever more apparent. With continued population growth in London went an eightfold increase in convictions for vagrancy in the period 1560 to 1601. The government, concerned by the threat to law and order posed by vagrants and masterless men, issued a proclamation in 1595 entitled 'Enforcing Curfews for Apprentices'. This reflected deep unease about disorder and potential revolt and placed the responsibility for control of troublesome apprentices on their masters. In June 1595 alone there were twelve disturbances in which apprentices, who had long had a reputation for fomenting or being involved in such incidents, had started riots against the Lord Mayor and against food prices. These riots have been described as the most dangerous and prolonged urban uprising in England from the beginning of the Tudors in 1485 to the calling of the Long Parliament in 1640 (Manning 1988: 208). The 1595 proclamation noted 'a very great outrage lately committed by some apprentices and others being masterless men and vagrant persons, in and about the suburbs of the city of London'. London apprentices were perceived to be lawless and truculent and it is therefore not surprising that they frequently appeared as victims at Tyburn, a point illustrated in Hogarth's famous engraving of the *Idle 'Prentice* on his way to Tyburn.

The associating of apprentices with prostitutes was seen as the beginning of the fall into greater sins. Prostitutes, 'lewd women', or nightwalkers, were blamed for leading not only apprentices but also servants and other dependent workers into immoral habits. Thomas Savage who was hanged at Tyburn in 1668 for murdering a fellow servant included the frequenting of bawdy houses as one of the reasons for his fall into sin:

> The first sin . . . was Sabbath breaking, thereby I got acquaintance with bad company, and so went to the alehouse and to the bawdy house: there I was perswaded [sic] to rob my master and also murder this poor innocent creature, for which I come to this shameful end.
>
> (Sharpe, 1985a:151)

Apprentices and servants made up half of the workforce in London. It is estimated that between 1640 and 1660 apprentices numbered some twenty thousand in London and domestic servants exceeded that number several times over. Both groups were vulnerable to being laid off during trade slumps and it was all too easy for them to turn to crime when times were bad. It is hardly surprising that sizeable numbers of apprentices and servants appeared on the scaffold at Tyburn.

The sixteenth and seventeenth centuries witnessed the production of cheap printed literature such as broadsides, newspapers, chapbooks, ballads and pamphlets and these constitute an important source for the study of early modern popular culture. Contemporary pamphlets gleefully described the gory details of executions and Foxe's *Book of Martyrs* which extolled the heroism and endurance of Protestant martyrs during Mary's reign, was used as official propaganda during that of Elizabeth. Broadsides provided information on a single sheet with a woodcut illustration at the top and a popular narrative or sometimes a scurrilous attack on a figure in the public eye. Broadsides and ballads sold particularly well at Tyburn and although only a few survive from the seventeenth century, they offer insights into those who went to witness the executions.

By the mid-seventeenth century, more people, particularly in London, had learned to read although not necessarily to write. Because London had a higher literacy rate than elsewhere, publishers were quick to take advantage of what became a lucrative market. Much of this ephemeral printed matter was cried round the streets by itinerant ballad-sellers of whom there may have been over three hundred in London in the 1640s. They had been regarded as vagabonds during Elizabeth's reign and were always of low social status. However, crowds of the size that gathered to witness many of the executions at Tyburn always provided a ready market for their wares. Although this street-literature was diverse in the topics it covered – romance, chivalry, bawdiness, heroism, the supernatural – crime was one of the most popular themes and especially when it involved murders or bizarre or salacious activities. Ballads focused with prurient relish on murders involving the aristocracy, on wives who murdered their husbands, on serial murderers, on murders where witchcraft or necrophilia was thought to be involved or on any unusual sexual practices. This street literature was generally loyal to the Crown and condemnatory of rebellions or conspiracies such as the Gunpowder Plot. It therefore played a role not unlike that of today's tabloid newspapers. Ballads flourished during the mid-sixteenth to the mid-seventeenth centuries but went into decline with the appearance of new kinds of prose writings which could be said to be the forerunners of the literary genre of the novel.

Another practice which developed in early modern England was the elaborate playing out of rituals of various kinds on or around the execution site. One of these was the last dying speech, a sixteenth-century innovation intended by the secular authorities, supported by the Church, to uphold their power through ideological means. It developed at a time when various statutes were broadening the range of offences for which the death penalty could be imposed (Sharpe, 1990: 31). Treason, homicide, coining, rape, horse-stealing, cutpursing and the theft of items valued at more than 40*s* now became capital offences. Dying speeches were intended to provide a very public articulation of the fact that crime did not pay and that those who heard them should realise how important it was to respect secular and religious authority. However, not all felons used their valedictory speeches in this way; sometimes they delivered speeches which mocked and debunked the authorities, thereby converting the activities around the scaffold into a parody, a popular, carnivalesque celebration which undermined the powers that be (Laqueur: 1989).

Public execution at Tyburn and elsewhere and the rituals surrounding it were intended by the authorities to emphasise the omnipotence of the law and the condign, inevitable punishments that would befall those who seriously transgressed it. In reality, what often happened was a burlesque, both on the way to and at the place of execution and the development in popular culture of a widespread belittling of and irreverence for the authorities. Evidence of this can be found in the many slang terms that emerged to describe both the hanging day and the hanging itself. These include: 'the hanging match'; 'collar day'; a 'hanging fair' or the 'Paddington Fair'; to 'dance the Paddington frisk'; 'jammed'; 'collared'; 'nubbed'; 'stretched'; 'tucked up' or 'turned off'. The noose was a 'horse's nightcap' or a 'Tyburn tippet'. Other slang references included: 'a man will piss when he cannot whistle' and 'there is nothing in being hang'd, but a wry neck and a wet pair of breeches' (Sharpe 1985a: 16).

That this attempt to browbeat the people into respect for law and authority was unsuccessful is indicated by the fact that the crowds that surrounded the scaffold often contained people who would later feature centre-stage at subsequent Tyburn Fairs. An early example of the fact that the prospect of barbaric punishment did not necessarily dissuade people from committing serious crimes was one Edmund Kirk who had stood in the crowd at Tyburn watching the execution of a man for murdering his wife. Two days later, Kirk murdered his own wife.

The awful punishment of hanging and quartering which involved disembowelling was confined to men. Sir William Blackstone (1723–80), the eminent jurist, offers a not very convincing reason why women were not subjected to the same public pain and humiliation: 'For as decency due to the sex forbids the exposing and public mangling of their bodies, their sentence is, to be drawn to the gallows, and there to be burned alive.' However, this explanation is difficult to sustain given the practice of 'carting' around London. This involved male and female criminals being led at a cart's tail around the streets and made the object of the onlookers' ridicule and abuse. In certain cases women who underwent this punishment were ordered to walk naked. For example in 1579, three women – Joan Sharpe, Edith Bannister and Clemence Belton – who had all abandoned their infants, were stripped naked, tied to a cart and whipped with rods around the City and into Southwark (Griffiths and Jenner, 2000: 141). The offence of a wife who murdered her husband had been defined as petty treason since 1351 but in the sixteenth century a more serious view tended to be taken of this crime which was now seen as undermining the social order, an order dominated by men. Women found guilty of this offence were fastened to a stake and had a rope tied around the neck whereupon they were strangled before the surrounding material was ignited.

Peter Ackroyd argues that women in sixteenth-century London played a subordinate role to men in a markedly hierarchical and patriarchal society. In a 'city of power and business, they retain a supportive invisible presence' (Ackroyd 2000: 628). Be that as it may, their largely invisible presence was often made visible on the scaffold at Tyburn, as with a formidable beldame and cutpurse who was executed in 1557, but not before she had greatly entertained the crowds by directing at the legal authorities one of the most sustained outbursts of obscene invective ever heard at Tyburn. Women certainly appeared before the courts less than men at this time. The legal system of early modern England very much reflected this male-dominated society and they were not permitted, for example, to serve as jurors or, of course, as magistrates. In fact their involvement, except sometimes as suspects, was largely limited to the examination of other women for evidence of pregnancy or marks which would indicate that they might be witches. They might also be called upon in investigations where female corpses needed to be examined for evidence of violence (Gaskill 2000: 256).

As London continued to expand, particularly in the late seventeenth and early eighteenth centuries, substantial numbers of women migrated there to seek work. Many of them were widowed, deserted or unmarried mothers. They were a very vulnerable group as is evident from the lives of some of those who ended their days at Tyburn. Peter Linebaugh's analysis shows that of ninety-two women executed at Tyburn between 1703 and 1772, two-thirds were born outside London and ten had been convicted of infanticide (Linebaugh 1993: 148). Women were employed in large numbers in unskilled and low-paid work in the sweated trades and in domestic service. Their employment was particularly at risk at times of economic slump when it was all too easy for them to drift into prostitution and its concomitant, crime.

However not all the women who died at Tyburn fell into the category of the unskilled and underprivileged. In 1523 Lady Alice

Hungerford was hanged at Tyburn and afterwards buried in Greyfriars. John Stow mentions a monument there to 'Alice Hungerford hanged at Tiburne for murdering her husband' (Stow 1999: 305). Although her name was given as Alice, it was in fact Agnes. She was the second wife of Sir Edward Hungerford, an influential West Country landowner and sheriff but it was her first husband, John Cotell, whom she was found guilty of murdering. This was a curious case because nobody suggested that she had committed the murder herself: those who actually carried it out were William Mathew and William Inges. After strangling Cotell, they had burnt his body in the furnace of Farleigh Castle kitchen. Agnes was charged with receiving, comforting and aiding the two murderers some months later when the incident came to light. William Inges, who was a servant of Agnes, pleaded benefit of clergy but this was not allowed. Her elevated social status did not prevent Agnes being found guilty, incarcerated in the Tower and eventually dying horribly at Tyburn.

The 1530s were a politically sensitive period and to speak out against Henry and his marriage to Anne Boleyn was regarded as treason. One who did so was Elizabeth Barton, a maidservant from Aldington in Kent who was known as the 'Holy Maid of Kent'. Since 1525 Mary had suffered from a form of epilepsy which gave rise to trances. For this reason she was credited with having some form of second sight and this 'divine gift' made her famous. Elizabeth entered the Benedictine nunnery of St Sepulchre at Canterbury in 1527 where Catholic priests made use of her condemnation of Luther's ideas. When Henry had formally divorced Catherine of Aragon in 1533, Elizabeth was outraged and was foolish enough to have predicted publicly that Henry would die within a month of his marriage to Anne Boleyn. Considering that it was Elizabeth, who was already well known, who had made this prediction, such an outburst could not be ignored and she was arrested for treason. She was taken to the Tower and tortured and hanged at Tyburn in April 1534. It is reputed that hers was the only female head ever to be spiked and exhibited on the drawbridge gate of London Bridge.

Another woman who died at Tyburn was Margaret Ward who helped a priest named Watson to escape from prison. She was flogged and suspended by her wrists for such a long time that she was crippled and temporarily paralysed. She was executed on 30 August 1588. We can be fairly certain that as well as the small number of recorded women who died at Tyburn, there must have been many others whose deaths scarcely warranted a mention. There is likely to have been a continuous procession of anonymous victims such as the 'five men and four women executed for theft' in June 1562 (Nichols 1848: 285).

The sixteenth century saw a great increase of trials and executions for witchcraft, especially after the Witchcraft Act of 1563. There then followed about a century during which this activity was widely prevalent. Middlesex and London did not have a Quarter Sessions and Assizes. Sessions of the Peace were held twice a year as well as Sessions of Inquiry. Hence those charged with witchcraft in Middlesex could be tried in the Session of Peace for Middlesex or Westminster, the Sessions of Gaol Delivery of prisoners from Newgate or the Old Bailey.

Among those hanged at Tyburn for witchcraft were Margaret Hackett in 1585, Anne Kerke in 1599, Elizabeth Sawyer in 1621 and Joan Petersen in 1652. Margaret Hackett, from Stanmore, was the servant of William Goodwinne and her case is recorded in the contemporary pamphlet *The Severall factes of Witch-crafte* where she was described as 'this ungodly woman . . . this witch'. She was a 60-year-old widow who had been accused of causing a series of incidents which were said to have brought misfortune on a number of her neighbours. Anne Kerke of Broken Wharf in the City was alleged to have used her skills in witchcraft to kill several children. When, in 1599, she attended the funeral of one Anne Taylor for whose mysterious death she had been blamed, she was offered no share in the traditional doles for the poor for which she was apparently 'sorely vexed' and in consequence is said to have directed her magic against a member of the family (Thomas 1971: 664). At her trial, in order to disprove the idea that a witch's hair could not be cut, the justice took some hairs from her head. However, a 'serjeant attempting to cut [the hairs] with a pair of scissors, they turned round in his hand, and the edges were so battered, turned and spoiled, that they would not cut anything'. When this was followed by an attempt to burn the hair, it was said that the fire flew away from it (Purkiss 1996: 126).

Elizabeth Sawyer was the subject of the play *The Witch of Edmonton*, first performed in 1621 at the Cockpit in Drury Lane. Her case is interesting because it throws light on the attitude of the courts to cases of witchcraft and also shows how an accusation could become distorted and fictionalised through popular ballads that were sold at the execution. Elizabeth was accused of causing the death of a neighbour by witchcraft. Curiously, the court seemed unsure how to proceed until a local magistrate, Arthur Robinson, intervened and told them that Elizabeth had a mark on her body which would confirm the suspicion that she was indeed a witch. The justices then ordered officers of the court to bring three women to conduct a body search of Elizabeth. The women reported that they had found a teat longer than a finger and this was considered to be sufficient evidence on which to find her guilty and condemn her to death. Elizabeth was visited by the Revd Henry Goodcole, the part-time Ordinary of Newgate, who not only wanted her to confess in order to shrive her soul but obviously hoped to pick up some juicy information which would sell well when Elizabeth's 'last dying confession' was put onto a broadsheet and touted round the crowd at Tyburn. Elizabeth cared little for co-operating with Goodcole, who had to admit that her confession was extracted with great labour. In fact it was said that she was constantly swearing, cursing and blaspheming, something which would only have confirmed in the minds of many that she was most certainly a witch. Her fame or notoriety went before her and assured a large turnout at Tyburn where several different versions of her last dying confession were circulating among the crowd. Henry Goodcole was seriously put out by the appearance of these alternative accounts and he compared his own account with 'the most base and false ballads, which were sung at the time of our returning from the witch's execution' (Purkiss 1996: 233).

In April 1652, Joan Petersen, the 'Wapping Witch', was hanged at Tyburn. Joan had been asked to provide an alibi for a complex series of deceits involving the mysterious death of Lady Powell. Joan refused to be involved but found herself arrested anyway. Her house was searched and despite any very convincing evidence, she was charged with using witchcraft to kill Lady Powell. Joan vehemently denied the charges and declared that she had never even met the murdered woman. At her trial Joan was searched and, predictably, was found to have a 'teat . . . in her secret parts' (Ewan 1929: 274). It seems that the trial was rigged because defence witnesses failed to appear, possibly because of intimidation, while prosecution witnesses may have been bribed to testify against her. Joan vigorously protested her innocence even when she was offered a pardon if she confessed. In fact, her response to this offer was perhaps not the best one in the circumstances – she hit an officer of the law and made his nose bleed. The Ordinary or chaplain who travelled with Joan to Tyburn was so unrelenting in his attempts to make her confess that even the executioner asked him to desist.

Anti-Catholic rhetoric was a feature of English society after the death of Mary in 1558. It was frequently presented in a way which tried to make Catholicism synonymous with criminality and also, more loosely, it was often used to demonise women and others who could be regarded as threats to authority and order. The pursuit of so-called 'witches', some of whom died at Tyburn, involved both Protestants and Catholics and was a part of this process. It was a response, frequently violent, by those in power to prevent social, economic and political changes which they thought were undermining and threatening the status quo. They were absolutely right because processes were evolving which over a period of two or more centuries would make Britain the crucible of a new order, an urbanised and industrial society. However, most of those who died at Tyburn in this period, both female and male, did not analyse or attempt to explain the circumstances in which they found themselves. They were unwitting victims in a process of historical change.

The majority of those executed in the period under review were not religious offenders but nameless felons. For example, Machyn records in his diary that in 1556 ten thieves were hanged for robbery, sixteen felons were hanged in 1590 and nineteen in 1598. He mentions also in 1598 that a hangman with a 'stump-lege' was executed for theft and it was noted with some glee that he had 'hangyd many a man and quartered many and beheaded many a noble man and other' (Nichols 1848: 109). There is brief mention of other felons such as Thomas Green, a goldsmith, executed in 1576 for clipping and coining and in 1598 of Richard Ainger who was executed for the murder of his father at Grays Inn. The body was found floating in the Thames and Ainger, after being placed in manacles and tortured, was hanged at Tyburn.

Many felons were found guilty of coining and clipping and appeared at the 'Triple Tree'. The shortage of coin by the late fourteenth century led to widespread clipping and counterfeiting which became particularly prevalent in the early modern period. Laws against coining were harsh and it was considered serious enough to be a treasonable offence. In 1540 four felons died at Tyburn for clipping gold coins, two men were executed in 1554 for the 'coining of naughty money' and three more in July 1555. Other coiners are recorded as dying at Tyburn in 1572, 1576 and 1586. The anonymity of these offenders suggests that their crimes and their characters made no great impact at the time.

FOUR

Religion, Civil War and Restoration: Tyburn in the Seventeenth Century

During the reign of the Stuarts between 1603 and 1714, London's built-up area was expanding westwards, particularly into the neighbourhoods of Bloomsbury, Marylebone and Mayfair, and advancing steadily and apparently inexorably towards Tyburn which, however, remained a predominantly rural location at the beginning of the eighteenth century. The 'Triple Tree' continued to bear its gory fruit. Among the many felons executed at Tyburn there was a continuing presence of Catholics dying for their beliefs even if the state designated them as traitors.

One such victim was Anne Line, disowned by her family for embracing Catholicism. She became the housekeeper of premises in London owned by Father John Gerard, a leading Jesuit. He had been arrested and placed in the Tower but had managed to escape in 1597. When the authorities began to suspect Anne's involvement with clandestine Catholic activities, she moved to another house which became a rallying point for recusants. On 2 February 1601 a group of Catholics was about to celebrate Mass in her house when the pursuivants or priest-catchers broke in. The altar prepared for the ceremony was all the evidence that was needed for the arrest of Anne, who was indicted for harbouring a priest. On 27 February 1601, she was taken to Tyburn and hanged with the Catholic priests Mark Barkworth and Roger Filcock. She continued vigorously to declare her faith right until the end.

In 1606 Robert Drury was offered his life if he would only take the new oath drawn up under the rule of James I which required him as a Catholic to swear allegiance to the King as Head of the

Church of England. Pope Paul V condemned the oath 'as containing many things contrary to the Faith and Salvation'. Drury felt that his conscience would not permit him to take the oath and he died a martyr at Tyburn on 26 February 1607. It was declared that he and other prisoners were to be

> Laid upon a hurdle and so drawne to the place of execution . . . then to have their secrets cut off and with their entrails thrown into the fire before their faces, their heads to be severed from their bodies, which severally should be divided into four quarters.
>
> (Harleian Misc. 1809: 46)

For the occasion of his public demise Drury wore a new black cassock and shoes. He declaimed somewhat unctuously from the gallows that he had never told a lie but then added, after a pause pregnant with second thoughts, 'not willingly'. A year later Thomas Garnet was also offered his life if he would take the oath but he refused. He was executed with several coiners but casting aside the slight to his religious beliefs that this involved, on the gallows he announced that he was 'the happiest man this day alive'. In 1610 John Roberts, a Benedictine priest who was found guilty of illegally ministering in England, was hanged and quartered at Tyburn with sixteen other prisoners who had committed a range of criminal offences and was supposedly buried with them in a common grave, although the story is that his remains were later recovered and eventually reinterred at Douai.

Although accounts of the last dying speeches and the actions of the condemned on the gallows were used by officialdom for propaganda purposes, they sometimes offer useful insights into the interaction between the prisoners, the officials and the crowd. John Roberts had used the gallows to preach a valedictory sermon which so impressed the sheriff that he rebuked hecklers in the crowd who wanted him to stop. The sheriff had made it clear that Roberts would be permitted to say anything that he wanted 'so long as he speaketh well of the Kinge'. Such concessions could be abused. In 1612 when the priest John Almond was about to be hanged, the sheriff was at first inclined to prevent him from speaking but on receiving an assurance from Almond that he would not say anything offensive to the King or the state, he relented. Almond then annoyed keen Protestants in the crowd by stating that salvation was only to be found within the Church of Rome. Although there were protests at this comment, he finished by mentioning repentance which was regarded as a crucial aspect of any last dying speech. After he had expired, it was said that his heart had leapt into the hands of a watching Jesuit (Lake and Questier 1996).

On the scaffold many condemned prisoners refused to confess and indeed some continued to protest their innocence right up to their deaths. Few went as far as Francis Newland who was hanged for murder at Tyburn in 1695. On the gallows he insisted on his innocence saying, 'I am at peace with all the world . . . I suffer a most just reward, for my past sinful life and conversion.' Edward Altham, executed for rape in 1688, stood on the gallows and declared his innocence so forcefully that he drew widespread sympathy from the crowd, 'every person seeming to be very sorry for his untimely end'. George Goffe executed at Tyburn in 1700 provided a variation on the normal dying speech by confessing to his earlier sinfulness and adding that his fate was the result of malicious prosecution by men rather than a just judgment by God.

Peter Linebaugh and V.A.C. Gatrell have written about the dynamics of the eighteenth-century gallows crowd but finding evidence of crowd reaction from earlier periods presents greater difficulty. It is clear, however, that the crowd's response to an execution often depended on the character of the victim. For example in 1571 the attitude shown towards John Story was hostile because he was a known persecutor of Protestants. The crowd's sympathies might be swayed by the way in which the condemned behaved in the procession and on the gallows and also by their last words, if any. After the priest Mark Barkworth had been quartered it was noticed that constant kneeling had hardened his knees. Someone in the crowd picked up one of his legs after he had been dismembered and not without some sympathy and admiration is said to have called out, 'Which of you Gospellers can show such a knee?'

The London gallows crowd was the subject of outrage and disgust voiced by various commentators and also sometimes of praise depending on the social, economic and political circumstances of the events in question. For example, the crowds who assembled around Westminster during the period prior to the Civil War in the early 1640s were described by an observer as 'rabble . . . porters and other dissolute rude fellows'. However, elsewhere they were said to be 'citizens and 'prentices' or comprising 'for the most part men of good fashion . . . many thousand of the most substantial of the citizens' (Manning 1978: 25).

The size of the crowd varied enormously and it seems that it was not necessarily those whose crimes or executions have been well documented or who have otherwise been remembered who drew the largest numbers. It is likely that there were huge crowds for some criminals now hardly known and that this reflects the dynamic complexity of public executions in the culture of the time. While the responses of the crowds may seem capricious, even inexplicable to us today, they probably made perfect sense in the context of the times.

In 1616 the Catholic priest Thomas Maxfield drew a crowd of just 4,000 at his execution. However, on the evening before his death the gallows at Tyburn were adorned with garlands and flowers and the ground strewn with bay leaves and sweet herbs, a mark of respect or reverence which does not seem to have been extended to other martyrs. Very large numbers were attracted to the execution of an apprentice, Nathaniel Butler, in 1657. His case generated enormous interest at the time and even while he was in prison many pamphlets were published dealing with it. In the condemned cell, he was visited by many Puritan divines who converted him on the strength of hopes of salvation and forgiveness. The Puritans then carefully stage-managed his appearance and performance on the gallows and used it as evidence of divine intervention. At Tyburn, Butler's speech described his fall from grace, his sense of redemption after conversion and ended with an appeal to the members of the crowd urgently to reform their own manners.

Crowds around the gallows were by no means always tolerant of expressions of pious contrition or other religious exhortations from condemned prisoners about to die. When a prisoner engaged in lengthy sessions of prayer or gave long admonitory sermons, the patience of the crowd could wear distinctly thin. John Nelson was heckled during his prayers with shouts of 'Away with thee' while the supplications of William Sherwood and Thomas Woodhouse were interrupted by cries of 'Hang him, hang him'.

Were such catcalls evidence of disapproval by the crowd of the religious beliefs of those on the gallows? It is likely that the demeanour of the prisoner on the gallows counted for more than protestations of religious conviction. V.A.C. Gatrell has drawn attention to the way in which the crowds could be won over by the defiance, the courage or the modesty of the condemned man. He also argues that during the periods of religious persecution, some last speeches had a telling effect. For example, the Venetian Ambassador described Henry Garnet as a man of 'moving eloquence' and said that the power of his speech could 'produce just the reverse of what they desire' (Gatrell 1994). However, while some individuals elicited sympathy and moral support by giving a good performance in the very public theatre of Tyburn, even where contentious religious issues were involved, the crowd could respond with mockery or hostility to signs of cowardice or arrogance on the gallows.

While the procession over the years of the nameless poor to Tyburn went largely unrecorded, crime in high places has always attracted interest and extensive coverage and the murder of Richard Overbury in 1613 was one such case. A writer and poet, courtier to James I and mentor to one of James's favourites, Robert Carr, Overbury became involved in writing love letters for Carr, who had fallen in love with Frances Howard, daughter of the Earl of Suffolk. There was a snag. Frances was already married to the Earl of Essex. Howard, with Carr's approval, attempted to get a divorce but Overbury objected. Carr was displeased and when James offered Overbury a prestigious foreign appointment, he perfidiously advised Overbury to refuse it. Carr then reported Overbury's refusal of the offer to the King and suggested that Overbury had rejected it with contempt. Overbury was seized and thrown into the Tower. Carr had not done with Overbury. With the assistance of some prison guards, he made sure that Overbury was fed with some tarts and jellies laced with poison mixed by a pliant physician called Franklin. The plan was successful and Overbury wasted away and died. The wished-for divorce went ahead and Carr, who became the Earl of Somerset, was married three months after Overbury's murder. However the plot was leaked by the physician's assistant. The outcome was the hanging of Richard Weston, the under-keeper of the Tower, at Tyburn in October 1615 followed, perhaps rather unfairly, by that of a Mrs Turner who had delivered the sweetmeats to the unsuspecting Overbury. The physician Franklin was executed at St Thomas a Waterings for his part in the murder.

A year later, Frances Howard and Carr were tried for murder but acquitted. There was much speculation about favouritism and inequality before the law and whether the King had intervened in the judicial process. Carr's position as a favourite of the King went into decline and he was overshadowed by the rise to eminence in the King's favours of George Villiers, Duke of Buckingham, whose later assassination was to play an indirect role in the history of Tyburn.

James was succeeded in 1625 by his son who became King Charles I. His marriage to the French Catholic, Henrietta Maria, was one of the factors in the growing tensions between the King and those who felt that the country was lurching back to Roman Catholicism. Henrietta Maria did nothing to allay these fears when on 26 June 1626 she visited Tyburn to offer prayers and devotions to the Catholic martyrs who had died there. The Queen had assembled a large entourage of courtiers, many of them French, and had agreed to the suggestion that she walk barefoot to the gallows to honour the souls of the martyrs. This gesture and indeed the whole affair sparked an immediate row. A commission set up to inquire into the incident stated that the courtiers had abused their influence on the Queen by leading her to a place where it was customary to execute infamous malefactors and criminals. The French Ambassador, Marshal de Bassompierre, declared grumpily that the Queen had not even been within fifty paces of the gallows. An attempt was made to clear the Queen's name and show her to have been the dupe of scheming courtiers but, given her commitment to the Catholic faith, it is unlikely that she needed much persuading to undertake the walk to Tyburn. A diplomatic incident occurred when the French courtiers were sent back to France, this in turn evoking an angry response from the French King.

Charles inherited his father's advisor and favourite George Villiers, Duke of Buckingham, who was described by the measured critic and great nineteenth-century historian S.R. Gardiner as being among the most incapable ministers of the seventeenth or any other century. Buckingham's rapid accumulation of power and wealth made him a deeply unpopular figure, an unpopularity exacerbated by his intimate relationship with James I and the fact that he was accused of dragging England into war with Spain and France during the early part of Charles's reign. In August 1628, Buckingham went to Portsmouth to see an expedition set sail for La Rochelle. Suddenly out of the crowd ran a naval officer, John Felton, who plunged a knife into Buckingham's chest, inflicting mortal injuries. Felton, whose grievances stemmed from failure to gain promotion, gave himself up and was brought to the Tower. He made a full confession and stated that he wished his right hand to be cut off as a testimony of his remorse. However it was discovered that Felton carried a letter of justification for the murder sewn into his hat because he feared he would be killed after the assassination. In it he stated that 'by killing the Duke he should do his country great service'. In November 1628, Felton was carted to Tyburn where he was hanged. Later his body was taken to Portsmouth and suspended in chains. While few mourned Buckingham and indeed crowds turned out in their thousands to cheer his funeral procession, Felton became a national hero and the political furore surrounding the case created something of a republican *cause célèbre* (Holston: 2000).

Two years after Buckingham's assassination an intriguing case brought together a number of sensitive issues concerning sexual abuse, rape and buggery. Mervin Touchet, Earl of Castlehaven, was denounced by his son James and was subsequently imprisoned in the Tower in December 1630. In the following April a grand jury brought three indictments against Castlehaven: accessory to rape against his own wife and two cases of buggery with his menservants. In relation to the charges of buggery, the Attorney-General denounced Castlehaven for rejecting God and giving himself over to lust. He was tried by twenty-seven of his peers, found guilty and executed at Tyburn in 1631 despite the fact that he claimed he was the victim of a conspiracy (Cobbett 1809 iii: cols 402–18).

The case, with its detailed accounts of orgies at Fonthill Gifford in Wiltshire, excited much salacious interest. However, it is the case of the two servants who had testified against Castlehaven which is more pertinent to the history of Tyburn. Their names were Lawrence Fitzpatrick and Giles Brodway and they were brought to trial in June 1631 despite earlier assurances that they would be immune from persecution. Fitzpatrick was accused of buggery and Brodway of rape. Giving evidence against Brodway was the Countess of Castlehaven, who declared that he had carnally known her and had entered her body. Fitzpatrick argued that the evidence that he had already given was for the King against Castlehaven and that he felt no obligation to offer any more. This counted for little and Fitzpatrick was charged with committing buggery. The Lord Chief Justice declared that Fitzpatrick was a voluntary prostitute who should have known better and that with his age and strength he should have resisted Castlehaven's advances (Cobbett 1809 iii: cols 419–26).

Brodway and Fitzpatrick were both found guilty and sentenced to be hanged at Tyburn on 16 July 1631. Both men made confessions and last speeches which provided a wealth of prurient and smutty material for the spellbound audience around the scaffold. Fitzpatrick declared his allegiance to the Catholic faith but then stated that he had been entrapped by the Privy Council into declaring Castlehaven guilty of buggery. He added, almost as an afterthought, that his lordship had buggered him and that he, in turn, had buggered his lordship. Supporting his co-defendant, he said that Brodway had done nothing to the Countess of his own volition but had been pressurised to do so by the Earl. This was a reference to evidence offered at the trial in which Brodway averred that Castlehaven had instructed him to get into bed with himself and his wife. He followed this with the revelation that the Earl had held his wife by her hands while Brodway had sex with her. Towards the end of his speech and presumably providing something of an anti-climax for his audience, Fitzpatrick acknowledged that he was sorry for the sinful life he had led which had involved drinking and whoring. He ended the speech typically, by blaming his sins on his failure to go to confession. He then prayed for the King.

Next Brodway delivered his speech. He confessed to all his sins and to breaking the Commandments in thought and deed and regretted that he had not observed the Sabbath or paid enough attention to sermons. He then read three prayers out loud, offered up another prayer and threw away his posy of flowers. The crowd, who were growing restive, perked up considerably when Brodway went on to say that he had only lain with the Countess once and only as a result of pressure from the Earl. He added that he had ejaculated but had not penetrated her body. All ears strained to hear as he added that the Earl had said to him: 'Brodway, thou art young, lusty and well-favoured . . . I am old and cannot live long, my wife wholly delighting in lust, which I am neither able or willing to satisfy, thou mayest do well to lie with her, and so pleasing her.'

After Charles had succeeded his father as King, he soon found himself in conflict with Parliament which he dissolved in 1629 and did not recall for a further eleven years. Turbulent years followed in which many Puritans and others deplored what they saw as 'popish plots' to restore Catholicism and the attempts of the King to rule without Parliament. The conflicts between Charles and Parliament escalated from 1640 and London played an important role in the approach to civil war. There was much support for Parliament among the citizens of London and it was the threat posed by the London crowds that made the situation unhealthy for Charles to remain. He therefore left in January 1642 and headed north. During the 1640s and 1650s London witnessed significant events including the executions of the Earl of Strafford, the King's adviser, of William Laud, the Archbishop of Canterbury and, in January 1649, of course, of the King himself. None of these executions took place at Tyburn.

The Civil War was declared in August 1642 and London was obviously a key factor in the considerations of both sides. Although the City was protected by a wall, London had expanded well beyond the boundaries of the old square mile. It was essential that London be protected so the building of fortifications began with the construction of 18 miles of trenches which connected twenty-four forts including a large bastion with four bulwarks at Hyde Park near the Tyburn gallows. The ditches and fortifications were unique in that they provided a circumvallation which united the cities of Westminster and London and extended to Hyde Park and Tyburn in the west, to the Tower in the east, Newington in the south and Hoxton in the north. These works were, however, never put to the military test.

Executed at Tyburn in 1640 was the highwayman Isaac Atkinson. The only son of a well-off country gentleman with an estate at Faringdon in Berkshire, such was his reputation for persistent womanising and for squandering the family's money that he was finally disinherited. Left without a legitimate source of income, he resorted to highway robbery. An early victim was the Attorney-General to Charles I. Atkinson made something of a speciality of robbing lawyers and it was alleged that in less than eight months he waylaid at least 160 attorneys on the roads of Norfolk alone, relieving them of around £3,000. While this was probably enough to make him a popular hero, a highwayman's career was usually short-lived and so it was with Atkinson. His downfall occurred when he attempted to rob a market-woman at Turnham Green. He was interested both in her looks and her money but when he accosted her she tossed her bag of takings over a hedge and ran off. Atkinson went to find the bag but while he did so his own horse which seems to have been as lecherously inclined as its master, took off after the woman's little mare. The woman quickly alerted the authorities and Atkinson had not gone far before he was arrested, albeit not without a struggle in which he killed four of his attackers. It was said that he behaved with 'intolerable insolence' during his trial and stay in Newgate. On the day of his execution he made an unsuccessful attempt to kill himself with a knife. He was taken to Tyburn and hanged at the age of just twenty-six. With typical bravado he declared in his last speech, 'Gentlemen, there's nothing like a merry life, and a short one.' Tyburn would witness the execution of many notorious and other less well-known highway robbers particularly after 1660.

Religion continued to be a highly sensitive issue during the period of the Civil War and there were many thought to be active Catholics or sympathisers who were taken to Tyburn during this time. On 21 January 1641 Bartholomew Roe, a Catholic priest who had already been imprisoned intermittently from 1618, was executed with another priest, Thomas Greene, who was eighty years of age when he went to the gallows, having lived under sentence of death for no less than fourteen of them. Both were drawn on the same hurdle and were hanged simultaneously to demonstrations of sympathy from the crowd. Later in 1641 Edward Morgan made his brief acquaintance with Tyburn but not before he had had his ears nailed to a pillory by order of the Star Chamber, as one of its last acts. He was executed at Tyburn on 26 April 1642. Thomas Holland was a long-standing Catholic activist who made a lengthy speech accompanied by prayers at Tyburn where he died on 12 December 1642.

On the day of Henry Morse's execution in 1645, four horses drew his hurdle to Tyburn and the French Ambassador attended with his entire suite, as did the Count of Egmont and the Portuguese Ambassador. Morse was hanged until dead and at the quartering of his body the footmen of the French Ambassador and of the Count came forward and dipped their handkerchiefs in his blood. When Peter Wright was executed for his religious views in 1651 along with thirteen felons on Whit Monday 1651, it was said that a crowd of over twenty thousand attended.

On 30 January 1649 King Charles I was publicly beheaded outside the Banqueting Hall in Whitehall. His execution was followed by a series of sweeping changes but Tyburn continued to require the application of the executioner's skills. In fact within four months of the creation of the new republic on 29 June 1649 it is said that Tyburn witnessed one of its largest number of simultaneous executions. The source for this account, 'A true and perfect Relation of the Tryall, Condemning of the 24 Prisoners . . . at Tyburn', tells us that the condemned were executed as convicted robbers and burglars. John Mercer, one of the condemned, spoke rather unexpectedly of his desire for unity in the kingdom and the desirability of bringing Charles II home and settling him into his rightful role. The twenty-four prisoners on this occasion included one woman and they were transported to Tyburn in eight carts.

Shortly after the upheavals of the Civil War more mundane events were taking place around the area of Tyburn. The land to the south – Hyde Park – was sold by order of Parliament in April 1652. The Park was divided into three lots, each fetching £17,000. The diarist John Evelyn recorded that the 'sordid fellow who had purchased part of it was charging one shilling for every coach to enter and 6*d* for each horse' (Weinreb and Hibbert 1983: 401).

After King Charles's execution republican hopes were raised that England would become a more godly and humane place. These hopes were heightened after 1653 when a number of thieves condemned to die at Tyburn were reprieved, an action which seemed to suggest that Cromwell was in accord with those who believed that the laws for trivial offences were too harsh. This optimism was unfulfilled and one Samuel Chidley wrote a letter to the Lord Protector and to Parliament expressing his disappointment at the fact that wicked laws were still taking people's lives away for a crime as relatively trivial as theft. Chidley printed his arguments in book form and a copy of this book was nailed to a tree which stood on a bank by the side of the Tyburn gallows.

The period between 1640 and 1660 had been a momentous one, in London and nationally. In 1660 Charles II returned to a rapturous welcome, the peeling of church bells and the joyful huzzahs of the crowds on the streets. Nonetheless, as Christopher Hill has stated, the political events which had occurred had reminded kings and archbishops that they had a joint in their necks and that in future they would have to pay due attention to the interests of the commercial and manufacturing classes in London and elsewhere. By the end of the century the traditional power structures around monarchy and religion were declining and the governing class increasingly depended on the law. Courts showed growing scepticism over evidence – appeals to dreams, the supernatural and spectral evidence were increasingly ignored. Witnesses needed to be reliable and those who were charged with offences were allowed a defence counsel. However, first and foremost scores had to be settled with those who had been complicit in the trial of Charles I and his death – the regicides.

FIVE

Changing Methods of Punishment: 1500 to 1800

At the end of the sixteenth century, there were fifty capital offences; by the end of the eighteenth century there were more than two hundred. How and why did perceptions of crime and the appropriate ways of punishing it alter over these centuries?

Crime, like the poor, has always been with us. Laws have been created to protect property and life, bodies of armed men have existed to implement law and order and methods have been devised to judge and to punish those deemed guilty of breaking the law. While 'law and order' is often referred to as an ideal, a concept transcending time and place, in reality it is a social construct. Laws are made, interpreted, applied and altered by people who are largely from the dominant social classes. The forms that law and order take change over time and in different societies, but their primary purpose is to ensure that those individuals and institutions that possess the bulk of power maintain their favoured position. In reality, the concepts of the rule of law and the equality of all before the law conflict with the actual distribution of wealth, power and influence in modern societies.

In Tudor and Stuart England the criminal justice system took on some resemblance to its modern counterpart. Henry VII (r. 1485–1509) was keen to strengthen the position of central government. At the same time he also wanted to continue the system whereby the dispensing of localised justice was largely in the hands of the magistrates. They were appointed on a county basis, met in quarter sessions and heard a wide range of less serious cases. Henry was also determined to establish a judicial system in which powerful barons and others could not pervert the course of justice by bribery and intimidation. He wanted, too, to provide a legal framework which would encourage the rising middle classes to pursue the wealth-creating efforts he thought essential to the country's development.

Henry VIII (r. 1509–47) took control of the Church and because of this, heresy and treason tended to conflate and the punishments extorted for these crimes became more severe. His daughter Mary (r. 1553–8) earned the nickname 'Bloody Mary' because of her forceful determination to restore the position of the Catholic Church in England. During her reign at least three hundred men and women died horribly at the hands of the state for infringing heresy laws enacted under her initiative. Most of these heretics were burnt at the stake. This was a fearful form of execution. The victim was often smeared with pitch or tar and then brushwood or other combustible materials would be placed around him or her. The executioner then employed a noose to render the prisoner unconscious before the flames reached him. This did not always work and agonising death resulted. Britain's last recorded burning at the stake occurred on 18 March 1789 when a woman was put to death outside Newgate Prison. Her crime was coining.

The quantity of business devolving on to the shoulders of parish constables increased in Tudor times. It was fashionable to lampoon these constables as officious incompetents and Shakespeare provides evidence of this with the characters of Dogberry in *Much Ado About Nothing* and Elbow in *Measure for Measure*. The constables resented the unpaid nature of their duties and often loftily dismissed the victims of crime if they were poor and without influence. One level below the constables ranked the watchmen. They were also something of a standing joke. Paid a pittance, they were usually portrayed as feeble old men who could not find any other work. Satirised because it was said that their instinct when trouble occurred was to ignore it or scurry away and hide in their little sentry boxes, it is unlikely that they were as useless as this caricature suggests. However, they were not the kind of force to be of much help in stemming the growing tide of lawlessness and violence in Stuart and Hanoverian London.

In the period between the start of the Tudor dynasty in 1485 and the restoration of the monarchy in 1660, a distinct change in attitudes to crime and how it should be dealt with can be perceived. The Crown, whose preoccupation had formerly been to keep powerful and ambitious nobles in their place, now felt seriously threatened by the less deferential and increasingly restive common people. This perception was shared by the well-to-do rising bourgeois classes who looked to the Crown and Parliament to protect their property and privileges. The criminal law became one means whereby the dominant classes imposed their control over what were seen as the irreverent, truculent and criminally inclined lower orders. A substantial increase in the population and a fall in real wages and living standards in the sixteenth century were accompanied by a number of popular uprisings, there being four in the period 1536 to 1554 alone. Additionally, the end of the monastic system and its charitable and welfare functions in the late 1530s was thought to have caused the emergence of that bogeyman of the Tudor and Stuart era, the able-bodied vagabond, the 'sturdy beggar'. In official circles, poverty and criminality became virtually synonymous.

Vagrancy was regarded as a major concern in Elizabethan times as minatory bands of sturdy beggars ranged across the countryside terrorising and robbing. In order to address the problem, in 1530 Henry VIII introduced the notorious Whipping Act which allowed the authorities to seize vagrants and take them to the nearest market town, where they would be whipped around the streets at the cart's tail. The savagery of this act was reduced slightly around fifty years later when the perambulation ceased and instead the victim was tied to a whipping post while punishment was inflicted. Vagrants were often branded with a letter 'V' after the first offence and from 1572 had a hole bored in the gristle of the ear. Houses of correction were built to punish vagrants and put idle people to work. Whipping posts soon appeared in towns and villages throughout England and in large numbers in London. This gave rise to the comments made by John Taylor (1578?–1653) the 'Water-Poet'. On a visit to the capital he was struck by the number of whipping posts and was led to pen the following lines:

In London, and within a mile, I ween,
There are jails and prisons full eighteen,
And sixty whipping-posts and stocks and cages.

Whipping became one of England's most common forms of punishment, not only used against vagrants but employed as the standard punishment for petty larceny, the theft of goods worth less than a shilling. In 1589 appropriateness was the criterion for decreeing the loss of ears for uttering seditious words and of the right hand for producing seditious writings. Such punishment left the offender with visible evidence of his guilt and dishonour.

Elizabeth I (r. 1558–1603) made England Protestant once more. In 1559, the Act of Supremacy abolished the power of the Pope in England while the Act of Uniformity made it illegal to hold any services other than those contained in the prayer book. The state argued that heresy was treasonable: heretics should be punished for treason because their religious activities and practices inevitably meant that they denied the monarch's supremacy. Torture was now being routinely used to obtain confessions, especially in cases where treason and religious heterodoxy were suspected. At the same time, increasingly severe punishments were thought necessary to tackle the perceived threat to law and order from rising crime. In a somewhat hysterical climate of opinion, nobody seemed surprised when a senior legal figure advocated pulling out the tongues of convicted criminals.

The concept of punishment embraced both physical pain and public humiliation. Petty offenders might be placed in the stocks or the pillory or fined or whipped. The pillory was extremely painful because the offender was held by the neck and the wrists, causing agonising cramps. Sometimes, to compound the punishment, the offender had his ears nailed to the hinged wooden board in which his neck was placed. This prevented him ducking when a hostile crowd pelted him with all manner of filth or, if they really disliked him, with stones. Sometimes offenders were fatally injured by such missiles. If their feet did not reach the platform on which they were placed, they could easily die as a result of slow throttling. Occasionally, if the authorities felt particularly vindictive, they would aggravate the punishment of standing in the pillory. In 1630 a Dr Leighton who had written a book lampooning royalty, the peerage and the upper echelons of the Church of England, was sentenced to be whipped severely and then to have an ear cut off before being placed in the pillory. His ordeal also included having the septum of his nose split and branding with the letters 'SS' which signified that he had stirred up sedition. Others sentenced to the pillory included sexual offenders, those caught cheating at cards for money and people selling substandard goods.

Although lock-ups, houses of correction and prisons existed, little use was made of custodial sentences for punitive and deterrent, let alone for reforming purposes. These places were used for people awaiting trial, appeals or sentencing, vagrants and the idle poor or in some cases for misfits and others who simply defied categorisation. However, from the early 1700s a wider assortment of petty offenders found themselves sent to perform hard labour in various houses of correction throughout the land. These might include poachers, petty thieves and those who uttered seditious slanders. The punishment for all felonies was, in theory if not actually in practice, death.

A form of torture was used on accused prisoners who refused to enter a plea. This might be an act of defiance or because the prisoner was literally dumb. If a prisoner could hold out without a plea until he died, he saved his property for his family. A prisoner refusing to plead meant that the trial could not begin. This greatly irked the authorities who would then subject him to the dreaded *peine forte et dure*, usually referred to as 'the press'. This was originally sanctioned in 1275 and extensive use was made of it in the sixteenth to the eighteenth centuries. The prisoner was stripped and placed on his back. A board was put on his chest with heavy weights on it. The agony of this meant that most prisoners quickly found their tongues and co-operated by entering a plea. A highwayman by the name of Thomas Spiggot held out for thirty agonising minutes with a weight of 400 lb on his chest. Sometimes the authorities dealing with a prisoner unwilling to plead simply twisted his thumbs with whipcord. That normally did the trick.

Nowhere did the perceived threat from crime seem as serious as in London. The capital offered unique opportunities to the criminally inclined. Its population was larger and growing because of inward migration. The result was the creation of a rootless and volatile population many of whom were unskilled and very much at the mercy of economic downturns and slumps. With few loyalties or moral restraints, many naturally turned to crime, at least when times were bad. London offered propitious conditions for crime because of the concentrations of wealth, its anonymity and the feebleness of its law-enforcement agencies. For the sixteenth and seventeenth centuries, no reliable quantitative evidence exists for levels of crime in London and historians have to rely instead on impressionistic contemporary material which strongly suggests social and political instability. Some particular events stand out. In 1554, fifty-nine rebels were hanged in London and Southwark after Wyatt's revolt. In the late 1590s a force of over five hundred unpaid soldiers threatened to loot Bartholomew Fair. Martial law was declared on this occasion.

During the Interregnum (1649–60), the heavy hand of Puritanism descended on the English people and many of their favourite activities and pastimes. 'Incontinence' now became punishable. This word was used in its sexual sense and made a misdemeanour out of fornication and a felony of adultery. In 1647 and 1648 actors could be punished for pursuing their trade as could in the latter year those who had turned out to watch them. In 1654 cock-fighting was banned less out of concern for the welfare of the animals than because it attracted ill-behaved crowds who gambled, drank, swore and might get out of hand. Abusing the sanctity of the Lord's Day became a misdemeanour, while various enactments tried to enforce attendance at worship on Sundays and prevent travelling and trading on that day. In the campaign against immorality, the uttering of profanities and gambling with cards became punishable, certain types of football were outlawed and for a period of six months, horse-racing was banned. With the Restoration in 1660 many of these recent enactments were repealed but savage punishments continued to be imposed for a wide range of offences. The state seemed determined to keep, literally, the whip-hand over a populace which, especially in London, was seen as increasingly fractious and insubordinate.

In rural England in the early eighteenth century the justices of the peace with their parish constables provided a reasonably effective system of law enforcement but things were very different in the towns. These contained few men of the propertied class from which the magistracy was normally drawn. Many towns were expanding rapidly and experiencing rising levels of lawlessness. The workload facing justices was growing and it became increasingly difficult to find men of the right calibre prepared to undertake the onerous duties that went with the unpaid job. In London especially this led to men who were not 'gentlemen', that is, reasonably well-to-do landowners, being appointed as what were known as 'trading justices'. They were paid to do the job and as the workload increased, many of them became professional, gaining their living from fees for the cases heard, the convictions obtained and various perks, mostly illicit. The opportunities for corruption and peculation are obvious.

London in particular provided the ideal conditions for a substantial growth in criminal activity which put the existing watch systems under considerable pressure. Few well-to-do citizens wanted to undertake the unpaid and sometimes hazardous duties that went with law-enforcement. They found proxies to perform these duties who, because they were poorly paid, were often inefficient and corrupt. The medieval idea of the *posse comitatus*, that is, communal responsibility for apprehending criminals and bringing them to justice, made no sense at all in the London of this period because any attempt to call a posse together would probably have been ignored or, possibly worse, have created an excitable crowd swiftly turning into a mob and going on a binge of violence and destruction.

The lack of an effective police system led to the emergence of the 'thief-takers'. These were men, only occasionally women, who captured and either delivered up to authority or themselves prosecuted wrong-doers for whom rewards had been offered. The most famous of these was Jonathan Wild. In the early eighteenth century he combined thief-taking with receiving stolen goods and organising a vast, complex and lucrative network of underworld activity in London. Thief-taking could be a highly profitable business when rewards of £40 from public funds were available for those whose actions led to the conviction of highwaymen, coiners and burglars, for example. In 1720 an added incentive was a sum of £100 offered for the successful conviction of those who committed robbery within 5 miles of Charing Cross. This sum was more than most working men received in wages in three or four years. Additionally the various societies concerned with the 'reformation of manners' from the 1690s offered rewards for those whose actions brought to justice blasphemers, Sabbath-breakers and others guilty of 'immoral acts'. The existence of these rewards encouraged corruption, blackmail and perjury. Informers and thief-takers destabilised and weakened the criminal world by sowing suspicion and disunity but also confused the boundaries between criminality and legality. The state was effectively recruiting criminals to act on its behalf.

A movement for reform began when Henry Fielding gathered together a group of constables noted for their relative integrity who reported directly to him on their activities. They were given a regular salary which reduced the temptations of bribery and corruption. 'Mr Fielding's People' as they were initially known evolved into the famous Bow Street Runners and mostly acted in cases where a reward was involved which encouraged their efforts. This primitive policing system helped the people of London to feel that the streets were safer. Henry Fielding and his blind half-brother Sir John Fielding owed much of their relative success to the compilation of what would now be called a database which gave them comprehensive information about London's criminals and their activities. The growing success of the Bow Street operation meant that it became the prototype for other forces such as a horse patrol established in 1763. This was a mounted force which patrolled the major routes into London and had some success in reducing the activities of highwaymen. In about 1780 the foot patrol was established which regularly made the rounds of the streets of the City and other parts of the metropolis. Also effective in tackling crime was the publication *Hue and Cry,* later renamed *Hue and Cry and Police Gazette,* which was published from Bow Street and distributed information about wanted offenders and their suspected crimes. This made it more difficult for criminals to evade detection by moving their operations around the country.

Mention should be made at this point of what became known as the 'Tyburn Ticket'. Sanctioned by Parliament in 1699, this was a document presented to a person who had successfully brought a prosecution ending with the execution of the felon concerned at Tyburn. With it he claimed exemption from various onerous or unwelcome public duties such as jury service. A Mr George Philips of Bloomsbury was the first person to receive one of these tickets after he had successfully brought two housebreakers to justice. The Act allowing this practice was repealed in the reign of George III, but as late as 1856 an armourer from Bond Street in London successfully claimed exemption from jury service upon producing a Tyburn Ticket. The judge involved had clearly forgotten that this privilege had been terminated. These tickets had become negotiable and were bought and sold surreptitiously at prices that could reach three figures.

Parliament created a very large increase in the list of capital offences during the eighteenth century in an attempt to tackle an apparently serious increase in the level of crime. What became known as the 'Waltham Black Act' of 1722 imposed the death penalty on those apprehended merely for being armed and disguised on the open road, open heath or in forests where there was game; for wounding cattle; for setting fire to crops; and various other rural crimes. Other legal enactments which sought to control the common people included the Riot Act, the Combination Act and the Workhouse Act. The Riot Act of 1715 proved to be a very useful measure against collective activity. Under its terms, any gathering of twelve or more people assembled for what were identified as 'unlawful purposes' had to disperse within an hour of its proclamation as a riot by a magistrate. Failure to disperse rendered all present guilty of felony. This hardening of attitudes saw some people declaring that hanging was too good for convicted felons who should be broken on the wheel instead.

In fact penal policy at this time was by no means straightforward. The early eighteenth century saw significant reforms to the criminal law and the ways in which it was enacted. While increasing the deterrent effects of the law, these reforms were also characterised by elements of humanity and practicality. Increasingly the courts imposed non-capital punishments on convicted felons. These might involve detention with hard labour or transportation to the American colonies. The victims of crime were encouraged to bring prosecutions themselves. Much has been written in the past about Britain's 'Bloody Code' with horror stories of how children of twelve or less were despatched to the gallows for shoplifting or transported for crimes that nowadays seem trivial. This suggests a brutally retributive penal system that was the desperate response of the authorities to levels of crime that were apparently getting out of control. The reality was more complex.

In London the spectacle of hanging at Tyburn occupied a central place in judicial and penal practice until the 1780s. However, simple discouragement of crime by terror was not an effective expedient against much of the crime that was perpetrated in London, and in practice eighteenth-century legal and penal policy was characterised by flexibility. It made considerable use of the royal prerogative of pardon and developed a pragmatic balance between deterrence and terror. J.M. Beattie sums up:

> An overriding pattern is clear, despite fluctuations over time and differences from place to place. The stern imperative of a criminal code in which, under the Tudors, execution appears to have become mandatory for a wide range of property crimes gave way in practice to a more moderate regime, the harsh sanctions of the law being blunted by jurors and judges alike. More acquittals and partial verdicts . . . resulted in falling rates of hanging and the elaboration of a number of alternative, non capital punishments.
>
> (Beattie 2001: 279)

Property became sacrosanct, elevated in law almost to the position of a deity. John Locke in *Two Treatises of Government*, published in 1690, acted as the ideologue and mouthpiece for the men who wanted a form of government which allowed them to maximise the wealth they could accrue from manufacturing, trade and finance. 'Government has no other end but the preservation of property', Locke said with disarming frankness. In order to safeguard wealth and property, governments over the next century created a penal code which, at least on paper, was of appalling ferocity. Those classes which dominated Parliament used the criminal law and the creation of more and more capital offences to support a redefinition of property and the purposes of government. As Douglas Hay said, 'the gentry and merchants and peers who sat in Parliament in the eighteenth century set new standards of legislative industry, as they passed act after act to keep the capital sanction up to date, to protect every conceivable kind of property from theft or malicious damage' (Hay et al. 1977: 22).

In the eighteenth century, the inadequacies of the police system meant that only small numbers of those who offended were apprehended and brought to justice. Therefore those who were caught were liable to be made an example of and treated with considerable ferocity. However, what initially appears to be a cruelly vindictive penal code turns out often to be something very different because of a considerable discrepancy between theory and practice. As J.M. Beattie argues: 'In the century after the Restoration, in a period in which the society and the culture of the metropolis were undergoing considerable change, the elements of an alternative means of dealing with crime in urban society were emerging in policing, in the practices and procedures of prosecution, and in the establishment of new forms of punishment' (Beattie 209: x).

Since Elizabethan times, juries had frequently practised what Sir William Blackstone called 'pious perjury'. This meant that the severity of the law was often mitigated by juries when prisoners were charged with capital offences. Where theft had been involved, for example, they sometimes undervalued the articles stolen so that the crime no longer constituted grand larceny, a capital felony, but instead petty larceny, a misdemeanour attracting a lesser punishment. Judges on their own initiative sometimes dismissed cases and reprieves were by no means uncommon. They often sentenced convicted felons to transportation rather than hanging. A number of women avoided the death penalty by pleading 'benefit of the belly'. This allowed them a respite until the baby was born and in practice usually meant they were ultimately pardoned. Women in Newgate awaiting trial or execution for capital offences often bribed the warders to allow men to visit them for the purpose of sex. The hoped-for outcome was, of course, pregnancy. The so-called 'Bloody Code' was actually highly flexible in practice.

When the prisoner in the dock was well-to-do, he might have recourse to bribery. False witnesses would be produced, happy to tell the grossest lies in court in return for payment. They might be associates of the accused or what were known as 'straw men', professional witnesses who sauntered around outside the court advertising their trade by sticking pieces of straw in the buckles of their shoes. They would lie on behalf of anyone or say absolutely anything for money. Corruption was deeply entrenched in all aspects of public life in the eighteenth century and the legal and judicial systems were no exception.

Juries, too, could be bribed. They came to their decisions very quickly by today's standards. Jurors were more socially cohesive than today, consisting of those who met certain property qualifications and usually had shared values. They often happily concurred with the recommendations of the foreman, an older and more experienced man. However, although jurors were not the social peers of most of the wretches over whose fate they deliberated, they could act with genuine compassion. People of previous good character or those who could convince the court of extenuating circumstances might well be treated leniently. For example, Ann Flynn appeared before a court in London in 1743 charged with stealing a shoulder of mutton. The court was told that she only committed the crime when her husband, the family breadwinner, became unable to work through illness and she did so in order to feed her starving children. The jury declared that she was indeed guilty but recommended clemency. The judge, combining professional discretion with compassion, proceeded to fine Anne the substantial sum of 1s. It was immediately paid by the jury itself.

Many serious offenders escaped hanging through the curious practice of benefit of clergy. This had its origins in the conflicts between the jurisdiction of the Church and that of the state in the Middle Ages and accorded clerics the right to be tried for certain types of felony in the ecclesiastical, rather than the royal, courts. Proof of clerical status was rather generously taken as the ability to read, a test which became increasingly meaningless as literacy became more widespread. During the reign of Henry VII, it was declared that those convicted of felony, in particular theft and manslaughter, might escape hanging in the case of a first conviction if they could demonstrate that they could read. In practice, if the prisoner could recite Psalm 51 or at least that part known as the 'neck verse', then he would be saved from the gallows. Judges even exercised discretion when benefit of clergy was claimed and might err towards clemency by ignoring a hopelessly unlettered mumble by a supplicant who could not even memorise the required, brief passage, let alone read it. In cases where a successful plea of benefit of clergy was submitted for the court's consideration, the judge and the jury could exercise considerable discretion. They might, for example, acquit the defendant of a non-clergiable offence but find him guilty of a lesser, clergiable crime. This came to be known as a 'partial verdict'.

An unpredictable, even capricious mixture of terror and apparent humanity and clemency exercised by the courts added powerfully to their mystique. The elaborate rituals whereby bewigged judges in ermine-tipped scarlet robes donned the black cap when death sentences were solemnly pronounced emphasised the majesty of the law and tended to overawe those who offended against it. Flexibility in the application of the law could mean inconsistency. The court's decision might therefore be unclear until the very last minute, heightening the tension. There were also 'general' or 'circuit' pardons. These were issued occasionally in celebration of particularly auspicious public events and could even result in hardened recidivists getting off scot-free.

The names of those condemned to death at the Old Bailey would be formally presented to the king for the possible exercise of his prerogative of mercy. In practice, especially after 1688, these cases were usually reviewed by the Cabinet Council at which the monarch might not necessarily be present. The prisoner would not appear himself although a petition might be offered up on his behalf. The Recorder of the City of London presented a report containing what he saw as the facts of the case to a Council meeting. He might have to answer questions but the petition was only one item in what was frequently a crowded agenda and there is no evidence that it was dealt with at greater length than any other item. The Council took a vote and the Recorder would make his way back to Newgate bearing what was known as the 'dead warrant' which gave the names of those who were to be hanged and the day to be set aside for the execution. It is likely that such factors as signs of remorse, of the felon having been duped by recidivist associates, his previous character and the nature of the offence would be taken into account. It was somewhat arbitrary.

From time to time, especially in the years immediately after the Restoration of 1660, substantial numbers of criminals were transported to the American colonies where there was a desperate shortage of labour. When they got there, they were sold to the highest bidder for whom they had to work while serving out their sentences under conditions virtually indistinguishable from those of slaves. Transportation suited the English authorities because it enabled them to be seen as exercising clemency while getting rid of some of the country's most anti-social elements, at least temporarily. Transportation to America ceased for a while because it was decided that England was already underpopulated and could not afford to lose so many able-bodied people, especially young men. However the practice was resumed after the Transportation Act of 1718 when it became very common to despatch convicted felons to the colonies for terms of seven or fourteen years. Many of these had been found guilty of capital offences but, on receiving a royal pardon, had had their sentences 'commuted' to transportation. Given the appalling conditions in the ships that carried them to the penal colonies and the living and working conditions when they arrived, the pardon was often tantamount to a death sentence anyway. The fact that this alternative to the capital sanction became available was one reason for a fall in the number of hangings over the following period.

American colonies ceased to be a destination for British criminals when they gained their independence in the 1770s and the authorities then started using superannuated wooden men o' war with their armament, rigging and other fittings removed, as floating prisons. These 'hulks' were moored on the River Thames and elsewhere and the convicts used as forced labour locally. The hulks were soon filled to bursting point and the authorities forced to look elsewhere. In 1786 they came up with the idea of transporting convicts to Australia, the first cargo of woebegone criminals arriving there in January 1788, near Botany Bay in New South Wales.

Whipping remained a common punishment for petty larceny into the eighteenth century. Petty larceny was the only form of theft for which the perpetrators were not liable for capital punishment. It was not uncommon for juries to reduce the crime of grand larceny before them to one of petty larceny, for which whipping was seen as an appropriate punishment, where goods of low value were concerned. Whipping involved physical pain and public humiliation. The victim was stripped to the waist and then whipped through the streets behind a horse-drawn cart. This was another piece of public theatre like the ride from Newgate to Tyburn and the hangings there and it attracted large and unruly crowds who often disrupted business activity in the City.

In the City of London the Lord Mayor headed the administration of justice and enforcement of the law. After 1741 all City aldermen were also magistrates. They had jurisdiction over Newgate Prison and over the courts at the Old Bailey, where the cases that were considered were from the City and from Middlesex, which constituted most of the metropolis north of the Thames that was not part of the City. The sessions over which the City and the Middlesex magistrates had jurisdiction took place eight times a year. More serious offences were heard before High Court judges also presiding at the Old Bailey. Although its population was declining as a proportion of the capital's overall numbers, the City was still immensely important because of historical precedent and its enormous wealth. While there was still much small-scale manufacturing in the City, it was now developing as the hub of a complicated web of overseas and colonial trading relations and as a major international centre of financial services. Because of its affluence and its attraction for those wanting fame and fortune, the City was plagued by crimes such as highway robbery and burglary, against which its citizens felt they had little protection and which they perceived as growing at an alarming rate.

High levels of crime were seen as evidence that the moral fabric of society was breaking down. As J.M. Beattie has commented:

> a great chain of immorality and illegality – a linking commonly conceptualized as a slippery slope that began with apparently minor acts of wilfulness and disobedience that were to be taken seriously because they gave rein to the passions and, if not checked, would lead to the erosion of moral sense and of the principles of right behaviour that derived from religious beliefs and practice.
>
> (Beattie 2001: 51)

Minor misdeeds such as Sabbath-breaking had to be taken seriously because they showed susceptibility to a downward spiral of moral depravity. Large numbers of artless young people flocked to London in search of wealth and fame. These vulnerable youngsters could so easily move from Sabbath-breaking to the manifold immoral and criminal attractions to be found in London's brothels, taverns, coffee houses, theatres, gaming houses and fairs. This analysis of the causes of crime highlighted the insidious role allegedly played by 'lewd women'. To enable them to enjoy the salacious pleasures they offered, men went on to commit robbery and all sorts of other offences. This attitude was part of a continuum which had long demonised women as evil sirens employing their lubricious charms in order to captivate and control the male sex. Dorothy George provides a corrective by explaining that:

there is little doubt that the hardships of the age bore with especial weight upon them [women]. Social conditions tended to produce a high proportion of widows, deserted wives, and unmarried mothers, while women's occupations were over-stocked, ill-paid and irregular.

(George 1966: 174)

Large numbers of young women did indeed come to London in search of employment but what they managed to obtain was likely to be ill-paid, unskilled or at best semi-skilled work that was vulnerable to economic and seasonal fluctuations. The justification for paying women low wages was that their employment was considered nothing more than a supplement to the earnings of the male breadwinner on whom they depended and that it was often spent on mere frivolities. The harsh reality is that for very many women, with or without male partners, the low wages and irregular employment left them largely destitute. When they had no work, poverty stared them in the face and it was all too easy for them to slip into illegal ways of making money. J.M. Beattie takes up this theme:

For single women especially, the capital offered a greater degree of independence and privacy – a certain freedom from the surveillance and controls of patriarchal and paternalistic social relationships. At the same time, however, and as an inevitable consequence, the urban world forced on them a greater need for self-reliance. This must have been true of single women and widows in particular, and it is hardly surprising that not only were larger numbers of women drawn into theft in London, but that fully eighty per cent of the women before the Old Bailey on property charges in this period were unmarried.

(Beattie, 2001: 71)

What then was the rationale that underpinned the penal system in the period up to the 1780s? Three main principles can be identified. One was the concept of deterrence. It was believed that the very public ceremonies involving the condemned prisoner's last journey to the place of execution and the rituals on the gallows including their confession and subsequent agonising death, were effective deterrents which would instil into those who witnessed them a sense of the omnipotence of the law and the terrible fate awaiting those who committed serious offences. Retribution was another principle. The suffering attached to the punishment should be proportional to the heinousness of the crime. Laws were made by the wealthy and powerful. For this reason the seriousness with which offences were regarded and punished reflected, although not absolutely, the values and mores of those in power and these could change in different circumstances. The third principle was that the offender, even one guilty of a minor crime, had shown his disregard, even his contempt, for the values around which society operated. Therefore when the punishment fell short of death, he had to undertake a ritual penance involving shame and humiliation in public.

By the middle of the eighteenth century it seems evident that there was concern that the carnivalesque nature of the journey from Newgate to Tyburn and the rituals that were enacted there were detracting from rather than enhancing the awfulness of the law. Reformers like John Howard were influenced by the ideas of the Enlightenment and argued that existing forms of punishment were arbitrary, barbaric and largely ineffective in countering crime. Reforms were needed which, by letting potential offenders know that they were much more likely to be caught and punished, actually deterred people from committing crime. The punishment for each crime should be consistent. It should act as a deterrent and should suit the crime committed and where custodial sentences were concerned, should try to limit future offending through a regime aimed at reforming the offender's character. Ideas along these lines were adopted in the century after hangings ceased at Tyburn.

The ultimate punishment for City of London and Middlesex criminals was public hanging at Tyburn. This provided an unequivocal statement of the state's legal monopoly of violence within civil society. The hanging of a malefactor was a carefully stage-managed affair. Since the vast majority of those hanged had offended against laws protecting property, each hanging was intended to send out a clear message that property and the law should be respected. Only few people possessed any significant wealth and so the use of this deterrent was evidence of the conflict of interests between the rich and powerful and the poor and disenfranchised. Additionally the very existence of judicial hanging staged in this fashion is evidence of the potency of myths. Was hanging really a deterrent when pickpockets employed their skills to profitable effect in the crowds around the gallows at Tyburn?

It could be argued that the use of punishment by the state is about maintaining power and social control. The form it takes depends not on abstract concepts such as mercy or compassion but on the strength of the forces of government and authority at any particular time and their ability to maintain control over society in the easiest and most economical way. The barbaric physical punishments that were a feature of England in earlier times were replaced in the eighteenth and nineteenth centuries because the state was confident that it no longer needed to use such openly ferocious ways in order to maintain its power and to safeguard property and the status quo.

Hangings at Tyburn ended not on account of increasing humanity or compassion on the part of those, rich and poor, who had previously thronged to watch and enjoy the dying agonies of London's convicted felons. They ceased because the well-heeled and influential occupants of the new and extremely prestigious residential areas adjacent to Tyburn objected to the noise, the revelry and the frequently drunken and violent behaviour of the huge crowds drawn to Tyburn Fair. In today's language, this was a case of 'Not in my back yard'. Tyburn attracted the riff-raff on hanging days and the rich folk of London's emerging West End did not want to be reminded of their existence. More than that, these crowds and the festivities associated with Tyburn Fair disrupted the business life of London as many as eight times a year. Additionally, these crowds always posed the threat of running riot and getting out of control. The transfer of hangings to the more confined surroundings of Newgate assisted the authorities to manage a public spectacle which, at this time, they presumably still thought deterred potential criminals.

SIX

Tyburn from the Restoration to 1700

The Restoration of the monarchy in 1660 inaugurated a very different period from the preceding decade. It saw, for example, the reopening of the theatres, the granting of a charter to establish the Royal Society in 1660 dedicated to the propagation of scientific experimentation and knowledge and the return to the throne of the 'Merry Monarch' from over the waters. There was a conscious repudiation of what was seen as the joyless austerity of the recent past. However, the initial heady euphoria soon gave way to business as usual. Tyburn would witness more criminal executions in addition to the execution of some of the regicides. Moreover, an increasing number of commentators would visit, write about and illustrate the gallows at Tyburn.

After 1660 there was a marked desire to break with the memory of the two previous decades of civil war, revolution and republicanism. To symbolise that break the regicides who had been responsible for the trial and execution of Charles I had to be brought to account. Of the fifty-nine men who had signed Charles's death warrant, forty-one were still alive and of these fifteen had fled the country. Those who had ended up in Europe were believed to hold an annual celebration at a tavern in Charing Cross and were known as the 'Calves' Head Club': on the anniversary of Charles I's execution, members of this club toasted the regicides and banqueted on calves' heads.

Three of the regicides who escaped at this late stage were John Okey, a London chandler, Miles Corbet who had reached Holland, and John Barkstead, son of a London goldsmith, who was living in Hanau near Frankfurt. All three were tracked down after being betrayed by a collaborator, George Downing, who had been chaplain in Okey's regiment. Downing turned Royalist when he deemed it the best way of serving his interests and subsequently pursued a career in the Foreign Office as well as serving as the King's representative in Holland. He went on to be knighted and in 1680 to build a cul-de-sac of rather plain brick terraced houses which became famous as Downing Street. Downing's star may have risen but Okey, Corbet and Barkstead were not so fortunate and all three were executed at Tyburn in April 1662. Okey displayed much penitence on the gallows and his severed quarters were allowed a decent burial. Corbet's head, however, was displayed over one of the City's gates and Barkstead's was spiked above Traitor's Gate at the Tower. Barkstead's death generated more interest than most because it was believed that he had hidden treasure in the form of gold packed into barrels somewhere within the precincts of the Tower. Many people, including Samuel Pepys, searched for this in vain.

Two years later other regicides met their fate at Tyburn. Colonel Daniel Axtell and Francis Hacker were brought to the gallows in October 1660. Axtell spoke briefly and Hacker stated that 'God hath not given me the gift of utterance': he then read out a paper stating that his conscience was clear (Hill 1984: 73). He and Axtell prayed for some time and then Axtell went on to be quartered and Hacker to be hanged. Condemned prisoners such as traitors and regicides were expected to confess their guilt and express remorse for their crimes and in so doing it was hoped that the theatrical aspects of their public execution would endorse a sense of law and order. However, this did not always go according to official plans. Roger L'Estrange who acted as a censor during Charles II's reign, commented somewhat querulously that 'Scarce any one regicide or traitor has been brought to public justice since your Majesty's blessed return whom either the pulpit has not canonised or the press recommended to be a patriot or a martyr' (Hill 1984: 75). Dying at a public execution was usually before large crowds and in the seventeenth century it was increasingly being widely reported elsewhere in the developing media. It was important for a traitor or a regicide to die bravely: gushing outbursts of contrition on the scaffold hardly reflected well on the cause for which one was being required to die.

The most eminent of the regicides and the man associated with both the Civil War and the period of republicanism was the Lord Protector, Oliver Cromwell, although he had died in September 1658 nearly two years before the restoration of the monarchy. Historians have long argued about the causes of Cromwell's death. At the time their explanations included ague and pneumonia although some modern medical historians assessing what is known of his symptoms contend that the cause of death was pyelonephritis (inflammation of the kidneys and renal pelvis) resulting in uraemia, complications with a vesical (bladder) stone and tertiary malaria. A recent view suggests that Cromwell was poisoned by his physician Dr Bate who was part of a plot to restore the throne to the Stuarts (MacMains 1999). Cromwell was seen at the time as instrumental in the act of regicide and despite his earlier death, it was felt that along with other leading regicides, revenge should be extracted on 30 January 1661, the anniversary of the death of Charles I.

Almost twelve years after the execution of King Charles, the exhumed bodies of the regicides Oliver Cromwell, Henry Ireton who was his son-in-law and John Bradshaw, the judge at the King's trial, were brought to the Red Lion at Holborn to rest overnight on their way to Tyburn. John Lewis, a mason, is said to have been paid 15s to carry out the exhumations. Some writers, including Howard MacMains, support the view that Cromwell's remains were in such an awful condition that they were secretly interred in Red Lion Square, possibly with the collusion of the poets John Milton and Andrew Marvell. MacMains believes that the corpse identified as that of Cromwell at the Tyburn gallows was actually that of an ordinary soldier. If this theory is correct then it throws doubt on the idea that the head that was buried in 1960 at Sidney Sussex College, Cambridge, was actually that of Cromwell.

On 30 January 1661 a fast was declared to commemorate the execution of Charles I. The crowds that turned out to rejoice at the restoration of the monarchy would doubtless have contained many who had cheered Cromwell on his triumphal way only a few years before.

That this was likely to happen was obvious to Cromwell himself, who earlier had prophetically declared that what were then adulatory republican crowds would even more readily turn out for his execution. At approximately ten in the morning of the fast, the three bodies were publicly hanged on the 'Triple Tree' at Tyburn and displayed until sundown when they were cut down, decapitated and, according to some accounts, thrown into a nearby pit. The *Mercurius Publicus* for 31 January to 7 February recorded that the day (30 January) was observed not only by the fast but also by the 'public dragging of those odious carcasses'. The *Mercurius* added that the carcasses were taken from their coffins and placed 'at several angles of that triple tree where they hanged till the sun was set'. Later that day, according to this account, the bodies were flung into a pit beneath the gallows at Tyburn. Cromwell and Ireton had been embalmed but Bradshaw's body was in a grisly state evident from the green seepage passing through his white funeral cloth. Another account tells us that Cromwell was covered in a green cloth and looked very freshly embalmed and Ireton, who had been buried since 1651, was hung like a 'dried rat'. One description spoke of Bradshaw's body casting 'a most odious scent all the way it went' (Pearson and Morant 1935: 45–6). In addition to the indignities heaped on the mortal remains of these three men, the bodies of Admiral Blake and John Pym, a leading Parliamentarian spokesman between 1640 and 1643, were removed from Westminster Abbey and thrown into a pit nearby.

Although the actual site of the Tyburn gallows is disputed, Connaught Place at the southern end of Edgware Road is thought by some to be its location and there have long been rumours that Cromwell's ghost haunts the house and garden of 1 Connaught Place. During rebuilding of the area in 1820, large numbers of human remains were discovered there.

Many found reason to celebrate or justify Cromwell's fate in 1661. George Fox, founder of the Quakers, was one of the many radicals who felt betrayed by Cromwell. He stated in his *Journal* that before the battle of Dunbar in 1650 Cromwell had 'promised to the Lord that if he gave him victory over his enemies he would take away tithes'. The abolition of tithes had been a consistent demand of many radicals. Clearly Cromwell did not stick to his promise and Fox writes that they 'took him up and hanged and buried him under Tyburn, where he was rolled into his grave with infamy . . . I saw his words justly come upon him'. The modern song of Tyburn Fair also comments on the bones of Cromwell at Tyburn:

> To Tyburn Fair
> On a Saturday
> Across the road a beam of wood.
> The bones of Cromwell
> Dangle in the fog,
> The Maid of Kent last stood
> At Tyburn Fair . . .

Despite the many and varied theories as to what really happened to Cromwell's body, it is likely that his eventual resting place was indeed a pit near to the gallows, a fate similar to that of many much less illustrious victims of 'Tyburn Tree'. A.J. Beresford who lived at the south-west corner of Edgware Road wrote to *The Times* on 9 May 1860 commenting on the excavations that had taken place in the area and which had uncovered many human bones. He added his opinion that these were 'obviously the relics of unhappy persons who were buried under the gallows'.

Remnants of the radical forces and groups that had emerged in the previous decades persisted after 1660 even though it was no longer very advisable to declare beliefs in republicanism or Puritanism too loudly. The Fifth Monarchists were a millenarian group who had been active, particularly in London, during the 1650s and even had a number of representatives in the short-lived Barebones Parliament of 1653. They believed that the Second Coming of Christ was imminent and saw it as their duty to create the conditions out of which Christ would rule for a thousand years. Their reaction to the Restoration was marked by an outburst of protest which saw one of their supporters, John James, a coal trader, executed at Tyburn. It is clear that James evoked some sympathy at his execution as the sheriff and the hangman allowed him to die by hanging before they proceeded to disembowel and quarter him. His head was placed on London Bridge and then moved to Whitechapel (Cobbett 1809 vi: 67–120). Little was heard of the Fifth Monarchists after the death of James.

A last attempt to resurrect the Commonwealth failed in 1662 when four men were accused of plotting to capture the Tower and Whitehall Palace and to seize the King. Thomas Tonge, George Phillips, Francis Stubbs and Nathaniel Gibbs were drawn to Tyburn on 22 December and hanged, beheaded and quartered with their heads set on poles on Tower Hill.

Tyburn continued to receive many notorious thieves and a growing number of highwaymen during this period. One such was 'Sawney' Douglas, a Scotsman born at Portpatrick in Galloway. Having served many years in the army, after the Restoration he took to highway robbery. His robberies were perpetrated over a very wide area but ended when his attempt to rob the Earl of Sandwich failed and he was arrested, tried, sentenced to death and housed in Newgate awaiting the next hanging day at Tyburn. The *Newgate Calendar*, a publication by no means averse to embroidering details, related that at St Sepulchre's on 10 September 1664, 'Sawney' shouted at the crowd that he would rather be hanged twice over without ceremony than once after this superstitious manner. He refused the Prayer Book but rather curiously carried *The Ballad of Chevy Chase* in his hand all the way to Tyburn. When he arrived at Tyburn, he ignored the clergyman and told the hangman to be speedy. At the age of fifty-three – old for a highwayman – 'Sawney' Douglas was duly hanged and buried close by.

Restoration London is strongly associated with death and destruction. While London was no stranger to visitations of plague, in 1665 an outbreak of unprecedented virulence occurred which started in the parish of St Giles-in-the-Fields, associated with Tyburn as a stopping place for prisoners on their way to the gallows. London was reeling from the horrors of plague when a devastating fire broke out which destroyed much of the City including eighty-seven churches as well as St Paul's Cathedral and over thirteen

Sir William de Marisco being drawn to the gallows in 1242. After being hauled through the dust and dirt and jolted over every rut, arrival at Tyburn must have come as something of a relief. *(Master and Fellows of Corpus Christi College, Cambridge/The Conway Library, Courtauld Institute of Art)*

Part of a map of London from 1607 showing the Tyburn stream flowing southwards to the Thames. Note the representation of Tyburn's Triple Tree to the east of Hyde Park.

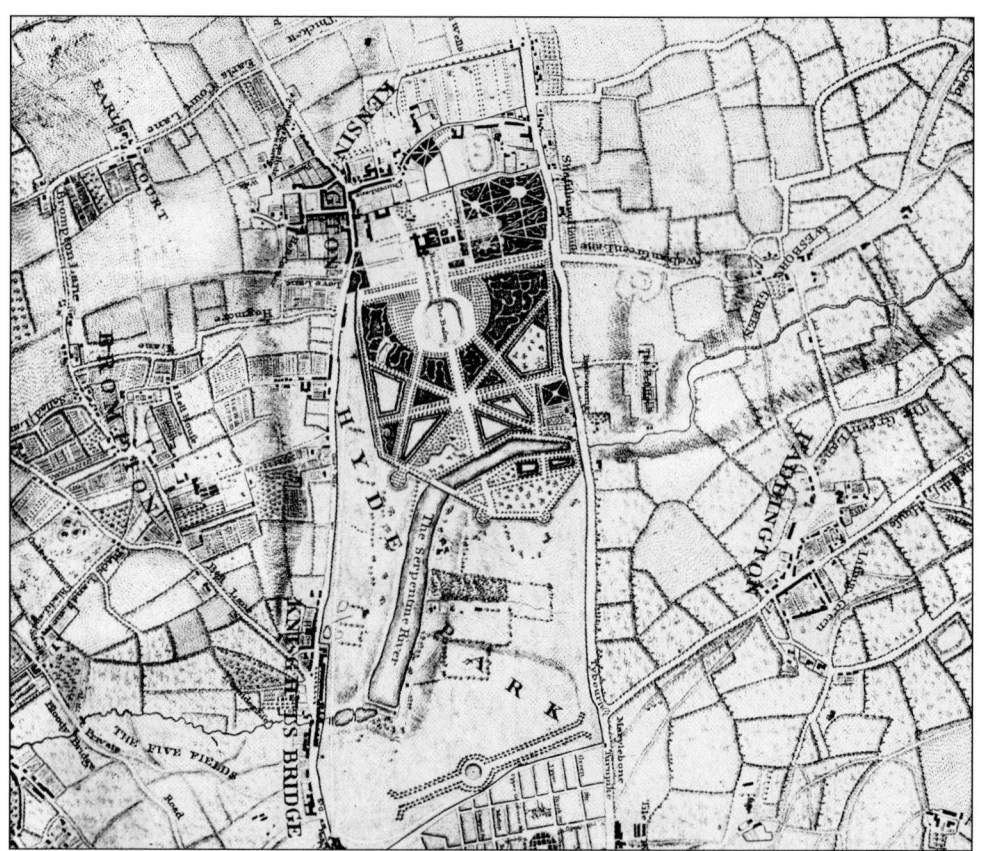

The Tyburn district in the 1740s. The gallows was close to the north-east corner of Hyde Park at the junction of what we know as Park Lane, Oxford Street, Edgware Road and Bayswater Road. *(Royal Borough of Kensington and Chelsea Library, London/Bridgeman Art Library)*

Beheadings with the sword were usually reserved for the high-born – a clear case of rank having its privileges. A sizeable crowd has been drawn to witness this spectacle. *(British Library/HIP/Topham Picturepoint)*

Executions taking place in Tudor times, probably in London but not necessarily at Tyburn. Only the person being hanged has the benefit of an audience. Note the man bustling away with a basketful of severed limbs.

The death at the stake of Robert Barns and others for their religious beliefs. The idea was that the victims were part-strangled and lost consciousness before the flames reached them. *(Bridgeman Art Library)*

Henrietta Maria, wife of Charles I, offering prayers at Tyburn for the Catholic martyrs who died there in the sixteenth century. This act aroused controversy because of fears that Catholicism might be restored as the official religion of England. *(Mary Evans Picture Library)*

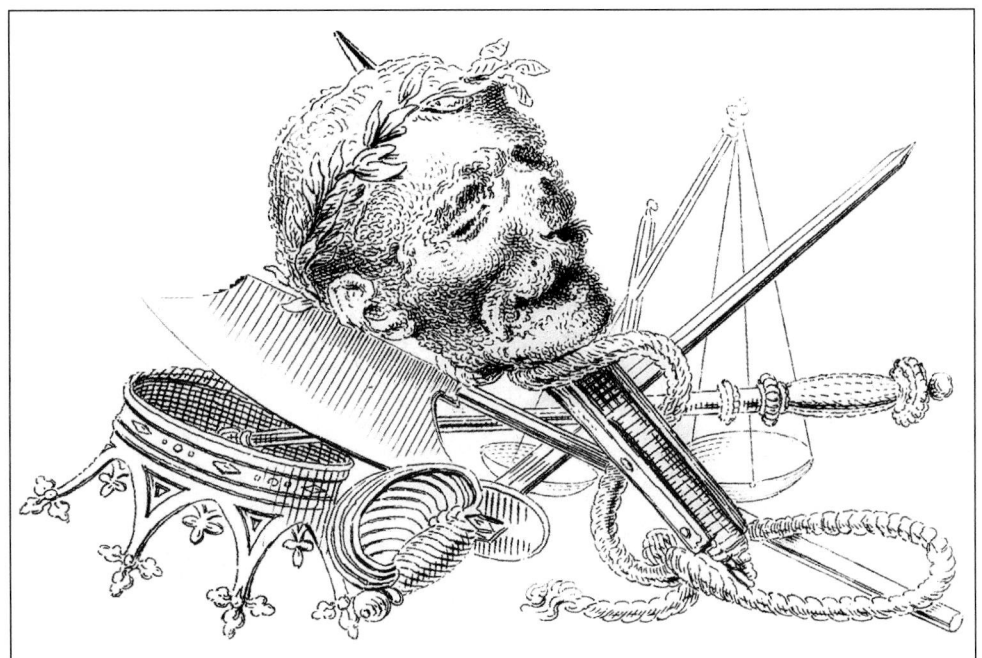

A mocking representation of Oliver Cromwell's severed head. The whereabouts of the head remains one of history's enigmas. *(Guildhall Library, Corporation of London)*

THE

Tyburn-Ghoſt:

OR,

The Strange DOWNFALL

OF THE

GALLOWS.

A moſt true RELATION

How the famous

TRIPLE-TREE

Neer *PADDINGTON*.

Was on Tueſday-night laſt (the third of this inſtant *September*) wonderfully pluckt up by the Roots, and demoliſht by certain EVIL-SPIRITS.

To which is added,

Squire *Ketch's* LAMENTATION

for the loſs of his Shop, &c.

With Allowance.

LONDON: Printed for *L.C.* 1678.

The front of a broadsheet sold in response to the curious destruction of the Tyburn gallows in 1678.

The Triple Tree at Tyburn, *c.* 1680. A maximum of eight prisoners could be executed on each 'branch'. Note the 'javelin men' on the right who guarded the prisoners en route from Newgate and at Tyburn itself.

On a trumped-up accusation by Titus Oates, Edward Coleman is drawn to Tyburn to be executed for his alleged part in a supposed Popish Plot; with him is Jack Ketch the executioner. *(Mary Evans Picture Library)*

Crowds gather to watch a hanging at Tyburn in 1696. The Triple Tree and cart used for hanging can be seen in the centre, while in the background to the left a drawing and quartering is being undertaken. The image erroneously shows London Bridge, the Thames and the City to be immediately opposite Tyburn. *(Corporation of London/HIP/Topham Picturepoint)*

A street brawl in seventeenth-century London. Although scraps on this scale were not everyday events, the streets of London were crowded, dirty, violent and dangerous.

The Enraged Musician, by William Hogarth, 1741. Here Hogarth emphasises the bawdiness and the cacophony that filled the streets of London. As well as the more obvious sources of noise, note the howling cats on the roof and the flag by the spire which indicates that bell-ringing is about to take place. *(Mary Evans Picture Library)*

The *Idle 'Prentice* hanged at Tyburn 1747. Hogarth provides us with probably the best representation of the scene at Tyburn as the crowds prepare for a hanging amid scenes of robust and bawdy revelry. *(Mary Evans Picture Library)*

hundred houses. Tyburn, still a rural spot west of the City, was untouched directly but it did claim a victim or, more appropriately, a scapegoat for the starting of the fire.

Many Londoners believed that Catholics, in league with the French, were responsible for starting the Great Fire. Robert Hubert, a French silversmith and watchmaker, became a convenient scapegoat when he confessed to starting the fire. It is difficult to accept that the judges at the Old Bailey believed Hubert was guilty but they sentenced him to be hanged at Tyburn. A curious twist came about a month after the Great Fire. The famous astrologer William Lilly was ordered to appear in the Speaker's Chamber of the House of Commons to give testimony before the special committee which was set up to examine the cause of the fire. It was claimed that Lilly had predicted its outbreak over a year before. Lilly persuaded the committee that there was nothing sinister in this prediction and that it had never been meant to be precise. He was allowed to go free and the unfortunate Hubert alone bore the brunt of London's cry for vengeance. However, the execution of a scapegoat did not silence rumours and anti-Catholic hysteria continued. 'Priests and Jesuits' were ordered to leave the kingdom or face penal sanctions. When further fires broke out in 1676, Catholics were suspected of starting them. In 1671 the Monument was erected to commemorate the Great Fire and it bore an inscription explaining that the fire was begun and carried on by the treachery and malice of the Catholics.

When it became clear that the Duke of York, the future James II, had become a Catholic by 1673, the spectre of 'popery' again became a real threat and a major issue in domestic politics. Various attempts to exclude James from the succession all failed and he became King in 1685. Three years later, in 1688, James was in exile in France and his nephew and son-in-law William of Orange succeeded to the throne as William III. In December 1688, London witnessed increasing disorder. The atmosphere was highly charged and anti-papal sermons, propaganda and rumour contributed to unsettle the population. The execution of six Catholics at Tyburn in September 1690 saw the condemned defiantly drinking the health of King James and making an appeal to the crowd to support his return.

Anti-Catholicism needed little encouragement and in 1678 another outbreak of hysteria had occurred as the result of rumours of a Popish Plot. At the centre of the rumour was Titus Oates (1649–1705), an Anglican priest and liar and perjurer of quite monumental proportions. With Israel Tonge he invented the story of the Popish Plot which involved a Jesuit-led plan to assassinate Charles II thereby hastening the accession of his fervently Catholic brother James. This story was a total fabrication. It was revealed first by Oates and Tonge to the magistrate for Westminster, Sir Edmund Berry Godfrey. When he died under mysterious circumstances shortly afterwards, many people were all too ready to conclude that the plot had begun. Catholics were always the prime target for popular retribution and three innocent Catholic men, Robert Green, Lawrence Hill and Henry Berry were framed, convicted and subsequently hanged at Tyburn in February 1679. Also implicated was William Staley, a banker and goldsmith, who was executed at Tyburn in 1678. His friends and relatives had pleaded that his body be given decent burial. His funeral service was held at St Paul's Church in Covent Garden but the King was said to be so angry at hearing the singing of the Masses and the funeral display of grief that he ordered the opening of Staley's coffin. The corpse was removed and dismembered and the quarters displayed on the City gates and the head on London Bridge. Staley's head was said to be the last to have been exposed there (Pierce 2001: 223).

These events sparked another wave of anti-Catholic hysteria and persecution with some thirty-five innocent people executed and hundreds of others suffering as a result of the perjured evidence of Oates and Tonge. Several more innocent men died at Tyburn including Edward Coleman, William Ireland, John Grove, Thomas Whitebread, John Fenwick and John Gavan. Some of those who went to the scaffold over this sorry affair suffered the aggravated punishment of having their genitals cut off. Public opinion can be capricious and Oates, who at one moment was hailed as a great patriot and saviour of the nation, later found himself convicted of perjury.

He was now reviled and fined, flogged and imprisoned. He was later imprisoned for life but the sentence was then changed to the very curious one of having to stand in the pillory five times a year at Tyburn, Westminster, Charing Cross, Temple Bar and the Royal Exchange. In June 1689 in an attempt to close the whole episode the King granted Oates an ill-warranted free pardon.

Removal of the genitalia had earlier been decreed for those convicted of treason in the Gunpowder Plot in 1605. The judges' verdict in Cobbett's *State Trials* gives an interesting explanation of the process of drawing, hanging and quartering which, as we have seen, was frequently applied to wretches who died at Tyburn. It states that the traitor:

> Must be drawn with his Head declining downward, and lying so near the Ground as may be, being thought unfit to take benefit of the common Air. For which Cause also he shall be strangled, being hanged up by the Neck between Heaven and Earth, as deemed unworthy of both, or either; as likewise, that the Eyes of Men may behold, and their Hearts condemn him. Then he is to be cut down alive, and to have his Privy Parts cut off and burnt before his Face, as being unworthily begotten, and unfit to leave any Generation after him. His Bowels and inlay'd Parts taken out and burnt, who inwardly had conceived and harboured in his heart such horrible Treason. After, to have his Head cut off, which had imagined the Mischief. And lastly, his Body to be quartered, and the Quarters set up in some high and eminent Place, to the View and Detestation of Men, and to become a Prey for the Fowls of the Air.
>
> (Cobbett 1809: ii. 184)

On 1 July 1681, Oliver Plunkett the Catholic Primate of Ireland met his fate at Tyburn. Over a decade earlier, in 1669, Pope Clement IX had promoted him to the see of Armagh. For most of his time Plunkett was forced to conduct his business in secret and hide in various places because Catholicism was then outlawed in Ireland. Plunkett was accused of being in league with the French government and of plotting to aid a French invasion of Ireland. He was arrested on 6 December 1679 and appeared six months later at a court at Dundalk where even the predominantly Protestant jury failed to convict him. By October 1680 he had been brought to Newgate where he suffered from kidney stones and eye infections as a consequence of the appalling conditions in which he was housed. Plunkett was accused of soliciting the invasion of Ireland by the French and of taking money from the Irish clergy for that purpose. Additionally, he was alleged to have incited the landlords of the north to take up arms to retrieve their confiscated estates. Plunkett was found guilty of treason and sentenced to death. He was sentenced to be drawn, hanged, disembowelled and quartered. His head was saved by friends and is preserved in the Catholic church of St Peter in Drogheda.

Rumours and plots were nurtured within the culture of the coffee houses and publicised by the newspapers which enjoyed increasing popularity and circulation in the latter half of the seventeenth century. These helped to develop a climate of opinion in favour of William on religious and political rather than personal grounds for he was not the kind of sovereign who would ever enjoy popular acclaim. In 1695 censorship ended and an even greater number of periodicals appeared on the market and helped to shape a new, popular reading public. The development of new media of communication and the spread of literacy enabled governments to play a more active role in moulding public opinion.

A curious incident occurred in July 1685 when Thomas Dangerfield, one of the informers associated with Titus Oates, was brought to trial and, like Oates, was sentenced to be whipped in the pillory. On the way back from Tyburn, Dangerfield who, rather unusually, was travelling in a coach, was jeered at by an onlooker, a Tory barrister by the name of Robert Francis. Dangerfield responded by insulting Francis who then stuck his cane in Dangerfield's face. Somehow the stick pierced his brain and he died the next day. Francis was found guilty of murder and was executed at Tyburn.

In 1670 Tyburn saw the execution of Claude Duval. This man was the very stuff of which legends about handsome, gallant highwaymen were made. Born in Normandy in 1643 of humble parentage, as a youth he had drifted to Paris where he made the acquaintance of English Royalist exiles ruefully licking their wounds over events back home and waiting to return when conditions became more propitious. In 1660 Charles II ascended the throne and this was a signal for these exiles to come back to England's shores. Duval came with them. Not for him a life of honest graft. The well-off wanted to flaunt their wealth after the drab austerity of the Interregnum and Duval soon found rich pickings from highway robbery for which he seems to have had a natural flair. He developed a reputation for the daring with which he carried out his robberies and for his Gallic good looks, of which he made good use in his encounters with female travellers. Credited with a host of female conquests, his reputation grew every time stories were told about him. With the incentive of a price on his head he was captured lying in a drunken stupor in a London tavern. He was convicted and sentenced to death. Although numerous women are reported to have attempted to intercede on his behalf, he was hanged at Tyburn aged just twenty-seven. A stone in the centre aisle of St Paul's Church, Covent Garden, carries a eulogistic epitaph over his remains although some claim that he is buried at St Giles-in-the-Fields, Holborn.

In 1678 much interest and speculation about supernatural interference were aroused when the gallows at Tyburn were uprooted one night and left in pieces on the ground. Without difficulty witnesses were found who solemnly declared that they had seen ghosts – undoubtedly those of some of Tyburn's past victims – squatting on the gallows and screeching before demolishing the structure. Others averred that it had been taken down by a company of quack doctors who had planned to remove it and use its magical properties in their patent medicines, but they had been disturbed and forced to leave the pieces on the ground. The mystery was never satisfactorily explained. As a result of this event a new triangular gallows was erected which claimed its first victims, three women and two men, on Friday 6 September 1678 (*The Confession . . . 1678*).

Around the late 1670s a broadside called *The Plotters Ballad* made the first reference to the infamous hangman Jack Ketch who often presided at Tyburn. The broadside talked of the 'Receipt for the Cure of Traytrous Recusants, or Wholesome Physicke for Popish Contagion' and included a woodcut showing Edward Coleman drawn on a hurdle to his execution at Tyburn in December 1678. Coleman is depicted as saying, 'I am sick of a traitorous disease'. Ketch is holding an axe in one hand and a rope in the other and exclaiming, 'Here's your cure sir' (Laurence 1932: 96). Richard Jacquett or John Catch became better known as Jack Ketch and his reputation is based on the generic use of his name for the executioners who followed him as well as on the Punch and Judy character inveigled into hanging himself by Mr Punch.

The procession of the largely unknown to Tyburn continued throughout these years. One little-known victim was Robert Foulkes who was hanged in 1679 for the murder of his new-born baby. Foulkes was a minister of the Church from Stanton Lacy in Shropshire. He was married with two children and had attempted to conceal the pregnancy which resulted from an extra-marital affair. Foulkes went clandestinely to London with the young woman and took lodgings in the Strand, murdering the baby when it was born. The *Newgate Calendar* states that some women of the neighbourhood became suspicious and began to question the girl who eventually confessed what had happened. Foulkes was charged with murder, committed to Newgate and taken thence to Tyburn on 31 January 1679.

There was a marked increase in prosecutions for infanticide at this time. In 1624 the Act to Prevent the Murdering of Bastard Children required the defendant to prove innocence rather than the prosecution to prove guilt. For a young girl to become pregnant could be a disaster especially if she worked in an occupation where she needed to be single, such as domestic service or prostitution. Women employed in domestic service were especially vulnerable to sexual advances by their masters and other males in the household. Peter Linebaugh has shown that between 1703 and 1772, of the women who died at Tyburn, 12 per cent were hanged for infanticide and a large number of them were domestic servants. As he states, the common themes of the women involved were poverty, loss of employment and irreligion (Linebaugh 1993: 148–9).

There were many victims of poverty who resorted to crime such as Mary 'Moll' Jones who was born in Chancery Lane where her parents lived in permanent debt and she worked as a hood-maker. Mary married an apprentice for whom she had a great love but he was so extravagant that Mary resorted to picking pockets in order to survive. She was caught stealing from Jacob Delafay who was a chocolate-maker to James II and William III. For her crime she was committed to Newgate and there received the common punishment for thieves of being branded on the hand. Although released, she turned to shoplifting for a further four years before being caught and branded once more. Mary was eventually executed for stealing a piece of satin from a shop on Ludgate Hill. She was hanged at Tyburn at the age of twenty-five on 18 December 1691.

The story of Mary Jones is a pathetic one of a downward spiral of deprivation and despair leading to crime, punishment and eventual hanging and it is one that can be replicated in the case of any number of other seemingly petty offenders who ended up as victims of the 'Triple Tree'. However, there were cases which saw justice done and the death penalty meted out to offenders whose activities were an affront to society. On 22 February 1681, Captain Richard Dudley was executed at Tyburn and it is hard to have much sympathy for the plight in which he found himself. He had obtained a captain's commission in a regiment of foot. One day he was inspecting the troops on parade when he noticed that one soldier was standing out of line. Dudley instructed his sergeant to strike the man. The sergeant obeyed, but not forcefully enough as far as Dudley was concerned. To show what he had meant, he grabbed a halberd and brought it down on the trooper's head, killing him instantly. This incident meant that Dudley was forced to leave the army and take to highway robbery. He had a longer career on the road than many but was finally arrested and paid the price at Tyburn.

The golden age of the highwayman was almost certainly the century or so after 1660 and many of these robbers found their way to Tyburn. Some were invested with an aura of romance and chivalry and others were popular because they had robbed the rich and powerful who in many cases hid peculation and graft behind their respectable public personas.

On 5 July 1691 Thomas Sadler was executed at Tyburn. A scapegrace and recidivist, Sadler had tried his hand at highway robbery but what proved to be his last crime, carried out with the help of two accomplices, involved stealing the Lord Chancellor's mace and official purse. In a symbolic parody, Sadler walked across Lincoln's Inn Fields with one of his colleagues in front of him parading the mace and the other behind acting the role of purse bearer. Officialdom was not amused by this burlesque and Sadler and his accomplices were arrested. To his credit, Sadler pleaded most forcefully that they were innocent and one was reprieved.

In 1669 Stephen Eaton, a confectioner, George Roades, described as a 'broker', and Sarah Swift were executed for the murder of the Revd John Talbot. A gang attacked Talbot and stole about 20s and a knife with which they attempted to kill him by cutting his throat. They botched this and so they stabbed him in the chest. The noise of this unseemly fracas roused the local dogs and neighbours soon emerged to find Talbot lying bleeding and seriously injured in the street. He was carried to the Star Inn in Shoreditch. The suspected assailants were quickly caught. Talbot died of his injuries shortly afterwards but not before he had identified three of his attackers. They were conveyed in a cart to Tyburn where they were executed on 14 July. They could not plead poverty or circumstances as a defence for what was a very squalid crime.

The *Newgate Calendar* records the almost unbelievable story of Mary Carleton who claimed to be a German aristocrat by the name of Princess von Wolway. In reality she was the daughter of a chorister at Canterbury Cathedral. She had been in Cologne between her second and third marriages to accept a proposal of matrimony from an old and wealthy German whom she then proceeded to rob and from whom she perhaps gained the inspiration for her outrageous name. She fled Germany and returned to England where she met John Carleton who believed her story of misfortune and from whom she managed to extract some more money. Mary was footloose and she set out again on the road to use her natural charms and to swindle more men. Her exploits were the stuff of Restoration comedy. She was arrested for theft but discharged whereupon she married a wealthy apothecary whom she robbed of over £300, for which she was arrested in January 1673. Continuing offences meant that her luck ran out and she was eventually arrested once too often, tried and sentenced to death. Her attempt to 'plead her belly' on the grounds that she was pregnant did not gain her a reprieve. On 22 January with a picture of her husband pinned to her sleeve, she rode in the cart to Tyburn. When she arrived, she told the people there that she had been a very vain woman and deserved punishment for her sins. She was thirty-eight years of age when she died.

In 1683 a conspiracy to assassinate Charles II failed, following which a number of men were arrested and executed. This was the Rye House Plot for which in July 1683 Thomas Walcott, William Hone and John Rouse were drawn to Tyburn as traitors and hanged and quartered. Another of those involved, Lord William Russell, was executed in Lincoln's Inn Fields. A fifth conspirator, Sir Thomas Armstrong, escaped to Holland but was captured in 1684. He also made the journey on a hurdle to Tyburn. He swung for about half an hour before being taken down and quartered. Another conspirator, James Burton, also escaped to Holland but became involved in the Monmouth Rebellion of 1685. This was an attempt by one of Charles II's natural sons, the Protestant James Scott, Duke of Monmouth, to wrest the throne from the Catholic James II. When the Rebellion was defeated, Burton got away and sought refuge in London where he was sheltered by his wife, his neighbour and a woman who had given him shelter previously, Elizabeth Gaunt. In order to save his neck, Burton rather ungratefully betrayed these people by testifying against them. They died at Tyburn on 23 October 1685. Elizabeth made a minor contribution to history. Her courage won the sympathy of the crowd and she was the last woman to be burnt for high treason.

Anti-Catholicism was still very much an issue at this time and was reflected in the execution for treason at Tyburn on 30 April 1684 of James Holloway. A dissident Bristol merchant and manufacturer, he was enraged by the election of Catholic Tory sheriffs in London and became involved in a planned uprising in the city in the summer of 1682. The plan was discovered in May 1683 and Holloway went on the run, firstly in disguise in the West Country and then, with the aid of his wife, he got away to France and later the West Indies. He was betrayed and brought back to England in chains and delivered a confession which was not believed. Holloway was convinced that he would be pardoned but the case went before Chief Justice Jeffreys who peremptorily ordered his execution for treason.

A last-minute reprieve was the desperate hope of many who took the route to Tyburn, there to have the noose placed around their necks. Visiting an execution in 1664, Pepys recorded that the condemned frequently delayed the fatal moment by engaging in long discourses and prayers in the hope of a reprieve or pardon. Thomas Laqueur has commented on the significance of pardons suggesting that they were part of an elaborate system of patronage and control and were a reminder of the King's power and his gratuitous gift of life (Laqueur 1989).

There were cases of a reprieve arriving quite literally at the last minute. Jonathan Simpson was an apprentice to a linen draper in Bristol. He moved to London where he set up a business but his marriage broke up, the business failed and he took to highway robbery. Within a short time he was caught but rich relations came to his rescue and managed to get him a reprieve just as he was about to hang at Tyburn. On his return to Newgate the gaoler refused to let him back because he was discharged, a free man unless a fresh warrant for his committal could be produced. Simpson pushed his luck and went back to his life of crime on the road, carrying out around forty robberies in Middlesex within six weeks of his discharge. His career came to its inevitable conclusion at Tyburn on 8 September 1686 when he was aged thirty-two. Simpson, incidentally, had earlier carved out a little niche for himself in the history of robbery by being the only recorded highwayman on skates! The winter of 1683–4 was exceptionally cold and pickings on the roads were poor because few people were travelling. The River Thames in London, however, was frozen for about two months and thousands thronged to the 'Frost Fair' and enjoyed the novel experience of standing on the river and seeing familiar landmarks from a different angle. Simpson equipped himself with skates and enjoyed rich pickings by simply bumping into people, knocking them over and robbing them in the ensuing confusion.

Changes in the power of granting pardons took place after the Glorious Revolution of 1688. As the old structures of religion and monarchy began to loosen their grip, the cabinet took greater responsibility for managing capital punishment at Tyburn by making pardons less a matter of arbitrary decision-making by the monarch. This reflected a style of governance more suited to the constitutional monarchy after 1688 as well as a change in the way power was exercised and managed (Beattie 1992: 218–33). Crime statistics for London and Middlesex between 1701 and 1785 show that out of 3,617 people condemned to death, 1,243 were actually executed; the rest were either pardoned, transported or died in gaol (Gatrell 1994: 616).

Deterring sexual immorality became the object of many seventeenth-century initiatives and was reflected in Acts attempting to regulate adultery and bastardy as well as campaigns for the reforming of manners. The Reformation of Manners campaigns witnessed the prosecution of thousands of people found guilty of 'lewd and disorderly conduct'. Homosexual practices carried the death sentence but records show that they were only rarely punished. It was crimes against property that took on a new dimension during this period. As property grew so did concerns about its preservation with a resulting proliferation in property-related offences.

Society was undergoing a process of secularisation and this is reflected in the last speeches made by condemned prisoners. These now made less reference to regret for having disobeyed divine law. By the eighteenth century those executed at Tyburn were expected to make a speech which involved commenting on a 'just end' for sins committed rather than showing religious penitence. The issue of repentance is seen in illustrations in the earlier popular ballads where images of Death and Judgment Day feature in a terrifying form. In the Elizabethan ballad 'The Doleful Dance and Song of

Death', Death is personified as a skeleton with trumpet and spade beckoning the lover, lawyer and merchant. Another ballad, 'The Great Assize', which is about Judgment Day, describes Satan waiting in the flames of Hell (Reay 1988: 219). Satan would also be described encouraging people to commit crimes in order to hasten their journey to the gallows or avenging angels would be portrayed sitting in judgment on those who had committed an offence.

The rituals leading up to and including the execution itself continued, as did the presence of large crowds around the gallows and along the route to Tyburn. Dying speeches, ballads and broadsides were hawked from Newgate to Tyburn and often contained lurid biographies of the condemned prisoners and a warning to those who bought them, not that they would incur the wrath of God but that they would die in the same painful and wretched fashion. Death on the scaffold at Tyburn was the price to pay not for irreligion but for the criminal acts which so often followed on a life of fecklessness, of drink and depravity. These doom-laden exhortations, however, did not lessen the festive mood of the crowds on execution days as the song Tyburn Fair makes clear:

> To Tyburn Fair
> I used to go,
> To watch the just procession,
> And eat the oranges
> The dead would throw,
> And hear their last confession.

The attempts of the state to stage-manage public executions to provide a warning of the awfulness of the law and the fate awaiting those who committed serious offences all too often foundered on the reality that the crowds who attended did so in an atmosphere sometimes resembling that of carnival. Some of the condemned turned the event into a special occasion by dressing for it. John Hall, the robber, said of some of the condemned 'that one would take them for bridegrooms going to espouse old Mrs Tyburn'. Henri Misson, a contemporary French observer, wrote:

> He that is to be hanged or otherwise executed first takes care to get himself . . . handsomely dressed. . . . When his suit of clothes, or night gown, his gloves, hat, periwig, nosegay, coffin, flannel dress for his corpse, and all those things are brought and prepared, the main point is taken care of, his mind is at peace and then he thinks of his conscience.
>
> (Waller 2000: 320–1)

Flamboyant and defiant displays on the way to and at the gallows provided just the kind of entertainment the crowds craved, but for all those who were able to carry off such bravado, there were far more who went to their deaths with numbed resignation or in a state of abject terror. Hypocrisy and pomposity on the gallows met with complete derision from the watching masses; prisoners who cursed the fates and lambasted the authorities were cheered and those who quipped humorously with the crowd drew forth approving laughter and good wishes. On occasions, however, the sight of a young prisoner sentenced to death for some trivial offence and totally, abjectly, convulsed with fear, might evoke a rough-and-ready but compassionate response from the onlookers. They wanted to provide some support for the last moments of those whom they considered the unjustified victims of a flawed judicial system. No sarcastic wisecracks were offered, no acerbic gibes were uttered. The gallows crowds on these occasions were hushed. Their demeanour was dignified and humane. A quiet gasp might be all that was heard when the awful deed was done.

In the seventeenth century, London's growing population added to the size of the crowds that turned out at Tyburn. It also meant a much larger pool of social deprivation and distress, new forms of crime, especially those related to property, and a heightened fear of criminality among the well-to-do. The government's response was to increase the number of capital offences. However, execution days took on an increasingly holiday spirit. They were in the strong tradition of festivity and misrule associated with carnivals and were the occasion for ribald humour, bawdy language and the subversion of authority through mockery and festive symbols such as wakes, dances, costumes, masks, processions and the composing of commemorative ballads. Mr Punch, the hunchbacked and bullying puppet of traditional English entertainment, represented one form of the carnival tradition. Punch expressed the mocking voice of the world turned upside down and an association with the scaffold in his subverting of the law by making the hangman, Jack Ketch, hang himself. The gallows crowd would also have been familiar with Mr Punch who, like some of the condemned prisoners on the scaffold, refused to accept the rules or to behave in a socially acceptable manner. His triumph over the hangman is expressed when he declares:

> I've done the trick!
> Jack Ketch is dead – I'm free.
> I do not care now, if Old Nick
> Himself should come for me.

Carnival or what might be called aspects of carnival – the carnivalesque – provided an opportunity to break away for a short time from the everyday demands and drudgery of ordinary life. Because of this, Tyburn Fair was an event deeply etched into the popular culture of London's citizens.

Public executions attracted the largest crowds of any public event and many people saw a hanging as a major social occasion to be attended in the company of friends and relations. The authorities intended the hanging to be a visible and spectacular warning, a deterrent, but it could be said that the public appropriated it and used it for their own purposes. During the early modern period a national and local calendar of events and festivals was still celebrated. These occasions can be found in almanacs of the period and most English county towns had days set aside for public executions which often coincided with fairs and festivities of various sorts. By the eighteenth century centralising forces were attempting to develop a sense of nationhood and a national political consensus. Carnivals, fairs, popular games and festivals were seen as undesirable throwbacks to earlier times and were 'politicised'. They became more closely controlled in an attempt to reduce their demotic and anarchic elements. Over the next century and a half, many of them were done away with altogether. Tyburn's removal in 1783 and the relocation of its functions outside Newgate on a more easily controlled site were part of that process as was the eventual ending of public executions altogether. The removal of the Tyburn spectacle represents the view that the 'history of political struggle has been the history of the attempts made to control significant sites of assembly' (Stallybrass and White 1986: 80). So the festive calendar was seen in official circles as too disruptive, too frivolous and also too likely to degenerate into a riot. The London middle class found alternatives to the Tyburn spectacle in the more rational enjoyments offered by the coffee houses and the spas.

However, as Alexander Pope (1688–1744) observed, hanging days still attracted crowds of both the 'high' and the 'low':

> A motley mixture in long wigs, in bags,
> In silks, crepes, in Garters and in rags,
> From drawing rooms, from colleges, from garrets,
> On horse, on foot, in hacks and gilded chariots.

The gallows crowd was traditionally cosmopolitan but in the eighteenth century there was an increasing tendency for those who considered themselves refined to stay away from Tyburn, whose gruesome spectacle did not accord with the evolving sophisticated culture of Augustan London. While writers such as Boswell wrote despairingly of the 'most prodigious crowd of spectators' at Tyburn and of how he was 'most terribly shocked and thrown into a very deep melancholy' by the whole scene, similar comments could as easily have been made about other places used for public pleasure. An eighteenth-century writer describes the disgusting environment of an alehouse: 'The vile obscene talk, noise and ribaldry discourses together with . . . belchings and breakings of wind . . . are enough to make any rational creature amongst them ashamed of his being' (Stallybrass and White 1986: 94).

The theatre came in for similar criticisms. In the 1690s, Jeremy Collier's *Short View of the Immorality and Profaneness of the English*

Stage attacked both the plays and the audiences for their blasphemy, impiety, indecency and riotous behaviour. The ancient annual Bartholomew Fair was greatly cut down in duration in the mid-eighteenth century but not before an observer had written about the 'fools, the drunkards, the madmen, the monsters, the pickpockets' and the various examples of 'lewdness and impurity' that were its presiding characteristics (Stallybrass and White 1986: 118).

The seventeenth century witnessed the last official hanging of a witch and the last burning of a heretic. It also saw what has been described as the 'emergence of the poor as an institutionalised presence' (Sharpe 1984: 183). It was a century of paradox. Many aspects of pre-industrial England were excised and new orthodoxies relevant to a different society were put into place, one of which was the absolute sanctity of private property. A start was made on creating an extensive raft of new laws designed to inflict severe penalties on thieves and robbers – those who attacked private property. A superficially more rational and enlightened attitude towards crime and methods of punishment contrasted with the development of what at first looks like a draconian penal code which threatened to overawe the masses by publicly hanging substantial numbers of its poorest, most desperate citizens simply for the crime of stealing. The so-called 'Bloody Code' however, as we shall see, was not always applied according to the letter of the law. Certainly Tyburn continued to be the place where many of London's miscreants ended their often miserable lives. In practice, the courts employed some compassion and humanity to try to ensure that not all those who committed capital offences paid the ultimate price on the 'Deadly Nevergreen'.

SEVEN

London Street Life in the Eighteenth Century

Many of those who died at Tyburn in the eighteenth century were residents, even if only recent ones, of the capital. What sights, sounds and smells assailed those living in London in this period and what were the various hazards to which the people passing through its streets might find themselves subjected? London was like a living organism and as such was dynamic and ever-changing. The last hangings at Tyburn took place in 1783. What factors had affected changes in crime and the ways in which it was dealt with in this period?

In 1700 England's population was around 5 million. Most people lived in the countryside and obtained their livelihood from agricultural activity. Something like 550,000 people lived in London in 1700. This number rose rapidly throughout the eighteenth century and constituted about one-tenth of the total population of England. During the century London's population grew largely because of inward migration. Its dominance over the rest of the kingdom is shown by the fact that Norwich, the second largest city in 1700, is estimated to have had a population of less than 30,000.

The eighteenth century did not get off to a propitious start when, in November 1703, London suffered the greatest storm on record. This appalling storm lasted nine hours without abating. During the night, many ships on the Thames were driven from their moorings and wrecked on the banks of the river; barges were driven against the arches of London Bridge and reduced to matchwood; four hundred watermen's wherries sank or were likewise smashed to smithereens. Two thousand chimneys crashed through roofs or fell into the streets and yards below. Churches lost their spires while

103

houses lost their roofs. Numerous buildings collapsed. Many of those foolish enough to be on the streets in these turbulent conditions were killed by falling debris. Tragedy and disaster were never far away on the streets of London.

London in the early part of the eighteenth century had two main centres, the City and Westminster. The continuously built-up area strikes today's observer as small in extent but densely occupied and overcrowded. It was filthy, pestilential, noisy and vibrant with activity. The mansions of the rich were cheek-by-jowl with the slums of the poor. Narrow, ill-lit and poorly paved, the streets were awash with filth of every description. The ordure which coated London's streets was valued by the market gardeners who used it as fertiliser. As Liza Picard put it, 'It was a rich, glutinous mixture of animal manure, dead cats and dogs, ashes, straw and human excrement' (Picard 2000: 10). Drinking water was contaminated and could be lethal. The mortality rate was higher than it had been a century earlier. Only one in two children survived beyond the age of fifteen. Diseases such as tuberculosis and smallpox prospered in the overcrowded, insanitary conditions. Dark, sinister alleys led off into rookeries or 'sanctuaries' where the underworld of the metropolis planned its criminal activities, divided the spoils and lived, procreated, drank and died. Such areas were rarely penetrated by the forces of law and order. When they were, every hand was against them. Animals, many of them semi-feral, were everywhere, rooting through the rubbish and adding to the cacophony and confusion. London, especially to the eyes of a provincial visitor, would have seemed exciting, confusing and threatening.

By daytime, the streets presented a curiously mixed picture of luxury and dirt, bright colours and ingrained grime, riches and rags. Wealthy men and women dressed in luxuriant finery and showed off their opulent gilded coaches, the often gaudy liveries of their footmen and their black African pages. Eye-catching signs hung above the doors of shops, taverns and drinking places and also of many houses. The splashes of colour created by all these elements contrasted with the layers of dust or mud – depending on the time of the year – which encrusted the streets and lower parts of the buildings. They would also have contrasted with the drab and ragged appearance of those who shuffled listlessly through the streets with nowhere to go. Others, moving quickly and with more sense of purpose, bawled and hawked their wares from door to door or went about other pressing business. Many were thieves and robbers who obtained rich rewards for their efforts in the teeming, chaotic thoroughfares.

These streets, the dangers of which during daylight hours included recklessly driven horse-drawn vehicles and careless riders, pugnacious young bucks keen to espy an insult and demand a duel to restore honour, and closely pressed crowds containing highly-skilled robbers and pickpockets, became infinitely more hazardous during the hours of darkness. While lighting in the major streets improved considerably during the eighteenth century, William Hogarth in 'Night', the last part of his series *The Four Times of the Day*, published in 1738, gives a realistic impression of a street scene on a moonlit night in the Charing Cross district. It is Oak Apple Day, celebrating the Restoration of the Monarchy in 1660, and acorns and oak leaves can be seen decorating shop signs and the hats of passers-by. Hogarth depicts a narrow, crowded street in which the Salisbury stagecoach has overturned on hitting a celebratory bonfire lit, with scant consideration for others, right in the middle of the street. While its woebegone occupants try to extricate themselves from the wreckage, a drunken and confused freemason is being led home from his lodge by an attendant only to be soused by the contents of a chamber-pot which has been jettisoned with characteristic abandon from an upper window. Like so many of the characters that Hogarth uses in these works, the freemason can be identified as Colonel Thomas de Veil, a magistrate and freemason of whom Hogarth disapproved.

Other dangers lurked in the streets. Costermongers and pedlars pushed their barrows through the streets with little concern for anyone else while noisily bawling their wares. Sometimes dangerous animals such as bulls ran amok and horses shied and got out of control. Pedestrians tried to walk as close as possible to the walls of the buildings lining the street. This could lead to acrimonious arguments and fights with others trying to do the same. Traffic jams of monumental proportions often blocked the way, not least when drovers chose to herd livestock such as flocks of turkeys or screeching geese through the general mêlée. Angry road-users yelled and shouted at each other. Iron-rimmed wheels resonated excruciatingly where the streets were composed of cobbles or setts. The cacophony on London's streets must have been almost intolerable.

Many more who gained their living by crime emerged as darkness descended, like the creatures of the night that they were. Pickpockets and robbers were everywhere. Even wigs were at risk. Ingenious thieves operating from upper windows employed devices of thin wire fitted with hooks with which they removed wigs and hats from those passing below. Men who were apparently porters would pass by carrying a basket on their shoulder. Invisible inside the basket was a small boy who, in the gloom, would reach out and grasp a wig before, in a flash, disappearing from view inside the basket again.

An anonymous poet gives a sense of the perils of being abroad in the night-time streets of London:

> The lurking thief, who, while the daylight shone,
> Made the walls echo with his begging tone.
> That crutch, which late compassion mov'd, shall wound
> Thy bleeding head and fell thee to the ground.
> Though thou art tempted by the linkman's call,
> Yet trust him not along the lonely wall;
> In the mid-way he'll quench the flaming brand,
> And share the bounty with the pilf'ring band.
>
> (Burke 1949: 72)

Another writer giving the same impression was Henry Fielding (1707–54) who described London and Westminster as 'a vast wood or forest, in which a thief may harbour with as great security as wild beasts do in the deserts of Africa and Arabia'.

Despite the fact that London was such a huge city by the standards of the time, to us it would have seemed small and semi-rural. London had spread far beyond the square mile of the City but open fields could still be seen north of Oxford Road at the beginning of the century. Chelsea, Islington and Camberwell, for example, were villages. Parts of present-day Soho were pastureland. In the Whitehall area, development of housing for the rich was taking place around St James's Square, Piccadilly and towards Hyde Park where it petered out. Concern was being expressed about the seemingly never-ending outward growth of London. Measures were enacted by Parliament in 1550, 1641, 1703 and again in 1785 to prevent suburban expansion outside the City. However, London seemed to have a life of its own, an unrelenting compulsion for growth that could not be prevented merely by passing legislation.

Nearly all newcomers to London quickly developed a chronic cough because the air was heavily polluted with the smoke from sea coal, burnt in innumerable domestic and industrial grates. Many soon succumbed, although not necessarily fatally, to the contagious endemic and epidemic diseases that flourished in London's airless, overcrowded and insanitary conditions. The lodgings they found provided cold comfort. As Dr Johnson said, 'falling houses thunder on your head'. Jerry-built dwellings sometimes suddenly collapsed into the street with fatal results. People headed for London because wages were better there than in the provinces but they often returned home as quickly as they could if opportunities presented themselves. This lent the population of London a fleeting, changing, volatile character. Provincial visitors commented on the moral dangers presented by life in London. They were disturbed by the fact that the seemingly eternal, reassuring certainties of English life elsewhere did not apply in the capital. London's 'lower orders' were masterless and largely lacking in the sense of deference to their social superiors that the latter thought provided the matrix necessary for social stability.

London was full of vigour and vitality. It never slept. It was extremely violent. In the city and its vicinity lurked the ever-present threat of assault by highwaymen, footpads and robbers of every description. Many popular recreations employed violence. Cock-fighting, throwing at cocks, the baiting of animals and bare-knuckle boxing attracted boisterous, drunken crowds almost demented with excitement, passions running so high that fighting frequently spread to the spectators. The London mob was irreverent towards authority, volatile, often ferocious and cruel. While the pretensions of fashionable dandies were mercilessly mocked, infirm and other vulnerable individuals such as foreigners found themselves the butt of derision and physical bullying. In the early part of the century the Mohocks, youngish men of the rich and leisured class, drank heavily and then roamed the streets looking for trouble. They seized women and forced them to stand upside down, often with their heads in barrels. Their skirts billowed down and caused them considerable embarrassment because few women at the time wore drawers. They might be pricked in their legs with swords or poked in their private parts. Sometimes they were raped. Men were often beaten up or had their noses broken or eyes bored out. Occasionally the Mohocks placed their victims in wooden casks and rolled them into the Thames.

Senseless violence and murder were everyday features of life in London. Life was considered cheap and pleasure was extracted from the sufferings of others. For a few pence, voyeurs could go and jeer at the antics of the crazed inmates of Bedlam, a repository for the mentally ill and for general misfits. They plied them with drink and incited them to perform obscene acts. Many people obtained great pleasure from a Sunday afternoon stroll to observe the rotting corpses of executed criminals hanging in cages on gibbets. Large crowds turned out to taunt people in the pillory, especially if their crimes excited popular disgust. They not only cast verbal insults but often subjected them to a ferocious rain of stones, bottles, rotting vegetables, decomposing domestic pets, excrement, mud and other noisome material. Best of all the entertainments was, of course, Tyburn Fair, the eight hanging days set aside each year when a carnival atmosphere prevailed and vast crowds turned out to watch the procession from Newgate to Tyburn and its eagerly anticipated climax, the death trauma on the scaffold of one or more criminals.

London possessed a distinctive 'criminal class', a substantial but not easily quantified minority that obtained its living largely or entirely by illegal activity. This class had its own subculture, mores and language, a criminal cant designed to allow communication while excluding outsiders. Highly organised, this underworld was rightfully seen by outsiders as threatening. A more nebulous grouping was that which moved between criminal and legal methods of making a living, depending on many factors, not least of which was the state of the economy. Elsewhere in Britain there was of course lawlessness but much of it, such as poaching and smuggling, enjoyed widespread public support. Such 'social crime' was very different from the anti-social activity of London's underworld whose depredations affected rich and poor alike.

The city was unlike anywhere else in the kingdom. Its size, the anonymity it offered, its cosmopolitan population, its rapidly growing wealth in the eighteenth century and its stark contrasts between generalised poverty and the conspicuous consumption of the rich all helped to make it the natural focus for criminals. In his *Enquiry into the Causes of the Late Increases of Robbers*, Henry Fielding neatly summed up London's uniqueness:

> Whoever indeed considers the cities of London and Westminster with the late vast additions of their suburbs, the great irregularity of their buildings, the immense number of lanes, alleys, courts and bye-places; must think that, had they been intended for the very purpose of concealment, they could scarcely have been better contrived.

In spite of a diverse economic base, London suffered severe trade fluctuations that brought unemployment and the hardship associated with it. These conditions lured into criminal activity numbers of people who otherwise lived largely within the law. There was also the more imprecise factors of anomie, of transience, of a sense of helplessness. London's sheer size, noise and constant activity may have created stresses among its population which added to the apparent inability of many of its inhabitants to exercise any real control over their lives.

Professional thieves found conditions in London in the early part of the eighteenth century particularly favourable. Their activities were supported by a sophisticated, efficient network of receivers who had few scruples concerning the provenance of the goods they were offered. The planning of robberies and negotiations with these receivers frequently took place in 'flash houses', usually drinking places located in the rookeries where all concerned enjoyed virtual immunity from the authorities.

Much crime, however, was opportunistic and the result of the dire conditions in which its perpetrators found themselves rather than the work of hardened recidivists. The ragged specimens of humanity that shuffled in front of the magistrates each working morning were hopeless and often helpless victims of circumstance. Desperation had led them to theft and robbery and many of them even lacked the skills to commit these effectively. Much of this miserable flotsam and jetsam consisted of women. There was a considerable if variable and capricious demand for female labour in London, especially in its extremely large service sector. Huge numbers of girls gravitated to the metropolis in search of work. A few made a success of things. Far more found that life was a hand-to-mouth, lonely struggle, in and out of poorly paid, unskilled work with periods of appalling deprivation threatening in the bad times. Many had little or no alternative but to turn to prostitution, crime or both.

In *Industry and Idleness* (1747), William Hogarth illustrates what he saw as the rewards that London offered the diligent and the temptations it presented to the easily led. He traces the divergent lives of Francis Goodchild, the industrious apprentice and Tom Idle, the feckless ne'er-do-well. Goodchild makes the most of his chances and rises to wealth and prestige. Idle, however, starts down the road to perdition by gambling on the Sabbath and then finds himself sucked into an awful maelstrom of degradation and despair. What Hogarth ignores is the fact that many of the nameless thousands of Londoners who lived in permanent want, misery and despair, had never had the opportunity to make anything of life in the first place.

The nature and volume of crime in London reflected wider socio-economic and cultural change. The eighteenth century was pre-eminently the age of drink and the effects of alcohol abuse on criminal activity were all too evident. From around 1690 to the

1750s the villain of the piece was gin. The Dutch were extremely fond of gin but hitherto it had been little known outside the Netherlands. In 1688 the highly unpopular King James II was deposed. The crown was offered to the most acceptable claimant in the circumstances who was James II's daughter Mary, along with her husband, Prince William of Orange, as consort. The accession to the throne of a Dutchman did not meet with universal approval but it led, among other things, to a revolution in drinking habits accompanied by an explosion of crime and, indirectly, to substantial numbers of miscreants meeting their Maker at Tyburn.

From 1690 onwards Parliament approved a number of measures directly encouraging the distilling of spirits made from English grain. King William provided a fine example to his new subjects and led from the front, consuming prodigious amounts of gin. Drinking gin showed loyalty to the new monarch and was patriotic. Soon gin overtook ale and beer as the drink of the people. It was cheaper and its inebriating effects were more immediate. In 1688 the English consumed about half a million gallons annually. By 1700 they drank four times as much. The government was happy because the sale of gin produced revenue for the government and benefited the farmers. It could not, however, have predicted what happened over the next fifty years. By 1733 in London alone 11 million gallons of gin were produced, this being about twenty-three times as much as had been produced throughout England and Wales in 1688. This figure, however, is only an official one and takes no account of the vast quantities of adulterated gin produced cheaply in innumerable illicit stills. This liquid filth had just two virtues: it was cheap and it brought quick oblivion.

Gin provided short-lived respite for people whose surroundings were comfortless and whose lives were characterised by deprivation and despair. In St Giles, one of the most notorious of London's rookeries, it was estimated that in 1750 one house in every four sold drink. All classes drank, there being no stigma attached to drunkenness, but the effects of the excessive drinking of the poorer sections of society were more likely to be seen in public and were therefore much more evident. Drunks reeled around the streets, colliding with obstacles, sometimes being run down by riders and carriages or collapsing insensible in the filth that was heaped up everywhere. Many, hopelessly addicted and deprived of the will to do anything positive, drank until they made themselves unconscious or the money ran out and then turned to casual crime in order to pay for the next drink.

In 1751 two powerful pieces of propaganda made a considerable impression on informed opinion. The first was William Hogarth's famous contrasting prints entitled *Gin Lane* and *Beer Street*. These provided a graphic portrayal of the moral and physical decay linked with the abuse of gin and the robust well-being associated with the moderate drinking of beer. Second was Henry Fielding's essay *An Enquiry into the Causes of the Late Increases of Robbers*. Fielding was a highly respected magistrate who explained clearly and simply that much of the criminality he dealt with was caused by the abuse of gin. In 1751 the government prohibited the sale of gin by distillers, by chandlers and grocers and workhouse-keepers. It also increased the duty on spirits thereby depriving gin of its price advantage over beer and ale. Gradually the amount of gin that was consumed declined as did the corresponding death rate.

Over the eighteenth century as a whole, many factors can be seen to have had an effect on levels and types of crime. The streets of London were better lit by the 1790s. This made street crime more hazardous for its perpetrators. By 1800 street robbery had declined while burglary was on the increase. Society as a whole was becoming less violent. Doubt was being cast on the efficacy of the 'Bloody Code', itself extremely violent, as a means of deterring crime. Ideas associated with the Enlightenment stressed the rational side of human nature and argued that increased knowledge could be applied to bring about substantial improvements in the human condition.

London underwent a massive transformation in the course of the century. Its population continued to grow although now at a slower rate than some of the places where manufacturing industries were being established. The area under bricks and mortar spread rapidly as many inhabitants of the City left for the more salubrious outer areas while there was a continuous migration into London by those seeking better financial prospects. London was the heart of the country's government and legal affairs, the focus of the country's finance and commerce, its literary and intellectual life, the centre of fashionable social activity and it offered the best shopping opportunities in England. However, the economic base of London was changing and while new industries continued to be established, manufacturing industry became relatively less important. London grew more rapidly as a financial centre, as a port and as the location for the developing apparatus of the state. This changed the composition of occupations and incomes and led to relative gentrification.

This process may have had a bearing on the marked contrast between the earlier and the later eighteenth century. The death rate, for example, began to fall gradually after 1750 and quite sharply from the 1780s. Visitors commented on an apparent reduction in the uncouth behaviour of those moving around London's streets, a phenomenon which may have had something to do with the work of inspirational magistrates such as Colonel de Veil and the Fielding brothers. These men tried to identify the causes of crime and advocated social reform as a means of tackling the poverty and deprivation which were at the root of much criminal activity. They also had a great deal to do with the establishment of a paid and permanent police force, a visible force on the streets to deter crime and provide citizens with some sense of security.

The organs of local government too underwent improvement in the eighteenth century. The vestries of the parishes surrounding the City obtained legal powers to enable them to raise money for watch purposes, to provide lighting and street-cleaning and to ameliorate the conditions of the poor. They effected a very considerable improvement, so much so that a guide book to London in 1802 stated: 'We venture to assert that no city in proportion to its trade and luxury is more free from danger to those who pass the streets at all hours, or from depredations, open or concealed, on property'.

In the early part of the eighteenth century, crime, disorder and violence had stalked the streets of London and the general belief was that crime was out of control. The weakness of the forces of law and order meant that few offenders were apprehended. Instead the law turned with apparently barbaric ferocity on those who were actually arrested and convicted. The penalty for an ever-increasing range of crimes was hanging, intended to act as a deterrent to potential offenders. At the end of the century, however, opinion in ruling circles was turning away from such an overtly vindictive penal code. Consideration was being given to alternative ways of dealing with what was seen as the continuing threat to life and property posed by the 'criminal classes'. Hangings at Tyburn and the ritual enactments associated with them had ceased and had been moved to the much more easily controlled area outside Newgate. Opinion had also moved against the systematic infliction of cruelty on animals. The Fielding brothers, the reforming magistrates, for example, had initiated action against throwing at cocks and increasingly such pastimes became punishable offences. The nineteenth century was to see the introduction of professional policing, the development of modern prisons and the concept of custodial sentencing. It also witnessed far-reaching efforts to control those occasions on which huge, boisterous and potentially unmanageable crowds congregated, be it as spectators of sporting activities or as participants in various forms of political activity. Change was the very dynamic of London life.

EIGHT

Some Victims of Tyburn in the Eighteenth Century

One constant in the otherwise ever-changing diversity of London life was the spectacle of the ride from Newgate to Tyburn where a wide range of miscreants kept the hangman busy and the crowd entertained right through until 1783 when executions there ceased. This chapter examines the lives and last moments of some of the felons who died at Tyburn during the period 1690 to 1783.

On 23 December 1690 Sir John Johnston was hanged. A Scot, native of Kirkcaldy, Johnston was a rogue who preferred seducing and swindling rich women to working for a living. He had set his sights on a young and wealthy Irish spinster and was winning the battle for her affections when her father found out. He hired a gang of ruffians who beat Johnston up so severely that he decided to abandon his courtship. With a group of accomplices Johnston then kidnapped a wealthy heiress who was forced to marry one of the gang, bringing with her a generous dowry. Johnston was identified as the ringleader and sentenced to death. This unedifying man made a long speech from the gallows in which, ahead of his time, he accused the press of misrepresenting his case!

In October 1693 six men guilty of clipping coin were hanged at Tyburn and in July 1694 'Wilkinson the Goldsmith' was executed for a similar offence. On this occasion one of his companions on the journey from Newgate endeared himself to the crowd by kicking the Ordinary out of the cart. In 1695 John More, described as a rich 'tripeman' who had achieved considerable wealth and acquired a country estate, was hanged for clipping coin of the realm. Coining was particularly prevalent at this time and in

December 1696 as many as ten men were executed at Tyburn for offences of this sort.

Thomas Cook was a condemned felon who in 1703 gained the uncalled-for distinction of having set off twice from Newgate on what was usually the once-in-a-lifetime journey to Tyburn. He believed a reprieve would arrive on the day before that set for the execution. It did not. He had travelled as far as Tyburn when, to his great joy, the reprieve arrived. Cook was returned to Newgate only to receive notice that the reprieve had been rescinded. He then had an uneasy wait of several weeks before the next Tyburn Fair when he set off from Newgate for the second and last time.

In 1714 Roderick Audrey died at Tyburn aged just sixteen. He had been found guilty of burglary and theft. His unusual modus operandi was to stroll around an area of fashionable houses searching for a convenient open window, carrying a sparrow with him. Looking in at the window, he would quickly ascertain whether the room contained any items worth stealing. If so, he would release the sparrow to fly into the room and climb in after it. Securing any easily removable items, he then climbed out, reunited with his unwitting accomplice, the sparrow. If apprehended in the house his explanation was that he was searching for his pet bird which had unfortunately flown in through the open window. Although this story does not sound very plausible, he apparently used it successfully several times. Eventually, however, he was caught, tried, sentenced and hanged. The records tell us nothing about how he coped with this ordeal. Nor do they reveal the fate of the sparrow.

In May 1723 the government hurried through one of the most far-reaching Acts in British legal history. This came to be commonly known as the 'Waltham Black Act' and it created fifty or more new capital offences. The Act's origins lay with the desire of those landowners who owned game and hunting rights to punish poachers who went to work armed and with their faces blackened or otherwise disguised. However, the Act was drafted in such a way that it could easily encompass a far wider range of offences. As sober an authority on English law as Sir Leon Radzinowicz commented about this Act:

There is hardly a criminal act which does not come within the provisions of the Black Act; offences against public order, against the administration of criminal justice, against property, against the person, malicious injuries to property of varying degree – all came under this statute and all were punishable by death. Thus the Act constituted in itself a complete and extremely severe criminal code. . . .

(Radzinowicz 1947: 77)

The initial victims of the Act were a group of deer-stealers from Hampshire who were also suspected of harbouring Jacobite sympathies. Seven of them were hanged at Tyburn on 4 December 1723. They realised that they were scapegoats. Why else, they asked, were they tried in London well away from a jury of their own Hampshire people who might have treated them with some sympathy? Their progress from Newgate and their deaths at Tyburn generated little interest. Clearly, those who turned out for Tyburn Fair had a preference for watching the demise of prisoners who had a local reputation.

One man with a lasting place in London's folklore who died at Tyburn was Jack Sheppard (1702–24). He became a popular hero starring in innumerable broadsheets and ballads, although much of this material was exaggerated and distorted. A fairly unexceptional thief and burglar, his name would have been forgotten had it not been for his extraordinary skill as an escapologist. Born in Spitalfields, a tough cosmopolitan community and the centre of London's weaving industry, at the age of fifteen he was apprenticed as a carpenter. The work lacked the excitement and glamour Sheppard craved but he was a quick learner and became highly skilled, not just as a carpenter but also as a locksmith. He drifted towards the criminal elements that frequented low drinking houses. In the Black Lion close to Drury Lane, he came under the tutelage of two experienced thieves, 'Edgeworth Bess' and Poll Maggot. Sheppard turned his back on carpentry and became a burglar and picklock. His fame, however, lay with his almost uncanny ability to get out of prison and the various other ingenious physical restraints into which he was placed.

Discovering that Edgeworth Bess was in St Giles's Roundhouse pending inquiries by the authorities concerning some stolen property, he walked in, knocked out the warder, took his keys, released Bess and then coolly walked out with her on his arm. Such is the stuff of which legends are made! Sheppard's brief but meteoric rise to fame had begun. Now with a price on his head, he was taken up by a constable in the notorious Seven Dials area and was deposited overnight in St Giles's Roundhouse. He had secreted a razor with which he made a hole in the plaster and lathe ceiling. He got out on to the roof and escaped using an improvised rope. Soon afterwards he was wrongly arrested for the theft of a watch and placed in the New Prison, Clerkenwell. To his great delight Bess turned up and was promptly detained by the authorities who placed her in the same cell. They were soon visited by one Joseph Blake, known in criminal circles as 'Blueskin'. He surreptitiously passed them a file which Sheppard used to remove his manacles, his fetters, two bars from the cell window, and Bess from her restraints. He made a knotted rope from blankets and sheets, attached it securely to the remaining window bar and with Bess stripped to her underwear, descended 30 feet into the courtyard below. After this, a climb of 22 feet to scale the outer wall was child's play. They dropped into the street and fled.

Sheppard and 'Blueskin' rather unwisely decided to carry out some robberies and sell the booty to a receiver called Field. They did this in defiance of Jonathan Wild, the acknowledged underworld leader who soon heard about this freelance activity and could not possibly overlook it. He persuaded Field to turn king's evidence. Sheppard and 'Blueskin' were arrested, tried at the Old Bailey and sentenced to death. They were then placed in Newgate awaiting execution. Edgeworth Bess accompanied by Poll Maggot soon turned up. The girls skilfully manoeuvred a file into Sheppard's cell while simultaneously titillating the gaolers and diverting their attention. Their mission accomplished, Bess and Poll left and a few days later so did Sheppard – over the roof and down the wall. Sheppard was adored by the populace because escapes from Newgate were almost unheard of and these dare-devil exploits made the authorities look stupid.

Soon Sheppard was caught once more and returned to Newgate where the warders took the unusual step of chaining him to the floor. Under the circumstances, they also banned visitors. Somehow Sheppard, flattered by this special treatment, acquired a crooked nail and expertly opening the locks, wriggled out of his handcuffs and remaining fetters. This time he escaped from Newgate covered in soot and via a narrow flue. The hero's welcome he received went to his head and he brazenly paraded around London with Bess on one arm and Poll on the other. The authorities arrested him as he sat carousing, much the worse for drink and revelling in the popular adulation. He was swiftly brought back through the now familiar gates of Newgate and placed in a set of restraining irons designed specifically for him. On looking at these, he must have realised that his luck was finally running out. However, he was a celebrity and many visitors, some of them very distinguished ones, came to assure him of their good wishes. Understandably, they were kept at a safe distance. However, just one file or even a crooked nail would have been more useful than all their well-intentioned felicitations. Somehow he managed to get hold of a sharp penknife but it was discovered by a vigilant gaoler. He also had a fall-back plan. He had arranged with associates to engage a surgeon at Tyburn in the hope that on being cut down, he could be whisked away and expertly resuscitated.

On 16 November 1724 Sheppard travelled in the customary cart from Newgate to Tyburn enjoying a triumphal progress. Rarely, if ever, did so many people turn out to cheer a condemned felon on his way and to shower him with posies of flowers. Revelling in the limelight, he smiled constantly and exchanged pleasantries and banter with friends and well-wishers in the crowd. Something must have struck him as funny because at one stage he burst out laughing. He stopped for a pint of mulled sack outside the City of Oxford tavern in Oxford Road, now Oxford Street, where the built-up area of London began to peter out and the route took on a semi-rural appearance. His posture continued to be brave but after Sheppard had been hanging for a quarter of an hour, a man described as a 'soldier' dashed through the crowds around the gallows, cut him down and made off with his slight body which still exhibited some signs of life. His accomplices set up a diversion so that his body could be whisked away to receive the urgent ministrations of the surgeon. However, in the excited crowd their cries were misunderstood and many onlookers thought that Sheppard's body was being taken away to be subjected to the attentions of the hated anatomists at Surgeons' Hall. A violent altercation broke out and if life had not been quite extinct before, it quickly became so as the body was seized, pulled about and fought over with well-meaning but misplaced zeal. One group of men succeeded in carrying the battered corpse off and taking it to the Barley Mow in Long Acre, Covent Garden. The rumour was that Sheppard's corpse was indeed destined for the surgeons but had been placed in the tavern until the furore died down. Soon an extremely angry mob was surging around Long Acre. Few had any real idea of what was going on except that the body of their hero Sheppard was in one of the buildings close by. Brickbats were flung indiscriminately, windows were smashed and doors knocked down as people, with the capriciousness that is the hallmark of the mob, quickly forgot the cause of the excitement and embarked on an orgy of looting and destruction. The Riot Act was read and order restored with some difficulty. Late the same night, a coach with an armed guard took Sheppard's mortal remains and interred them in the churchyard of St Martin-in-the-Fields. He was just twenty-two years of age.

The profession of thief-taker had effectively been created by the Act for Encouraging the Apprehending of Highwaymen, passed in 1692. England was then unique in Western Europe in having neither a public prosecutor nor a professional police force, relying instead on the cheaper expedient of leaving the enforcement of the law to private enterprise. Such a system encouraged common informers to bring offenders to justice with the incentive of cash rewards. 'The Highwayman Act' as it was called, offered a reward of £40 for the arrest and successful prosecution of any highwayman plus the useful bonus of his horse, harness, weapons and any other possessions unless these had been stolen. Those supplying the necessary evidence were also given a free pardon for any crimes they had committed.

This 'blood money' attracted large numbers of criminals to thief-taking. The law was subsequently extended to include a wider range of crimes and sliding scales of payment were introduced, depending on the perceived seriousness of each particular crime. The dangers inherent in thief-taking were recognised because a thief-taker's dependants were entitled to the reward if he was killed while attempting an arrest. It was obviously dangerous to tackle someone with a price on his head and there was a very real threat of revenge, little protection being offered to the thief-taker in what was basically a policeless state. Thief-takers enjoyed little popularity either with criminals or the law-abiding public.

The most notorious thief-taker was Jonathan Wild. Like Jack Sheppard, his story has often been told and again only an outline will be provided. Born at Wolverhampton in 1683, he became a buckle-maker. In about 1708 he moved to London and was soon placed in the Wood Street Compter for debt. Institutions like this were virtually academies of crime. Those who had embarked for the first time on crime as well as the most hardened recidivists mixed indiscriminately, swapping ideas and expertise. During the four years he spent there, Wild listened intently and made sure that he got to know those who might be useful to him in the future. His imprisonment was made easier to bear in the last few months because of the arrival of a prostitute named Mary Milliner. She became Wild's mistress and was doubly useful because she had plenty of underworld contacts. They left prison together and set up home in modest premises in Covent Garden. At first Wild returned to the trade of buckle-making but he also acted as Mary's 'minder' in a criminal partnership known as the 'buttock-and-twang'. In simple terms, Mary lured men into dark alleys for stand-up sex. Her victims were vulnerable with their breeches around their ankles. While they were in the transports of lustful pleasure Wild found it a simple matter to rob them.

The partnership prospered and the couple took over a drinking house which was a well known 'flash-house' or resort of criminals. Soon Wild was buying items stolen by his customers, going on to combine the work of a receiver and a thief-taker. He opened an office and invited victims of theft and robbery to give him details of what they had had stolen. He then promised to try to locate the items and to bring the robbers to justice. The robbers themselves had probably already knocked at the back door of Wild's premises and sold him the very same goods. He acted as a go-between, gaining an enviable reputation from the robbers for giving them a fair price and from the victims for his seemingly extraordinary ability to return their lost goods to them at a reasonable fee. This way he pleased everyone and prospered himself. However, Wild had further ambitions. He divided London and its environs into districts and allocated separate gangs to each of these. Any villain who crossed him risked being apprehended and framed with the assistance of witnesses who were Wild's creatures. On conviction as felons they could not testify against Wild himself in any subsequent court case.

Wild was intelligent, ruthless and worldly. The rewards for bringing offenders to justice brought in useful income and helped him to consolidate his position in the underworld, eliminating possible rivals. Wild became London's first 'Napoleon of Crime'. He had an exceptionally retentive brain in which he stored information about all those active in the underworld. Favours done for him were never forgotten and he was very loyal to those who earned his respect. However, treachery was never overlooked. He was absolutely merciless. Eventually he came unstuck when Sir William Thompson, the Recorder of London, became Solicitor-General in 1717. He had the measure of Wild and was instrumental in securing an Act of Parliament which made it a capital offence to take a reward under the pretence of helping the owner to recover stolen goods. This piece of legislation was, with good reason, known as 'Jonathan Wild's Act' because it was designed specifically with his activities in mind.

Initially Wild had little difficulty in finding ways around this legislation. However he overreached himself in 1723 when he decided to petition the Lord Mayor of the City of London with a view to being given the formal Freedom of the City. To back up this brazen submission, he explained that his efforts had resulted in the despatch of no less than sixty criminals to the gallows. Certainly, he had cleared some of the most notorious gangs from the streets of London and ironically was able to claim, like the Kray brothers many years later, that he had made the streets safer. Many of London's wealthier citizens were impressed by his promotion of himself as a public benefactor and saw him as their only defence against the apparently inexorable rise in lawlessness. Had he not consistently restored their stolen property to them and at a very reasonable price? Did not accounts of the criminals he rounded up appear every week in the newspapers? However, Wild was eventually arrested under the terms of the new Act for procuring the return of some stolen lace, to the value of just £40. As with many others before and since, Wild found that public opinion was cruel and capricious. As one revelation followed another, he found that the public quickly moved from seeing him as their main hope against crime to believing him to be the major perpetrator of it and calling for his blood. Unluckily for him he found that Thompson was presiding as judge when his case came to court. Wild defended himself vigorously and ably but he was found guilty. With an air of vindictive relish Thompson sentenced him to death. He was hanged at Tyburn on 24 May 1725.

The night before his execution, Wild tried to commit suicide with an overdose of laudanum. In the morning he was in a greatly weakened state and partly insensible to what was going on. The crowd along the route from Newgate to Tyburn gave him a terrible time. He was booed, verbally abused and pelted with a wide variety of missiles, including excrement and the festering corpses of long-dead cats and dogs. He himself was apparently in tears as well he might have been when hit in the face by a sharp stone which caused considerable bleeding. Tyburn that day attracted one of its largest-ever crowds. The people rejoiced to see the once omnipotent Wild brought down, humiliated and destroyed. They hated him for his bullying, for his mercilessness and for his hypocritical social pretensions.

Wild rode in the cart with two highwaymen and a coiner. The highwaymen were executed first. Wild, not totally *compos mentis*, listened bemused while the coiner, Robert Harpham, used the opportunity to tell the vast crowd about how he repented his life of sin and to urge them to eschew criminal ways. He then went calmly and with dignity to his death. By this time the onlookers were getting impatient. After all, it was Wild's death they had come to see; the others were merely the supporting cast. Still confused by the drugs given to revive him the previous night, Wild died without making either a pathetic admission of guilt or execrating the fates which had put him where he was. In this sense, Wild provided poor value for money. His body was cut down and before the surgeons' men could seize it, it was spirited away and buried in St Pancras Churchyard next to Elizabeth Mann, his favourite mistress. The grave was surreptitiously opened up a few days later and his body removed. The coffin was found at nearby Kentish Town. What exactly happened to his body has never been established. Some people believe that the surgeons got their hands on it. However, a few days later the *Daily Journal* reported that an unidentified body had been washed up on the bank of the Thames near Whitehall and had been consigned to the burial ground for the poor after examination by a coroner and jury. The extreme hairiness of the chest suggested that it might indeed be the body of Jonathan Wild. Little dignity in death!

Wild was a scoundrel and he paid the ultimate price for his multifarious criminal activities. But it has to be said that he lived in a period of the greatest venality in public life. Around the time of Wild's trial and execution, the Lord Chancellor, the Earl of Macclesfield, had been found guilty of taking £100,000 worth of bribes and of various other corrupt activities. His punishment was a substantial fine. Somewhat earlier Robert Walpole had not been brought to account for a massive unexplained deficit in Exchequer funds. This does not relieve Wild of guilt but calls into question the selective attitude of people in positions of power and influence towards crime and wrongdoing and their perpetrators. They looked after their own. Were Wild's crimes really more dastardly than those committed by people mostly born to wealth and influence who had used their official positions corruptly to enrich themselves even further and at the public expense?

On 12 April 1726 Emanuel Dickenson was executed at Tyburn for murder. Like many other wretches who went to meet their Maker there, it is easy to conclude that he was every bit as much a victim as many of those on whom he preyed every day in London's streets and alleys. The son of an army officer, his father had died early leaving his mother in dire poverty to care for him and his three sisters. The children all turned to robbery and Dickenson himself, caught stealing a gentleman's hat in the Strand, was sentenced to transportation but pardoned when his mother's privations were revealed. This experience did not, however, bring him back from the brink of a life of crime. He fell in with a gang of criminals who numbered street robbery, pickpocketing and house-breaking among their activities. They were violent and dangerous, prepared to use firearms and to murder informers. An associate of the gang informed on them and one by one they were picked off, tried for various felonies and sentenced to death. As with many of the more notorious criminals, Dickenson's body was placed in a gibbet, in this case on Kennington Common, after he had been hanged at Tyburn. Curiously, his body was taken down and buried after just one day when it became known that his father had died in active service for his country. His early ill-fortune in losing the family breadwinner, his swift descent into crime and equally swift absorption into the underworld, his brief notoriety and squalid fate are undoubtedly replicated many times in the annals of London's underworld and the biographies of those who died at Tyburn.

We have said that far fewer women than men ended their days at Tyburn but Catherine Hayes, 'Jenny Diver' and Elizabeth Brownrigg stand among the pantheon of English criminals on an equal footing with any of their male counterparts. Catherine Hayes was executed at Tyburn in 1726 for what nowadays seems the curious crime of 'petit treason'. This offence dated back to the reign of Edward III (1327–77) and involved the killing by a servant of his master, by a wife of her husband or by a lay person or junior cleric of a prelate. Catherine killed her husband and the law saw this as treason because she was, in effect, killing her lord and master. Born near Birmingham, Catherine had left home at about the age of fifteen after arguing with her parents. She had winsome looks and some soldiers who met her on the road asked her to go back to their quarters in Worcestershire. Quite what role she played there can only be guessed at but eventually she moved on and became a servant working for a Warwickshire farmer by the name of Hayes. His son promptly fell head over heels in love with her and proposed that they marry secretly because his parents would not approve. The wedding was celebrated at Worcester where the couple's connubial bliss was disturbed by the same group of soldiers who had befriended Catherine previously. They threatened the young man with forced enlistment. Swallowing his pride, he contacted his father who spoke to the magistrates. They in turn persuaded the soldiers to surrender the errant son. Hayes Senior may not have approved of the marriage but he gave his son money with which to start up in business. The young man seems to have been an honest, willing drudge. Catherine, however, quickly and very publicly started denouncing him for being parsimonious. She became increasingly ill-tempered and offensive but he seems to have been patient and when she demanded that they move to London, he complied willingly enough.

Hayes Junior prospered greatly from his various business interests in London. Catherine was curiously inconsistent in her attitude towards her husband. Sometimes she lambasted him when talking with neighbours but on other occasions she spoke of him with the greatest affection. Her reputation spread, neighbours taking offence at her quick temper and apparent capriciousness. The couple moved to what was then Tyburn Road which eventually became Oxford Street. They took a lodger by the name of Billings who quickly became Catherine's lover, the couple making sport when Hayes was away on business. They were not particularly discreet and neighbours told Hayes what was happening in his absence. He had a flaming row with Catherine who probably by now intended to kill him. Another lodger, named Wood, took up residence in the Hayes household. All four of them indulged in a massive drinking bout during which Hayes became insensible and his wife prevailed on the others to help her murder him. Billings and Wood killed Hayes with a hatchet and then chopped off his head, which was carried in a pail to the Thames and thrown into the river near the Horseferry at Westminster. It was found the next morning. The conspirators dismembered the body, parcelled it up and threw it into a pond in the Marylebone area.

Meanwhile the local magistrates had cleaned up Hayes's head and placed it on a pole in St Margaret's churchyard at Westminster in the hope that someone would identify it. This gory trophy predictably attracted a large crowd and was recognised by one Bennet, an apprentice organ-builder who hurried off to tell Mrs Hayes that he had just seen her husband's disembodied head on public display. Seemingly unconcerned by this revelation, she told Bennet that her husband had looked healthy enough last time she had seen him. When Bennet repeated that he didn't look too healthy now, Catherine's response was to threaten him not to take the matter further. She then moved to new lodgings with a female acquaintance and Billings and Wood. As more people claimed to recognise the head which by now had been treated with a preservative, she concocted the rather unconvincing story that Hayes had murdered a man to whom he owed money and had gone on the run, to Portugal. She told others that he had gone to Hertfordshire. Two neighbours apprised a magistrate of their growing suspicions that Hayes was the victim of foul play. A warrant was issued for the arrest of Catherine, Wood and Billings.

The magistrate and his attendants then hurried round to Catherine's lodgings and broke the door down. Catherine was hastily putting on her clothes while Billings was sitting, bare-legged on the side of her bed. When asked whether they had been making love, Catherine replied that Billings had been mending his stockings. Responding to this rather feeble explanation, the magistrate commented dryly that her companion's eyesight must be quite exceptional since he was doing the darning in the dark. All the suspects except Wood were taken away and examined. Wood himself was out of town but arrested soon afterwards. The next day Catherine requested to see the head in question and on doing so gave vent to a histrionic display of grief. At about the same time two men reported that that they had found what seemed to be a dismembered body near Marylebone. It had no head. Wood and Billings made full confessions. Catherine could not be induced to confess and went to court where she was found guilty although only after blaming Wood and Billings for the whole thing. Wood rather conveniently died and Billings, who expressed the deepest remorse, was hanged in Upper Wimpole Street near where Hayes's remains were found. Catherine was made of sterner stuff. Not for her a cringing admission of guilt and contrition. Somehow she got hold of a phial of poison but was unable to swallow it. For her particular offence of petit treason, she was drawn uncomfortably on a hurdle to Tyburn. She was then burnt. The usual procedure was for the executioner to strangle the victim with a rope around the neck so that she was dead before having to endure the unspeakable agony of dying in the flames. On this occasion, however, the executioner bungled things and let the rope go too quickly. Catherine therefore was still alive when she became engulfed in the flames. Her screams of agony rent the air as the crowd watched, at once both appalled and fascinated by the sight and sound of Catherine's death agonies. The date was 9 May 1726.

Hayes's crime was particularly heinous but this did not mean that these events escaped the attention of the humorists. These verses provide a flavour:

> In Tyburn road, a man there liv'd
> A just and honest life;
> And there he might have lived still,
> If it had pleased his wife.
>
> But she to vicious ways inclin'd,
> A life most wicked led;
> With tailors and with tinkers too,
> She oft defiled his bed. . .

Mary Young, also known as 'Jenny Diver', was one of London's most gifted pickpockets. A native of Northern Ireland, at the age of fifteen she attracted the amorous attentions of a young man and having decided that London was the place of opportunity, she let him know that she would confer her favours on him if he took her there. Overjoyed at the prospect, he made the necessary sailing arrangements. He also stole a gold watch and 80 guineas from his master. They got to Liverpool and took temporary lodgings but he was apprehended for the robbery. Mary was not implicated and showed her true feelings for her swain by proceeding to London while he was taken back to Northern Ireland to stand trial and eventually to be transported. She found lodgings in Covent Garden and tried to get honest employment as a seamstress but like so many before and since, she found herself destitute and desperate. Another woman lodger took her under her wing and introduced her to a gang of pickpockets operating out of the nearby St Giles Rookery. These thieves were well organised and highly skilled and Mary quickly won their respect, being naturally adept at pickpocketing. A genius in her own way, she invented a pair of false arms and hands. Equipped with these she would take her place in a pew for divine service and sit during the sermon with her false arms and hands crossed in her lap, gazing demurely at the parson. Meanwhile with her real hands she dextrously removed the valuables from her unsuspecting neighbours. Caught and transported to the Virginian colonies, she managed to serve her time and to make her way back, by which time the gang had dispersed. She returned to picking pockets, was caught, transported yet again and once more managed to return to England. Reverting to her wicked ways, she was caught again and this time condemned to death. She was hanged at Tyburn on 18 March 1740, having greatly irritated the crowd by the lengthy time she spent on the gallows engaged in prayer. She was interred in St Pancras churchyard.

In 1748 John Lancaster met his end at Tyburn. A Londoner, born in 1726 in the East End, he became apprenticed to a velvet-maker and combined that work with part-time education at a Methodist charity school and gambling with dissolute companions in disreputable alehouses. He stole some material from his master, sold it and ran away to sea. Eventually he returned and went back to the velvet-making trade. He carried out a second theft but was caught, convicted and sentenced to death. While awaiting execution, his teacher at the Methodist school appeared and persuaded him of the error of his ways and converted him to Christianity. Lancaster took to his new, if brief, way of life with great zeal. He is reputed to have ridden with ten other condemned prisoners from Newgate and led them in an impromptu recital of prayers and hymns. According to reports, this had a sobering effect on the spectators around the gallows at Tyburn. His body was being taken away for the use of the surgeons when a group of men described as 'mariners' elbowed their way through the crowd. They seized Lancaster's corpse and delivered it with great reverence to his mother, several miles away. She gave him a decent burial some days later. Lancaster's case is interesting not only because of his late conversion to evangelical Christianity but because his rescuers were believed to be sailors. Seafarers were known to have a strong aversion to surgeons at sea – they were widely regarded as the most dissipated, drunken and incompetent representatives of their profession. Did they seize the dead Lancaster in some kind of protest against the surgeons or simply because they were old shipmates of his?

James Maclaine is the archetypal 'gentleman highwayman'. Maclaine's father, a parson, died leaving his son a sizeable inheritance when he was just eighteen. He got through this speedily and then took a job as a butler. Maclaine thought this demeaning and enjoying an expensive lifestyle he could not afford, started stealing from his employer; he was caught and dismissed. Moving to London, he tried to find further domestic employment while developing a sideline in seducing rich women. This latter endeavour was partially successful because he married one such woman, a widow, lured by the prospect of the sizeable dowry she commanded. Maclaine pragmatically took on the grocery business that she brought with her. It bored him to distraction until she very obligingly died. With the remains of her money he bought himself several suits of fine clothes and decided to try his luck as an eligible widower at fashionable spas like Bath and Tunbridge Wells. Maclaine had charm and style and he used these to seduce a substantial number of women and to try to persuade them to part with their money. He found the former much easier to achieve than the latter. Although the occupation had its compensations he was disappointed to find that the money was usually only available after a public promise of matrimony. This did not accord with Maclaine's strategy. He employed a bankrupt apothecary called Plunkett to act as his footman. Keeping up appearances and treating the ladies in the way they expected was extremely expensive and funds became scarce. When Plunkett politely suggested that they should enhance their income by a little highway robbery, Maclaine jumped at the idea.

They made an ill-assorted pair out on the road because Maclaine was a total coward and the prospect of physical danger made his face twitch and his knees knock. He therefore lurked close by while Plunkett undertook the actual robberies. Maclaine found the seduction part of the business much more congenial and several times nearly contracted marriages which would have brought large dowries with them. However, the ladies concerned always seemed to smell a rat at the last minute and so Maclaine was left with nothing material to show for his efforts. Nevertheless, the pair continued to have their successes on the road and one of their best-known encounters was with the writer Horace Walpole (1717–97), the son of the man usually regarded as Britain's first Prime Minister. This robbery took place on a moonlit night in Hyde Park in 1749, and this time Maclaine must have plucked up courage because it was he who carried it out. Walpole wrote a daily journal in which he made much of the encounter. He was shot at by Maclaine and wrote that Maclaine's pistol, 'going off accidentally, grazed the skin under my eye, left some marks of shot on my face, and stunned me. The ball went through the top of the chariot, and if I had sat an inch nearer to the left side, must have gone through my head.' Next morning he received a very polite, even apologetic letter from Maclaine saying that he was sorry for the unpleasantness and inconvenience he had caused. Walpole commented that the encounter with the highwayman was carried out 'with the greatest good breeding on both sides'. Plunkett and Maclaine's genteel depredations on the King's Highway could not last forever and eventually Maclaine was arrested. Plunkett simply disappeared. Maclaine declared that he had never intended to rob anyone but had been forced to do so by his greedy and belligerent partner. He called numerous witnesses, all society ladies with whom he had enjoyed intimate relations, who attested to his character and probity although he himself made a very poor impression. After being found guilty, he was lodged in Newgate where he received numerous visitors, the majority, true to form, being dowager lady socialites. Large crowds turned out to watch him on his way to Tyburn in 1750 but he proved a great disappointment. He gave no rousing speech to provide a piquant taster for the main item of the day's entertainment which, of course, was the hanging, nor were his sufferings on the gallows prolonged.

On 7 June 1753, a Doctor Cameron died at Tyburn, his being the last judicial killing associated with the uprising of the so-called 'Young Pretender' Bonnie Prince Charlie. In 1744–5 Louis XV of France, then at war with the British, encouraged the Prince to launch a war from Scotland in an attempt to reclaim the British throne for the Stuarts and, at the same time, confound the British by opening up hostilities on another front. He duly landed in the Hebrides in July 1745, defeated a government force at Prestonpans near Edinburgh and advanced on England, hoping to pick up support as he went. But few rallied to his banner and by the time he got as far south as Derby, it was evident that his cause was lost. He retreated northwards, pursued hotfoot by the Duke of Cumberland who inflicted a crushing defeat on Prince Charlie's clansmen at the battle of Culloden on 16 April 1746. This ended any hopes he might have had of winning the throne. Dr Cameron had been a medical practitioner in the small town of Lochaber in the Highlands when the Rebellion of '45 broke out. Despite the advice of his brother, he attended the Young Pretender as his physician. Although he had not fought, he was clearly a wanted man and after the debacle of Culloden, he made his escape to France. Cameron failed to prosper there and in 1752 returned to England, believing that past events had been forgotten and trying to contact friends who might help him regain his position in society. However, bygones were not bygones and he was captured and placed in the Tower of London.

He was charged with treason and found guilty. His case had attracted a great deal of interest and large, not unsympathetic crowds lined his route to Tyburn. They were greatly impressed with his dignity and general fortitude.

On 5 May 1760 Lord Ferrers was hanged at Tyburn. In any list of British rotters, Ferrers can be assured a mention. Born into a rich and aristocratic family and grossly indulged as a child and youth, he grew up wilful, spoilt, idle and a bully. When drunk, which he was for much of the time, he could become extremely violent. On one occasion his horse lost a race and Ferrers horsewhipped his groom. When a barrel of oysters was identified as the probable source of an outbreak of food poisoning, the servant who had bought them was stabbed in the chest by Ferrers, beaten unconscious with a heavy candlestick and kicked repeatedly in the groin. The hapless man never completely recovered from the injuries he sustained. Ferrers married for the second time in 1752 and then subjected this wife to six years of systematic violence and cruelty which only ended when she left him after he had knocked her senseless. The household passed into the stewardship of an old and faithful family retainer called John Johnson. Ferrers, seeing plots against him everywhere, then accused Johnson of cheating with the accounts. Johnson protested his innocence. Ferrers told him to get on his knees and beg forgiveness and then shot him, fatally wounding him. A doctor was called who, ascertaining that he could do nothing for the expiring Johnson, contacted the authorities. Ferrers was arrested and tried before his peers in the House of Lords. In his arrogant way, he seems to have assumed that they would acquit him. However his reputation had gone before him. His manner was thoroughly unpleasant; he showed absolutely no remorse and the facts of the case were clear. He was condemned to death. Large crowds gathered to boo him as he made his way to Tyburn in a black coach and wearing a white satin wedding suit. He was the first nobleman to be executed on the common gallows. In fact he was clearly impressed by the size of the crowds, possibly because they had never seen a lord going to be executed.

On 9 January 1765 John Wesket was hanged at Tyburn for the murder of his master the Earl of Harrington. He treated the crowd to one of the best displays ever of sangfroid, dressing in an eye-catching blue and gold frock coat and wearing, as an emblem of his innocence, a white cockade in his hat. Standing up in the cart for most of the journey to Tyburn, he was applauded by the crowd for his apparent insouciance which he emphasised by eating several oranges as he went and casually throwing the peel into the street.

The case of Elizabeth Brownrigg has gone down in criminal history as one of the worst examples of cruelty and physical abuse to children. Elizabeth was probably the most hated woman to be hanged at Tyburn. She lived in Fleur-de-Lys Court, Fetter Lane, off Fleet Street. She married a plumber and house-painter by whom she had sixteen children and her employment – an apt one given her considerable personal experience of childbirth – was as a midwife. However, it was for her sadistic cruelty to the female servants in her employ that she is best remembered. As the midwife at St Dunstan's workhouse she was able to use her position to win the confidence of young vulnerable girl inmates. She brought them back as apprentices to her unsavoury home where they were kept as virtual slaves, although ostensibly working as family servants. Their living quarters were the cellars which they shared with pigs and in which they were systematically starved, whipped, tortured and otherwise abused. One girl had her tongue cut through with scissors and others died from a combination of extreme neglect and physical and mental distress. Elizabeth took the lead in perpetrating this gratuitous sadism but her husband and the one son remaining at home sometimes joined in. The authorities were alerted by the neighbours who heard the girls' cries of distress over a long period but they took an unconscionable time getting around to doing anything about it. The three Brownriggs were tried at the Old Bailey and convicted of murder. The appalling suffering they inflicted on these unfortunate girls was punished by the husband and son – incredibly – receiving a sentence of just six months' imprisonment each while Elizabeth was condemned to death. The outrageous nature of these crimes, even at a time when life was held as cheap, incurred widespread anger and Elizabeth had to run the gauntlet of verbal abuse and a hail of dangerous missiles from a huge crowd as she travelled to Tyburn where she ended her days on 14 September 1767. Her body was taken to Surgeons' Hall, dissected and anatomised. Her skeleton was preserved.

On 11 March 1768 James Sampson was hanged at Tyburn. In his youth, Sampson had shown evidence of precocious talent as an artist and had been able to attract the patronage of rich and powerful men like the Duke of Richmond and General Conway. They encouraged the development of his talent by paying for him to receive tutoring from some of the most successful artists of the day. His future seemed assured when he married a well-thought-of young lady in the general's service and he was so highly regarded by the general himself that he was allowed free and full access to the General's library. The problem was that Sampson, like so many other flawed geniuses before and since, was in thrall to the sins of the flesh. He carried on a number of illicit relationships with women maintaining whose affections depended on him constantly showering them with expensive gifts. This strained his financial resources beyond the limits of his income. Aware that valuable items were kept in a desk in the library, he resolved to steal these and cover his tracks by setting fire to the house. In this he was only partly successful because although he managed to set fire to the library, the desk was recovered and it was evident that some bank notes had been taken and that the fire was far from accidental. Sampson was recognised negotiating a number of cheques. He was arrested, convicted and sentenced to be hanged. His journey in the cart to Tyburn was unusual because it had to be diverted for what are now known as road works. It therefore passed through Smithfield, Cowcross and Turnmill Streets before regaining the usual route. A cringing confession on the scaffold and the prayers he offered up provided poor entertainment for the day's crowd.

Samuel Roberts came from the small county town of Shrewsbury where he completed an apprenticeship as a baker. He then decided to improve his career prospects by moving to London where, with the ease so typical of young men up from the country, he fell into bad company. In this case his new companions were a family of coiners by the name of Bacchus. He and Thomas Bacchus were found guilty of coining offences and were sentenced to death, as were all convicted coiners, for treason. They were therefore drawn to Tyburn on hurdles. This otherwise unremarkable pair of felons held forth most eloquently both on the way from Newgate and at Tyburn about how the authorities were totally justified in hanging them for the heinous crimes they had committed. They kept up a constant stream of this obsequious babble and with tears in their eyes implored the crowds to note their fate, respect the law and abjure all criminal temptations. This aroused the scorn and the ire of the crowd who showered them with verbal abuse and urged the hangman to despatch them quickly, if only to shut them up. They died on 31 May 1772.

'Jack' Rann was born near Bath in 1750 and christened John. A cheerful, quick-witted child, after entering service at the age of twelve he received rapid promotions in recognition of his ability and his pleasing manner. He became a coachman in London and, as a servant in fashionable society, acquired a taste for the good life. He also developed a liking for attractive girls. Unfortunately, a coachman's pay could not provide him with the lifestyle to which he aspired and so he decided to try his luck as a highway man. Quickly he gained an enviable notoriety for the audacity of his robberies, the courtesy and politeness he employed when demanding that his victims part with their valuables and for the distinctive way in which he dressed. A born extrovert, he acquired the strange nickname 'Sixteen-String Jack' in recognition of the breeches of silk with their sixteen strings attached at the knees which he wore when out on the road. This leg gear must have made him rather conspicuous but although he was arrested on many occasions and charged with highway robbery, he was, rather surprisingly, acquitted because the witnesses failed to confirm his identity.

Rann positively relished the bright lights. On one occasion he was in the crowd attending a hanging at Tyburn and was dressed in such outrageous clothes that he almost stole the show from the condemned prisoners. Reputedly he laughed and joked with admiring onlookers and told them with some pride that one day they would be looking up at him as he stood on the scaffold. Jack was both charming and engaging. He was caught red-handed carrying out a burglary and when his case came up the magistrate was John Fielding, the 'Blind Beak'. Although he could expect little sympathy from such a man he went ahead and spun a yarn about how he had not intended to rob the house he had broken into but had actually been keeping a tryst with a young lady by the name of Dolly Frampton. She was a servant girl and the hour was late, well after her employers would allow any admirers to come and go. To support his case, he got Dolly to appear as a witness. This she did sporting a remarkably low-cut and well-filled bodice with which she made a considerable impact in the court, creating an atmosphere which mollified even Fielding's mood even though, of course, he could not actually see her. To everyone's amazement, he let Rann off with a warning as to his future conduct. Rann remained cheery to the end. When he was finally in the condemned cell at Newgate, he was visited by an unusually large number of well-wishers, most of them women. He exchanged pleasantries with them as if he did not have a care in the world. He was executed at Tyburn in November 1774 treating the large and hugely appreciative crowd to his latest sartorial creation – a suit of pea-green clothes, equipped with sixteen strings on his breeches of course, and with a large nosegay as an accessory. His carefree manner won him many friends that day.

In 1777 Tyburn witnessed the end of Dr William Dodd. He was in holy orders but boosted his income by extensive writing and by tutoring. Educated and cultured, he was a genial and popular society host. His main problem was that in order to keep up appearances, he lived way beyond his means. The debts piled up, but when the pressure finally became too much he tried to find a way out of his money problems by forging the signature of his patron on a promissory note. The sum concerned was a then massive £4,300. When the deception was discovered, his patron decided against prosecution but the Lord Mayor of the time, who happened to be a banker, decided that an example should be made of Dodd and he was despatched for trial at the Old Bailey. He spoke up very eloquently in his own defence using a speech written for the occasion by Dr Johnson, who also appealed to the King for clemency for Dodd. The subsequent hanging attracted one of the largest crowds ever seen at Tyburn. The occasion was a sobering one because of the dignified way in which Dodd comforted the other felon who was to be hanged at the same time. Dodd curiously put on a nightcap once he mounted the scaffold. Then perhaps even more curiously, an attendant held an umbrella over him. One wag in the crowd was heard to observe that an umbrella at this stage was quite unnecessary since it was so hot in hell that he would soon be dry! Most striking, however, was the otherwise eerie silence that accompanied these sights. Rumours were circulating that Dodd would be resuscitated after an arrangement with the hangman, Dennis, who figures in the novel *Barnaby Rudge* by Charles Dickens. The idea was that Dodd would be taken down as soon as possible and rushed away to an undertaker in Goodge Street where it was hoped that his life could be restored. Treatment involved a physician trying to pump up his lungs to revive him and to administer doses of various supposedly stimulating substances such as peppermint water, extract of horseradish and essence of turpentine. However, despite these efforts, nothing availed to bring Dodd back to life. Dodd's companion on the gallows that day had no rich friends and received no such attention. He was a fifteen-year-old boy called Harris who had been stupid enough to rob a stagecoach. His takings were less than £2 and he had been swiftly apprehended. The price he had to pay was infinitely higher.

James Hackman was a native of Gosport in Hampshire and his parents bought him a commission in an infantry regiment. While on recruiting duty he made the acquaintance of a Miss Martha Reay who had served an apprenticeship as a mantua-maker. Being both of good character and pleasing manner, she attracted the patronage of one of the country's richest aristocrats who took her into his household. Hackman fell desperately in love with her and, deciding that he was not cut out for the army, took holy orders. He became a curate in a very rural benefice. It is not obvious why he took this drastic step because it meant that his financial state was as dire as that of the proverbial church mouse. If he thought that his lady-love would be impressed by such piety, he was mistaken. It eventually dawned on him that he was the victim of unrequited love and that she would not abandon her secure employment and pleasant lifestyle to live with an impoverished priest. One night Hackman saw Miss Reay going to the opera in Covent Garden in her patron's coach. In a sudden insane burst of frustrated passion, he rushed to his lodgings for his pistols – strange possessions for a man of the cloth. He then made his way to the theatre, shot Miss Reay, fatally wounding her and turning one of the pistols on himself, tried to take his own life. He was unsuccessful and was quickly arrested and lodged in Newgate. There were no mitigating circumstances to take into account although Hackman was so full of contrition that it seemed as if he almost welcomed the attentions of the hangman. He was hanged on 19 April 1779. Some wag penned a piece of doggerel to commemorate this sorry chain of events:

> O clergyman! O wicked one!
> In Covent Garden shot her.
> No time to cry upon her God –
> It's hoped he's not forgot her.

It was unusual for brothers to act as partners in highway robbery which alone makes George and Joseph Weston of particular interest. They were hanged at Tyburn on 3 September 1782. Young men from the provinces who drifted to London in search of wealth and fame, they were seduced by the raffish but expensive delights of the metropolis, turning to crime to be able to engage in them more fully. Horse-stealing, confidence tricks, forgery and smuggling were all attempted before the pair decided to chance their luck as highwaymen. They started by robbing a coach conveying the Royal Mail and successfully made off with bills of exchange and banknotes to an estimated value of £15,000. Time was not on the side of the Weston brothers because they had to cash these bills as quickly as possible before the details were circulated throughout the country. Accordingly, they set off on a high-speed dash around the country in a post-chaise with George disguised as a naval captain and Joseph dressed as his servant. A team of Bow Street Runners was deployed to bring them to justice and set off in hot pursuit every time they heard that the Westons had been recognised trying to negotiate the bills. However, the brothers managed to elude their pursuers and eventually it became obvious that the trail had gone cold. In fact with their ill-gotten gains the Westons had acquired property in the small Sussex town of Winchelsea. There they posed as men of respectability and substance, entering local society. George even managed to be elected a churchwarden, carving himself a unique place in the history of highwaymen by so doing. However, they lived beyond their means and their creditors eventually called on the authorities to help them recover what they owed. This threat to their little idyll on the Sussex coast made them panic and they fled to London where they were soon run to ground by the persistent men from Bow Street. They were locked up in Newgate but their friends managed to smuggle a file and a brace of pistols in to them. The brothers broke out of their fetters, overpowered a warder and managed to get out of the prison but they were recaptured soon after and found guilty of a number of capital offences. They were immortalised, albeit as a pair of scoundrels who thoroughly deserved their fate, by William Makepeace Thackeray (1811–63) in his unfinished and now largely forgotten novel *Denis Duval*.

There is some confusion as to exactly who was the last person to die on the scaffold at Tyburn. Some sources cite a William Ryland, forger, hanged at Tyburn on 29 August 1783 but others claim the dubious distinction belongs to John Austin, hanged on the same day. The ending of executions at Tyburn had come about not because of more humane or enlightened attitudes towards penal policy. Far from it. They had ceased because the disorder they created disrupted trade and commerce in the City and along the route from Newgate. They also offended against the even tenor of life and affected property prices in the highly fashionable streets and squares that were being built in the neighbourhood of Tyburn.

Calls for the relocation of the Tyburn gallows began to be heard early in the eighteenth century and it was in 1719 that a move to Stamford Hill was mentioned. Another site which was considered for the location of a replacement gallows was Camden Town and the crossroads near the Mother Redcap Inn which was on the road to Hampstead. However, the decision was made to transfer Tyburn's hangings to a space outside Newgate Prison. The disruption to London's business that occurred at every Tyburn Fair could now be largely avoided. Even so, this decision did not meet with universal approval. In particular Dr Johnson fulminated:

> No sir; they object that the old method drew together a number of spectators. If they do not draw spectators, they do not answer their purpose. The old method was most satisfactory for all parties: the public was gratified by a procession; the criminal was supported by it. Why has all this to be swept away?

In large part, this chapter has focused on some of Tyburn's best-known victims and curious or notorious cases. It is important, however, to dispel any impression that Tyburn was the destination only of those whose lifestyles and activities marked them out from the crowd. The felons themselves and the crimes they had committed were usually nothing other than mundane. Many were thieves and robbers. The items they stole were often of little value. They were life's losers and London's forgotten criminals.

NINE

Newgate to Tyburn in the Eighteenth Century

The three miles from Newgate to Tyburn was the last journey on earth for the condemned felons. Although most are unlikely to have been noting their surroundings with any great interest – other than perhaps to look for a way of escaping – they travelled a route imbued with many interesting features. What were some of the major historical and topographical features along or close to the route from Newgate to Tyburn which could have been seen around 1783, the last year in which felons made this dismal one-way journey?

Newgate was an ancient gaol that took its name from the adjacent building of the same name, erected around AD 200. This was the nearest of London's six landward gates to the powerful fort that the Romans had constructed in the north-western corner of their settlement, Londinium, in about AD 120. Close by was Ludgate and the area between the two gates came to be known as 'The Bailey', a bailey denoting a ward or court within an enclosed space. The name 'Old Bailey' was applied for the first time about 1760 to a new street that resulted from the demolition of several small alleys in this area. Newgate had a turbulent history but survived until 1777, being the last of the City's gates to be demolished. It looked rather odd in its last years because it was topped with a curious ventilating device invented by a Dr Hales.

Newgate, the prison, stood some distance to the east of the Fleet River which flowed close to the west wall of the City. Although its origins may have been earlier, it was certainly used as a prison around 1130 for housing people thought to be dangerous to the Crown. It was also the prison for the County of Middlesex and the City of London and was supervised by their respective sheriffs, they in turn appointing the keeper. It gained a fearful reputation both for the horrors of its accommodation and the corrupt and cruel behaviour of its keepers. It is therefore no coincidence that Wat Tyler's rebels attacked and partly demolished it in 1381. Attacks aside, the fabric was frequently neglected and it had to be extensively rebuilt several times. In 1770 a massive reconstruction programme was embarked upon which was not completed before large parts of it were demolished during the Gordon Riots of 1780 when the mob let the prisoners go free. It was quickly rebuilt but with little improvement to its facilities.

Emerging from Newgate into Old Bailey, the procession turned westwards at the junction with Newgate Street and Giltspur Street. Newgate Street was once known as Blow Bladder Lane because of the butcher's shambles in that area and the common practice of inserting the bladders of sheep into carcases in order to make them swell. They therefore looked bigger and prices could quite literally be inflated. Giltspur Street had previously been known as Knightrider Street because knights probably used this thoroughfare on their way to do mock battle at the Smithfield tournaments. At a later stage it is likely that gilt spurs were actually made there. The procession then passed through the site of the Newgate itself and stopped outside the church of St Sepulchre on the north side. The full name of this building was the Church of the Holy Sepulchre without Newgate, the name referring to the Church of the Holy Sepulchre in Jerusalem and probably adopted at about the time of the Crusades. The Great Fire burnt itself out almost exactly on this spot and the church was severely damaged. At midnight before an execution, the sexton of St Sepulchre's traversed an underground passage from the church to Newgate, rang his handbell outside the prisoner's cell and offered some salutary advice in verse form. What the other inmates thought about being woken up by this performance has unfortunately not been recorded.

The procession now entered Snow Hill, which wound sharply down to 'Oldbourne' or Holborn Bridge over the Fleet. In the eighteenth century Snow Hill gained some notoriety as one of the places where vicious gangs of young rakes congregated. At this point the Fleet was alternatively known as the 'Holebourne' or 'stream in the hollow', meaning the significant valley that the Fleet had carved for itself at this point shortly before joining the Thames. St Andrews Church, Holborn, situated at the top of Holborn Hill, would have looked down on the passing procession. While resembling many other Wren churches, it had escaped the Great Fire but was so decayed that it was largely rebuilt by the great man himself between 1684 and 1687.

Having crossed the bridge over the Fleet, the procession then made its way up the steep western bank past the junction with Saffron Hill coming from the north. This name commemorates an estate in the vicinity where the Bishops of Ely once had a palace and which became famous for the cultivation of saffron (*Crocus sativus*). This spice has long been valued as an aromatic flavouring for cakes, sauces and rice dishes, as a colouring agent and for a variety of medicinal purposes. The Bishops' Palace had been demolished in about 1772 and by the second half of the seventeenth century large amounts of the land on which it had stood had been built upon. It soon became notorious for its ramshackle housing and the criminal tendencies and practices of its inhabitants.

Soon after gaining Holborn itself, Fetter Lane was passed on the left. The origins of this name may have been from the Old French *faitor*, a lawyer, because of the numbers of those practising law in the area. However, it appears that members of the legal profession were not always held in high esteem and that 'faitor' eventually came to mean idler or vagabond and the lane and its vicinity became a notorious criminal rookery. Another explanation is that the name originates with the fetters worn on the cuirasses of fighting men in the Middle Ages which were made by armourers in workshops in this area. Close to the Holborn end of Fetter Lane had lived Nathaniel Tomkins, the brother-in-law of Edmund Waller who was implicated in Waller's Plot of 1643 for which he was hanged outside the front door of his residence, no. 5. Other punishments and executions took place in Fetter Lane from time to time. From the middle of the eighteenth century, Fetter Lane became known for its conventicles or clandestine religious meetings and meeting places. The Fetter Lane Independent Chapel was established in 1660 and over the years the voices of many famous preachers, including John Wesley, echoed through its halls. True to the heterodox religious traditions of the area, the first Moravian Chapel in London was erected there. Others who lived in Fetter Lane included Thomas Hobbes (1588–1679), the political philosopher, the poet John Dryden (1631–1700) and Tom Paine (1737–1809), the maverick polemicist.

Leather Lane met Holborn on the north side. A famous thoroughfare with a street market even then, its name was probably derived from *leveroun*, an old French word for greyhound which possibly referred to an inn that once stood in the area. Another explanation is that leather-sellers who obtained their raw material from Smithfield Market nearby had established businesses in the area. Shortly after Leather Lane, Gray's Inn Lane (as it was known until 1862) joined Holborn from the north. This was the main route from the north to the various city markets and therefore always a thoroughfare of considerable importance. Gray's Inn itself on the north side of Holborn recalled the name of the de Greys who resided in the vicinity in the thirteenth century. This important family numbered among its members Walter de Grey who was Chancellor to King John between 1206 and 1214 and Reginald, the Chief Justice of Chester under Edward I at the time he was trying to subdue the Welsh. In the early fourteenth century the family moved away and Gray's Inn began its long association with the legal profession although its records of this date back only to 1569. The route through the Holborn area passed innumerable hostelries including on the north side the Black Bull, the Bell, the Three Cups and on the south the Black Swan and the George. These did a roaring trade on Tyburn Fair days.

The Inns of Court were, and indeed still are, training institutions and professional associations for barristers. They began to have a corporate existence in the fifteenth century and played a vital role in the development of a secular legal profession. In this sense the word 'inn' means a hostel for barristers and students of the law. The latter lived in and studied a curriculum on aspects of law as well as taking classes in history, music and dancing to round them out and prepare them for a prestigious role in society. The Inns of Chancery were in effect institutions that housed and prepared those aspiring to enter the Inns of Court. By the middle of the eighteenth century, the educational function of the Inns of Chancery was just about defunct. Several of these Inns would have acted as mute witnesses to the procession to Tyburn. Barnard's Inn was established in 1435 close to Fetter Lane on the south side of Holborn and nearby was Furnival's Inn (1383), close to Lincoln's Inn on the north side of Holborn. Staple Inn at the junction of Holborn and Gray's Inn Lane had been founded in 1378 and had perhaps gained its name because it was at one time a wool warehouse. This point was known as Holborn Bars and marked the western extremity of the City of London. Here tolls and commercial duties were exacted and measures taken to prevent undesirables from entering the City. A gallows once existed at this point.

Innumerable famous men were associated with Gray's Inn including Archbishops Whitgift and Laud; Sir Nicholas Bacon and Francis Bacon; Thomas Cromwell; Sir Thomas Gresham; William Cecil; Lord Burghley and William Camden, the eminent antiquarian. On the south side of Holborn, the procession would have passed Lincoln's Inn. Founded in the mid-fourteenth century, it took its name either from Henry de Lacy, 3rd Earl of Lincoln, a close adviser of Edward I, or from one Thomas de Lyncoln described as the King's Serjeant of Holborn. Lincoln's Inn is likely to have been on this site since around 1420, when the land on which it now stands was leased from the Bishops of Chichester. The playwright Ben Jonson may have worked as a bricklayer when the Chapel was being built in the 1620s. Leading alumni of Lincoln's Inn by 1783 included Sir Thomas More; Jeremy Bentham; Robert Walpole, Britain's first Prime Minister; John Donne, the metaphysical poet, and David Garrick.

Lincoln's Inn Fields had long been a popular place of resort and recreation for the citizenry of London. In 1586 Anthony Babington and some of his fellow conspirators were executed there in a fashion so barbaric as to cause even Queen Elizabeth qualms of conscience. Sentenced to death for conspiring to assassinate her and to place

Mary, Queen of Scots, on the throne, they were hanged, drawn and quartered. However, Babington and the first batch of conspirators were still fully conscious when taken down and then eviscerated. Lincoln's Inn Fields was chosen for this brutal demonstration of the power of the state because a figure of Elizabeth made of wax and stuck with pins was said to have been found there. The area certainly had something of a reputation for harbouring Catholic recusants in the dark days of religious persecution. Close by in Sardinia Street were buildings occupied by the Franciscan Order which were attacked and set on fire by an anti-Catholic mob in 1688 at the time that James II was making his ill-judged attempts to reimpose Roman Catholicism on his subjects. Although the Franciscans had abandoned this building, it was once again wrecked during the anti-Catholic Gordon Riots of 1780.

In 1683 the execution of Lord William Russell had taken place in Lincoln's Inn Fields. He had been implicated in the Rye House Plot, a hare-brained scheme to block the road close to Rye House outside Hoddesdon in Hertfordshire and assassinate Charles II and the Duke of York when they were forced to stop at the obstacle. These plans were rendered meaningless when the intended victims passed by considerably earlier than expected. In 1711 Newcastle House at the corner of Great Queen Street became the home of Thomas Pelham-Holles, later better known as the Duke of Newcastle and a Whig Prime Minister. As Prime Minister he was obviously in a position to dispense favours. One man, by the name of Sir Thomas Robinson, frequently called round to curry favour and the Duke tired of having to receive him. He instructed his servants to tell Robinson whenever he called that their master was out. This did not deter him and he coolly invited himself into the kitchen to wait for the moment when the Duke might become available. While he was waiting, he apparently kept glancing at the clock and playing with a pet monkey. This behaviour irritated the Duke and so the household servants were eventually instructed to send Robinson away with a flea in his ear after reciting this neat little epigram: 'Sir, his Grace has gone out, the clock has stopped and the monkey is dead'.

Continuing along Holborn, the procession now approached the dominant bulk of St Giles-in-the-Fields which originated as the chapel of a leper hospital founded in 1101 by Matilda, the Queen of Henry I. The chapel only became a parish church in 1547 after the hospital was dissolved by Henry VIII. In a ruinous state in the early 1620s, the church was rebuilt only to deteriorate again to the extent that money had to be raised for its total rebuilding. This was carried out by the comparatively obscure Henry Flitcroft between 1730 and 1734. Flitcroft was better known as a gardener than as an architect but he drew extensively on what might be called the 'Wren and Gibbs' tradition which had provided the City with so many handsome rebuilt churches after the Great Fire. St Giles was only subsumed within the encroaching urban spread of London in the earlier part of the eighteenth century and indeed some areas of the parish especially in the north were still not fully developed by the 1780s. The church and the small rural settlement around it were therefore something of a landmark on the road to Tyburn.

In much earlier times there had been a gallows standing at the north-western end of St Giles High Street. This location had been chosen as suitably distant from London and Westminster but as the built-up districts spread northwards and westwards, hangings were moved to Tyburn, which was still a rural spot. It was entirely appropriate that the church was dedicated to St Giles because he was the patron saint of the indigent, of cripples, outcasts and social pariahs and there were many of these among the wretched felons who passed this way while travelling to Tyburn. At the gate of the former hospital the procession would stop briefly while the condemned criminals were presented with a bowl of ale. When St Giles itself had been the end of the journey from Newgate this had been literally their last refreshment but when executions were moved to Tyburn an enterprising publican set up a tavern called the Bowl. According to some accounts the present Angel in St Giles High Street is a reincarnation of the Bowl. The landlord and his successors provided ale free to the felons and did a brisk trade with the crowds on the days of Tyburn Fair. Jack Sheppard is said to have partaken of a drink at this point. He was unable to finish it and is reputed to have quipped with those around him, 'Give the remainder to Jonathan Wild'. The Crown was another inn said to have dispensed drinks at St Giles. A sense of solemnity suitable for the processions was lent by the tolling of its great bell. Money to pay for this custom had been provided through the munificence of Alice Dudley, the saintly daughter-in-law of Robert Dudley, the less-than-saintly Earl of Leicester, in the 1640s.

Eventually the procession got on its way once more, passing out of St Giles to the junction with the Tottenham Court Road. This led north to what had once been the manor of Tothele or Tottenheale. By the 1780s the open countryside there was being threatened by the new east to west road that had been built around the northern extremities of London from Islington and the Battle Bridge area towards Marylebone and Paddington. The procession continued westwards along what had become known as Oxford Street. This was a very ancient road, long used for commerce and by armies marching westwards. On old maps it is sometimes indicated as the 'Road to Oxford', as 'Tyburn Road', 'Tyburn Way' or 'Tyburn Lane' and indeed various other names. By the middle of the eighteenth century, however, the eastern portion had acquired the name 'Oxford Street' because land on the north side of the road had been bought by Edward Harley, Earl of Oxford. Residential property for the rich was spreading along both sides of Oxford Street but it was fronted by high quality shops catering for the affluent inhabitants of this growing residential quarter. One conspicuous building roughly half way between Tottenham Court Road and Tyburn was the Oxford Market built in the early eighteenth century to serve these new residential districts. It was now possible to see the countryside ahead and the procession began to pass through a quarter of London which was either recently constructed or still being developed. Completely open country, however, was only reached when the procession arrived at Tyburn. As recently as the 1700s, the way to Tyburn passing through this area was described as 'a deep hollow road and full of sloughs; with here and there a ragged house, the lurking place of cutthroats'.

Tyburn was not the only location for executions in the London area. Here the executioner displays a severed head to a rapt crowd. Although this is supposed to be Kennington Common, the Triple Tree that can be seen calls this into question.

Jonathan Wild travels from Newgate to Tyburn. If ever a London criminal was feared and loathed it was Wild, and the crowd gleefully pelt him with missiles. *(Billie Love Historical Collection)*

Some of Wild's victims. Wild used his exhaustive knowledge of London's underworld to rid himself of enemies and rivals, many of whom he framed. They were indicted for felonies and went on to be hanged at Tyburn.

A mock invitation to Wild's hanging in 1725. He was the self-styled 'Thief Taker General' and his pretensions to be a public benefactor and his mercilessness to those who crossed his path meant that the day of his execution was one of jubilation and relief. *(Mary Evans Picture Library)*

Thomas Turlis, executioner, was busy at Tyburn in the 1760s and among his victims was the hated murderer Elizabeth Brownrigg. He also had the strange duty of publicly burning issue No. 45 of the *North Briton*, the political journal published by the maverick MP, John Wilkes. This particular issue contained a seditious libel against the King.

Elizabeth Brownrigg in her cell in Newgate. She systematically mistreated and abused her servant girls, one of whom, Mary Clifford, died as a result. Elizabeth was hanged at Tyburn and her body anatomised and displayed for many years at Surgeons' Hall. *(Mary Evans Picture Library)*

With accomplices, Catherine Hayes murdered her husband, his severed head being thrown into the Thames. It was recovered, publicly displayed and recognised. Elizabeth was hanged at Tyburn in 1726.

The execution of Earl Ferrers, an aristocratic scapegrace, who died at Tyburn on 5 May 1760 for murdering a faithful family retainer. Note the grandstand and the fact that the crowds are being kept at a distance. *(Museum of London/HIP/Topham Picturepoint)*

Sir John Fielding (1721–80), the 'Blind Beak', succeeded his half-brother Henry as magistrate at Bow Street. A man of energy and integrity, he was said to be able to recognise 3,000 London thieves by their voices alone. He enthusiastically advocated street lighting as a deterrent to crime. *(National Portrait Gallery)*

Newgate Prison ablaze during the Gordon Riots of 1780. This hated prison had been extensively rebuilt in the 1770s and scarcely had work been completed than it was attacked and destroyed by the rioters. Rebuilding started almost immediately. *(Corporation of London/HIP/Topham Picturepoint)*

A hanging outside the debtor's door at Newgate, *c.* 1809. When hangings ceased at Tyburn in 1783, they were transferred to a site close to the rebuilt Newgate Prison where the size and behaviour of the crowd could be more easily controlled. Hangings continued there until the end of public executions in 1868. *(Museum of London/HIP/Topham Picturepoint)*

A view of Tyburn Turnpike with the tollhouse and the gate prominent. This is close to where Marble Arch now stands at a point which had been an important road junction since time immemorial. A movable gallows was used in the last years of hangings at Tyburn, so it is impossible to say exactly where each hanging took place. *(Mary Evans Picture Library)*

A floor plaque purporting to mark the site of the Tyburn Tree. This plaque is placed at the bottom of Edgware Road, a location that does not encourage quiet contemplation of the sights and sounds of the past. *(Hulton Archive)*

On leaving the junction with Tottenham Court Road, the procession had skirted the northern extremity of the Soho area. The word 'Soho' was a hunting cry and indeed this area had been used for hunting purposes until building development started in the seventeenth century. A number of mansions with large grounds such as Monmouth House and Leicester House had been a feature of the area but by the 1670s and 1680s the district was changing and a mix of humble housing and small industrial workshops had appeared. The area attracted foreign immigrants in large numbers, especially French Huguenots, who bestowed on it the cosmopolitan character that had already become one of its distinguishing characteristics by the middle of the eighteenth century. It had also become a somewhat bohemian quarter, attracting considerable numbers of artists, some on their way to fame and glory but most going nowhere at all. Parts of Soho such as Dean Street, Wardour Street and Poland Street were slowly losing their exclusive cachet by the 1780s. Dean Street had been built in the 1680s and at first had numbered many titled families among its inhabitants before Huguenots began moving in, while Wardour Street was becoming the haunt of antique dealers and furniture-makers, but Poland Street managed to maintain its relative exclusivity rather longer. The street took its name from the King of Poland tavern which stood at its junction with Oxford Street and which the procession would have passed on its way to Tyburn. Berwick Street to the west, built slightly later, was probably named after the Duke of Berwick, an illegitimate son of James II, and seems to have attracted French immigrants from the start – so much so, in fact, that there were two French churches in the street.

Large-scale planned development had taken place in the Mayfair district bounded by Oxford Street to the north and Hyde Park to the west and centred on Grosvenor Square. In 1735 Grosvenor Street was described as 'a spacious well-built street, inhabited chiefly by people of distinction'. At that time about a third of its inhabitants were titled. The 'Grosvenor Estate' as it came to be known encompassed land acquired in 1677 when Sir Thomas Grosvenor, a baronet from Cheshire, made an advantageous marriage to a Mary Davies. She was the heiress of a nouveau riche London scrivener who had inherited substantial amounts of undeveloped land close to Westminster. The wedding took place in 1677 when Mary was just twelve years of age. The match ensured Grosvenor's own and his family's future prosperity but Mary's subsequent behaviour must have caused him a few headaches. In 1685 she announced to her stunned family that she had decided to convert to Catholicism. As if this were not bad enough for a staunchly Protestant family, Mary then began to display signs of increasing mental instability, one of her favourite activities being to lock her servants into cupboards. This excitement apart, development of the area on land where the May Fair had once been held was largely completed in the 1770s. Ned Ward in his *The London Spy* provided a rather jaundiced view of the May Fair: 'In all the multitudes that I ever beheld, I never in my life saw such a number of lazy rascals, and so hateful a throng of beggarly, sluttish strumpets, who were a scandal to the Creation'.

To the north of Oxford Street busy periods of building activity had culminated in the development of the area around Portland Place, Cavendish Square and Wigmore Street on the Portman and Portland estates among others. These districts to the north and others south of Oxford Street, were composed of high-class, elegant residential property and their development had begun early in the eighteenth century. Portland Place can with some justification be described as the grandest street of eighteenth-century London and it had been laid out by Robert and James Adam around 1778. It is said to owe its remarkable width to a promise made to Lord Foley that the view northwards from his house that blocked the southern end of the street would never be obscured. The land in this area lent itself to comprehensive development because, unlike much land in the east of the City, it was divided into large estates mostly owned by a very small number of individuals. They needed little encouragement to embark on the lucrative development of this land for fashionable housing. There would have been a piquant contrast between the refined and affluent appearance of the inhabitants of these streets and squares and the rag-tag and bobtail who turned out in substantial numbers to watch or follow the procession to Tyburn.

The influential residents of the increasingly fashionable West End may well have been morbidly fascinated by the sight of the procession and the hangings but they did not like the regular presence in their neighbourhood of large numbers of boisterous, uncouth and often drunken members of the *hoi polloi*.

At 173 Oxford Street the procession would have passed the 'Pantheon' which had been opened in 1772. This was a fashionable resort for affluent Londoners and was described as 'a winter Ranelagh', the latter being one of London's best-known pleasure gardens. It was a kind of winter garden, performing many of the same functions as Ranelagh but open all the year round and with the advantage of being entirely protected from the elements. Concerts and masked balls were among the favourite activities. Among its early patrons were literary figures of stature such as Oliver Goldsmith, Fanny Burney and Edward Gibbon. In its heyday the Pantheon excited comments verging on the hyperbolic. Horace Walpole declared it 'the most beautiful edifice in England'; Gibbon thought it the wonder of the eighteenth century and of the British Empire. The socialites of fashionable London were a capricious lot, however, and by the time of the last procession to Tyburn, they were drifting off elsewhere in search of new experiences and sensations with which to counter their ennui. At 441 Oxford Street the procession passed a hostelry called the Man Loaded with Mischief, which at one time displayed a sign painted by none other than William Hogarth depicting a man staggering along bearing on his back a woman, a magpie and a monkey.

The procession crossed a somewhat rickety bridge over the Tyburn stream itself and then the outer fringes of the built-up area were reached. Ahead was the large expanse of Hyde Park, part of a tract of land bequeathed to Westminster Abbey in the eleventh century. It was sequestered by Henry VIII at the dissolution of the monasteries and used for hunting, deer still being hunted there by royalty as late as 1768. The park was opened to the public early in the seventeenth century. Its strategic position on London's north-western extremity meant that it had been used periodically for military purposes and as recently as 1780 troops had been encamped there during the Gordon Riots. It had become a place attracting fashionable society and those who were well-heeled but had more raffish propensities. An observer around 1700 described a bevy of showily dressed ladies enjoying refreshments that had been brought to them in their coaches. He reported that some of them were loudly and ostentatiously 'singing, others laughing, others tickling one another, and all of them Toying and devouring Cheese Cakes, Marchpane and China Oranges'. Strenuous efforts were made to encourage a greater sense of decorum among those seeking their pleasures in Hyde Park. It seems that these endeavours were doomed to failure because in the 1770s the *Westminster Gazette* wrote rather disapprovingly of the men of fashion who disported themselves in the park. According to the correspondent, 'The men imitate the women in almost everything. Perfumes, paint, and effeminate baubles engross most of their time, and now learning is looked upon as an unworthy attainment.' The writer waxed even more indignant when he caught sight of a Guards officer who, while engaged in military exercises, had the temerity to wear a white frock coat, generously ornamented with gold cord, over a waistcoat and breeches of blue satin. To cap it all, the same officer brandished a scented handkerchief to offset the unpleasant smell of gunpowder. As the writer despairs at the behaviour of the younger generation, he ruminates gloomily over the amount of tea-drinking he saw taking place. According to him the habit was degenerate, unmanly and undermined the virility of commissioned officers.

The park and the area around it had a bad reputation because of the activities of highwaymen and footpads. It also became notorious as the place where bored, tetchy and vainglorious so-called gentlemen of the eighteenth century sought to resolve their differences by duelling. Although quick to take offence, those who participated in duels usually conducted them with great mutual courtesy. In 1762, John Wilkes, the controversial political maverick known for his irreverent and acerbic wit, fought Samuel Martin, a notoriously cantankerous MP who had referred to him in the House as 'a stabber in the dark, a cowardly and malignant scoundrel'. Seething with injured pride and lusting for revenge, Wilkes called Martin out immediately after the speech and they made their way to Hyde Park. In both cases their opening shots missed their targets but then Wilkes fell, wounded in the abdomen. Martin, full of concern, hurried over as Wilkes lay writhing on the ground. The latter, determined not to be outdone so far as courtesy was concerned, then urged Martin to hurry away from the scene before the authorities arrived. Most duels in Hyde Park were carried out in a circular area called the Ring in the northeast of the Park close to the Tyburn gallows.

At the Tyburn corner of Hyde Park was the 'Donkeys' Dairies'. Here several dozen mother asses were kept and their milk bottled for sale to the residents of the fashionable streets and squares developing in the district. Asses' milk was highly thought of and sold at twice the price of cows' milk. This was also available, being taken straight from cows that grazed in Hyde Park. Its vendors would have been busy on Tyburn Fair days.

Proceeding south from the site of the gallows was Park Lane, a narrow rutted lane which for centuries had been bounded on its west side by the high brick wall enclosing the east side of Hyde Park. By the 1780s some select development had taken place in Park Lane which included Somerset House at the corner of Oxford Street which had been built for Viscount Bateman in 1770.

This, then, was the well-beaten route from Newgate to Tyburn. It was followed by the regular processions of condemned felons, riding in the cart with their coffins, their armed guards and the necessary functionaries, until 1783. The ending of Tyburn Fair deprived London of one of its most popular spectacles, albeit one which is now thought of as utterly distasteful and pointless. Its passing marked the end of centuries of a ritualised exhibition and was mourned by many, applauded by a few. London would never be quite the same again.

TEN

Some Hangmen of Tyburn

It is possible that the use of hanging as a legal execution was introduced to England by the Anglo-Saxons. Sparse records make some reference to hanging in Norman and Plantagenet times and suggest that the profession of hangman did not emerge until later. Indeed, it appears that when a miscreant was condemned to death, the individual prosecuting had to obtain the services of an executioner or, if none was available, do the job himself. Failure to do so could render the prosecutor himself liable to imprisonment. Playing a supporting role to the gallows was decapitation with the axe and block which was generally reserved for the execution of the high-born and those found guilty of treason and sedition.

Given England's established reputation for hanging, it is perhaps understandable that when Anne Boleyn went to the block in 1536, a headsman had to be brought over from Calais to do the job. In Tudor times large numbers were executed, usually for their heterodox political or religious views. Many of them were burned at the stake. A hangman would partly strangle the victims and then ignite the faggots around them. Others were hanged, drawn and quartered, which required of the hangman some elementary skills in butchery. Records of executioners from the Tudor period are scanty, but there was one in the reign of Henry VIII (1509–47) by the name of Cratwell. Although his professional duties probably kept him busy, like so many other executioners he was unable to resist some illegal freelance work and was eventually hanged for theft.

Derrick, forename apparently unknown, was an important hangman around the end of the sixteenth century. Etymological dictionaries claim that Derrick gave his name to the device still used as a hoist which bears some resemblance to a gallows. He is likely to have had a hand in torturing and executing Guy Fawkes. The torture was extremely thorough and the unfortunate Fawkes was so enfeebled that he could only ascend the scaffold with assistance. Derrick had an assistant by the name of Gregory Brandon who served as a hangman, combining this function when required with that of axeman and torturer. Gregory passed on his trade to his son Richard, who is reputed to have prepared assiduously for his role in life by cutting the heads off live cats and dogs. Richard Brandon was certainly one of England's most famous executioners and numbered among his illustrious victims Thomas Wentworth, Earl of Strafford, executed for treason in 1641, and the Archbishop of Canterbury, William Laud, who was executed in 1645. Brandon reached the peak of his career when he removed Charles I's head in 1649. Although the axeman was disguised, the dextrous way in which the job was done bore the hallmarks of the skill for which Brandon was renowned. He is said to have suffered such feelings of remorse for his work as a regicide that he died shortly afterwards.

'The Deadly Nevergreen' at Tyburn was fully occupied in the summer of 1649 when twenty-three men and one woman were hanged on the same occasion by William Lowen, of whom little is known except that his main occupation was that of refuse collector. He was replaced by Edward Dun whose notoriety lies in his almost certainly having been the executioner ordered to disinter the bodies of Cromwell, Ireton and Bradshaw from Henry VII's Chapel in Westminster Abbey and place them in full view on poles on the roof of Westminster Hall. Cromwell's head remained there until the death of Charles II in 1685 but his torso had been thrown contemptuously into a pit near Tyburn. To Dun probably also fell the task in 1660 of publicly burning John Milton's work *The Tenure of Kings and Magistrates*. Published in 1649, in it Milton had defended the execution of Charles I.

Upon Dun's death in 1663 John Ketch, commonly known as Jack, took over. As with many other members of his profession, he had earlier found himself on the wrong side of the authorities but this did not prevent him plying his trade for twenty-three years, which is surprising because he was universally regarded as both brutal and incompetent. In 1682 he is supposed to have gone on strike for better wages – and obtained them – before going on to end his career in a blaze of notoriety. One celebrity whom he despatched with an axe was Lord William Russell, arraigned for high treason in connection with the Rye House Plot to assassinate Charles II. The date set for the execution was 21 July 1683 and the place Lincoln's Inn Fields. As was traditional when dealing with the high-born, Ketch as executioner asked his victim to forgive him. Having obtained Russell's pardon, Ketch then received 10 guineas as an incentive to do the job quickly and effectively. Even with this cash bonus he bungled the job. The first blow of the axe merely wounded Russell who had to endure three more blows before his head was severed from his body. Rumours circulated to the effect that Ketch had been bribed not to kill Russell with the first blow of the axe. Ketch denied this strenuously, blaming his victim for moving his head at the last moment. In 1685 Ketch was given the task of beheading the Duke of Monmouth on Tower Hill. Again money changed hands but did not guarantee the quality of Ketch's work. Gallows lore is unreliable historical evidence, but Monmouth is supposed to have asked to handle the axe. Running his finger along the blade he reputedly commented that it was not sharp enough for the job it had to do. In the event five blows were required to end Monmouth's life and Ketch had to finish the job by using a knife to sever the unfortunate man's head. Monmouth was no darling of the crowd but they were so incensed by Ketch's incompetent butchery that he had to be escorted away under military guard to avoid the possibility of being lynched.

To Ketch also fell the job of inflicting punishment on the egregious Titus Oates, a monumental perjurer whose false accusations sent many innocent people to an unjustified judicial death for being implicated in the so-called 'Popish Plot' of 1678–9. Oates's initial punishment was to be pilloried and then whipped at the cart's tail the relatively short distance from Aldgate to Newgate and, a couple of days later, to be whipped the considerably longer distance from Newgate to Tyburn. Ketch seems to have inflicted floggings on Oates with a malignant relish and efficiency markedly missing from his work with the axe, but it may have helped that this time he had the watching crowds eagerly urging him on. They did not like Ketch but they positively loathed Oates. The treatment Oates received nearly killed him. This episode only added to the innumerable tales, both true and false, which centred on Ketch. Ironically, he had already been involved in the hanging, drawing and quartering of various Catholic men, implicated for their involvement in the plot by none other than Oates himself. As well as the Punch character Ketch's name lived on as a bogeyman with which to frighten children.

A later hangman for the City of London and the County of Middlesex was John Price, who took on the role in 1714. Following the example of others of his kind he got into debt and spent time in the Marshalsea Prison in Southwark. He managed to escape in 1718 but a few weeks later attempted to rape an elderly woman at Bunhill Fields. She was selling apples and it may be that Price mistook this for a cover for prostitution, which indeed it frequently was. That did not, however, excuse him. He assaulted her so brutally that she died four days later of her injuries. This crime excited popular revulsion and large hostile crowds turned out to abuse him as he was transported from Newgate to Bunhill Fields, 'going east' rather than the more customary 'going west' of a condemned felon. It was a common practice to execute some convicts at the scene of their crimes, especially if their offences were seen as particularly heinous. Apparently Price met his end at the hand of a hangman named Banks, who was then given the job of placing Price's inert remains on a gibbet which was put on display at Holloway.

Price's successor was noted less for his professional expertise than because he had a hand in executing some of the very last Jacobite rebels in the early eighteenth century. His name was William Marvell and he was yet another executioner who had previously fallen foul of the law. Criminal antecedents apart, Marvell was well equipped for the job. His experience as a blacksmith had allowed him to build up the physique and bulging biceps which must have impressed both victims and spectators. He executed two of the leading Jacobites, Lord Kenmure and the Earl of Derwentwater, at Tower Hill and not only collected a useful fee from the authorities but another from the victims who tried to ensure that he did his work quickly and efficiently. Lord Kenmure would have been justified in asking for a refund because Marvell had to use two blows to sever his head from his body. Marvell's greatest claim to fame is probably that he himself was arrested while riding in a cart at the head of a procession to Tyburn to hang three condemned criminals. Executioners were not popular people and it mattered little to the exultant crowd that his arrest was for debt rather than a serious crime. They seized him, gave him a good thrashing and threw him into a pond before the authorities restored order. Marvell was dismissed a few days later and soon ended up in court charged with theft. He was transported to the American penal colonies and disappeared from the records.

His replacement went by the name of Banks (mentioned overleaf) and he was appointed in November 1717. He hanged the Marquis de Paleotti at Tyburn in March 1718. This unsavoury young man was an Italian who had an argument with his servant which ended when he ran him through with a sword, killing him. Banks seems to have served as hangman for only a short time because the records show a Richard Arnet acting as executioner in 1719. It may have been Arnet who hanged Jack Sheppard. This would have made him extremely unpopular with the London crowds who adored the slippery and resourceful Sheppard. It was probably Arnet who hanged and burned Barbara Spencer in 1721. Her crime was coining, which was punishable as high treason. In 1726 Arnet carried out the same method of execution on the killer Catherine Hayes. In 1725 Arnet had hanged an extortionist named Smith. This would have been a fairly run-of-the-mill event but it was much enlivened when Smith, who had chosen to wear a shroud on the journey from Newgate to Tyburn as a symbol of his penitence, tried to escape. He jumped out of the cart and, elbowing members of the crowd aside, attempted to get away. Unfortunately a running man dressed in a shroud was rather conspicuous and he was quickly recaptured. He was put back in the cart and the procession continued to Tyburn, where Arnet made short work of him. The crowd, however, would have been well satisfied with the day's entertainment.

John Hooper was appointed hangman in August 1728. There was much that was literally butchery in the work of men like Hooper at this time. In 1731, for example, he was required to inflict punishment on a forger named Japhet Crook. He was placed in the pillory at Charing Cross for an hour after which Hooper had to slice off his ears with a sharp knife and then hold them up triumphantly to the watching crowd. As if this was not punishment enough, Hooper then had to slit Crook's nostrils with scissors whereupon a surgeon cauterised the wound. It could be argued that anyone whose job required them to carry out such appalling barbarities needed a sense of humour and Hooper was indeed famous for his. Nicknamed 'the Laughing Hangman', he had a reputation for clowning on the scaffold and for his fund of humorous repartee. It is unlikely that his victims appreciated a flood of jokes and witty banter on the scaffold when they were forced to make Hooper's acquaintance. Towards the end of his career, Hooper was disciplined for selling corpses to surgeons who ran private teaching schools. Like so many others in his trade, he had made the most of all the possible perquisites on offer.

His successor was John Thrift whose career lasted almost eighteen years, a long time to spend in such a fraught occupation. What makes it more extraordinary is that Thrift was a man of very nervous temperament who had even more active criminal tendencies than most in his trade. Trouble seemed to follow him wherever he went. On one occasion he hanged a man called Thomas Reynolds. When his life was reckoned extinct, Reynolds was cut down and placed in his waiting coffin. No sooner was this done than to the crowd's great delight he sat up! Thrift's response was to get him back on to the scaffold and have another go at hanging him. The crowd was incensed by this, adhering to the old-fashioned idea that you should not be punished twice for the same crime. They charged the scaffold, beat Thrift up and, seizing Reynolds, carried him off to seek medical attention, although he died soon afterwards. There was at least one other occasion on which a felon hanged by Thrift returned to life afterwards. Thrift was involved in the hanging of convicted pirates at Execution Dock and in meting out retribution to supporters of Charles Edward Stuart (1720–88), known as 'Bonnie Prince Charlie'. The latter's attempt to win the throne by force of arms was finally suppressed in 1746 and it fell to Thrift to execute many of the rebels. In July 1746 nine of them were hanged, drawn and quartered by Thrift on Kennington Common. He seems to have coped with this task perfectly well but it was another matter when it came to beheading Lords Kilmarnock and Balmerino on Tower Hill. It seems that Thrift was quite happy to browbeat and bully those who were of plebeian origins but it was quite another matter when it came to patricians. His behaviour then turned into a nervous and cringing obsequiousness. He was drunk and nauseatingly apologetic. He did, however, manage to draw on his professional expertise to remove Lord Kilmarnock's noble head with just one blow. Lord Balmerino fared less well. Thrift took three blows to sever his head. Shortly afterwards it fell to Thrift to execute the egregious rapist Lord Lovat. Perhaps it was the knowledge that Lovat, in spite of his title, was of less than aristocratic origins or that the crowd were wholeheartedly repelled by him, that enabled Thrift to treat the crowd to a copy-book decapitation. Over his long career, Thrift made many enemies and in 1750 became involved in a scuffle with a hostile and insulting crowd. In the confusion, someone in the crowd was killed and Thrift found himself charged with murder. Although found guilty, he was sentenced to transportation rather than hanging and finally given a free pardon. He seems to have resumed his duties but to have died not long afterwards.

Thomas Turlis succeeded Thrift and he had the job of hanging that aristocratic scapegrace, Laurence Shirley, the 4th Earl Ferrers. This man was totally without redeeming features but is remembered in penal history as the only English peer who was hanged for murder rather than being beheaded. He died at Tyburn on 5 May 1760. In 1761 Turlis hanged a Swiss artist called Theodore Gardelle who murdered his landlady and after dismembering her, unsuccessfully tried to dispose of the pieces. Gardelle was hanged in the Haymarket. In 1763 Turlis had the strange job of publicly burning an edition of the radical journal *North Briton*. This was published and largely written by John Wilkes (1727–97) and was virulently critical of the King, the church hierarchy and many of the politicians of the day. Its iconoclastic zeal reached a peak in issue No.45 when Wilkes accused King George III of systematic lying. Wilkes was prosecuted for seditious libel and imprisoned. Londoners, however, loved him for his irreverent attitudes and acerbic wit. The burning was intended to symbolise an execution and a large and angry crowd turned out in front of the Royal Exchange yelling insults at the authorities. A fire was started on to which Turlis began to drop pages from the *North Briton* but this enraged the crowd, who started bombarding everybody who looked official with mud and stones. Turlis just about managed to do the job before having to run for his life. Wilkes, incidentally, was renowned for the speed of his repartee. On one occasion an eminent and powerful political enemy warned him, 'You will either die of a pox or on the gallows.' Wilkes's lightning riposte is reputed to have been, 'That depends, my Lord, on whether I embrace your mistress or your principles.' It was Turlis who hanged the savage murderess Elizabeth Brownrigg at Tyburn on 14 September 1767. He died unexpectedly in April 1771 just after he had carried out a hanging at Kingston-on-Thames.

Turlis was followed by Edward Dennis. He had only held office for a short time when he was required to hang a young woman called Mary Jones at Tyburn. Her crime was that of stealing muslin valued at £5 5s. She was destitute and her children starving. The tragedy of the premature and savage end to her tragic life encapsulates the brutality of the 'Bloody Code' as it impinged on the poor and largely powerless victims of Britain's transformation into an urban and industrial society. The most famous victim of Dennis was almost certainly the Revd William Dodd who had been sentenced to death for forgery but whose reputation as the perpetrator of good works meant that many eminent people had rallied to his defence. Dennis must have acquired something of a taste for despatching clergymen, because two years later, in 1779, he officiated at the hanging of the Revd James Hackman. In a fit of uncontrollable jealousy Hackman had murdered a young woman who, as they said in those days, had 'thrown him over'. The tendency of hangmen to find themselves on the wrong side of the law has already been commented upon and Dennis was no exception. Implicated in the looting of a Catholic shopkeeper's premises in High Holborn during the Gordon Riots of 1780, he was found guilty and sentenced to death but eventually pardoned. This may have had less to do with clemency and more with expediency because it seems that the hangmen brought in to replace Dennis were hopelessly incompetent. He was restored to his role and probably acted as hangman at the last executions performed at Tyburn.

There was a multitude of other sites in London used regularly, occasionally or in some cases only once, for executions. On 8 February 1570 John Felton was dragged on a hurdle to St Paul's churchyard where he was hanged, drawn and quartered. His crime had been brazenly to walk up to the gate of the Bishop of London's palace and affix to it a copy of Pope Pius V's bull excommunicating Elizabeth I. This absolutely infuriated the Queen and her ministers, whose spies quickly got to work and identified Felton as the perpetrator of this affront. He was set on the rack, as a consequence of which he confessed and the vicinity of St Paul's was deemed an appropriate place for him to be punished and executed. Other heretics went to their deaths at the same place.

Sometimes executions were held close to where the crimes themselves had been committed. This was intended to impress on the neighbourhood the majesty of the law and its power of retribution. A well-known example occurred in 1517 after the so-called 'Evil May Day'. There had been extensive riots in the City aimed primarily at the growing number of foreign merchants and craftsmen who were establishing businesses in the area. Over a dozen of the ringleaders were hanged, drawn and quartered in such places as Aldersgate, Gracechurch Street, Bishopsgate and Aldgate where their crimes had allegedly been carried out.

In his *Diary* Samuel Pepys (1633–1703) described a large crowd in Leadenhall Street that had turned out to watch the execution of Colonel Turner. The onlookers were becoming extremely restive because of the tediously lengthy valedictory speech that Turner was delivering. Pepys himself complained about Turner's wordiness and because he had paid good money to stand on a cartwheel to obtain a better view of the proceedings. So drawn-out was the speech that he suffered painful cramps, had to climb down and missed the denouement.

In Cheapside close to the church of St Mary-le-Bow was a fountain called the Standard which was an important place for the meting out of punishment. In 1293 three men had their right hands cut off there because they had rescued a prisoner from the clutches of the authorities. In 1326 Walter de Stapleton, Treasurer to Edward II, was beheaded. In 1340 two fishmongers were executed for striking the Lord Mayor of London during a riot. During the Peasants' Revolt of 1381 Wat Tyler beheaded Richard Lions at Cheapside, and similarly in Cade's Rebellion, in 1450, Jack Cade decapitated Lord Saye and Sele. The heads of executed felons were frequently exhibited briefly at Cheapside before being despatched to London Bridge or the Tower for longer-term display.

'Execution Dock' was not a dock at all but gained that ironic name because it was the location where many of the most notorious pirates ended their days. It was on the north side of the Thames about a mile downstream from the Tower. The gallows were erected on the shore close to the low-tide mark. The pirates were hanged and their bodies were left to be overwhelmed by the incoming tide. The custom was to allow three tides to pass over them, after which the bodies were removed. This may seem a curious custom but it was to stress that the crimes for which they had been punished had been perpetrated in tidal waters which were under the jurisdiction of the Admiralty. Among those who died at Execution Dock were the notorious Captain Kidd and a less well-known pirate called John Gow who was immortalised by Sir Walter Scott, the prolific Scottish writer of historical fiction, who made Gow the central figure in his novel *The Pirate*.

The Neckinger is a short, small stream now flowing underground from the Elephant and Castle area through Bermondsey to enter the Thames a few hundred yards east of Tower Bridge at a tidal inlet that was known as St Saviour's Dock. It is one of the few of

London's hidden rivers easily accessible to the public at the point where it enters the Thames. A walkway now crosses the rather uninspiring muddy creek where the Neckinger and the Thames become one. The Neckinger gained its curious name from the fact that it also was used as a place for the execution of pirates, perhaps those who plundered shipping on the Thames rather than on the high seas. The rope with which they were hanged was known as the 'Devil's neckcloth' or 'neckinger'.

The executions carried out at Smithfield have mostly been dealt with elsewhere. However, it is worth mentioning the appalling fate undergone in about 1530 by a cook by the name of Rose or Roose who was boiled to death at Smithfield for allegedly having placed poison in gruel prepared for the household of the Bishop of Rochester. Two of the company died and seventeen were taken seriously ill. Roose was placed in a cauldron and the water gradually heated over a great fire. Later executions by this method were designed to be more humane – they placed the offender in the cauldron when the water was already boiling!

The Tower of London is probably the best-known castle in the world. Over the centuries the Tower has acted as a royal residence, a military stronghold, an arsenal and armoury, a mint, an observatory, a menagerie, a prison and a place of execution. Many nobles and others have been executed within its precincts. Some died by royal command surreptitiously and away from prying eyes in one or other of the buildings which make up this enormously complex structure. Others, more openly but still not subject to public scrutiny, died on Tower Green. The first to die there was probably Lord Hastings in 1483. He was a powerful advocate of the infant Edward V against the monarchial ambitions of Richard, Duke of Gloucester, who had him executed once he felt his own position was strong enough to get away with it. Close by Anne Boleyn breathed her last in 1536, executed with a sword.

Few executions in the Tower have been more undignified than that of Margaret, Countess of Salisbury, who was the last of the Plantagenet family and was seventy-one years of age when she was put to death in 1541. A woman of formidable spirit as well as remarkable fleetness of foot for one of her years, she absolutely refused to lay her head on the executioner's block and, dodging the guards, was pursued round and round the scaffold by the executioner who hacked pieces off her whenever his axe could make contact. He completed the job in the end, a new type of death by a thousand cuts.

In 1542 Jane, Viscountess Rochford, fell foul of Henry VIII, who believed that she had assisted his fifth wife, Catherine Howard, to carry on various adulterous affairs. Both women were executed within minutes of each other on Tower Green. It is said that Henry had been so incensed when he heard of Catherine's sexual adventures that his first instinct had been to rush for his sword and execute her there and then. Lady Jane Grey, 'the Nine Days' Queen', was executed at the same spot in 1554. In 1743 three soldiers of the regiment which became the Black Watch were executed on Tower Green having been found guilty of inciting disaffection. As late as the twentieth century, spies were executed within the precincts of the Tower.

Many executions took place publicly on Tower Hill. The victims were usually traitors or the high-born. Possibly the first to die there was Richard Wyche, in 1440. Condemned to death for being a Lollard, that is, a religious zealot of subversive views, he was very popular and became a revered martyr after being burned at the stake. In his memory a cross and small cairn were erected which attracted substantial numbers of pilgrims. Many of them showed their devotion by buying some of his ashes. Interestingly, even after a hectic day selling these ashes to eager pilgrims, there was always a plentiful supply for renewed trading the next day. The glorification of Wyche irked the authorities who had the cross and the cairn removed.

Among those who died at Tower Hill was Sir Thomas More. Not normally known for his levity, he made a jest as he ascended the scaffold in 1535. He is purported to have said, 'See me safely up, for my coming down I can shift for myself.' Other notables who died there included the Earl of Strafford in 1641 and Archbishop Laud in 1645. So hated was Strafford that an estimated 100,000 people are said to have watched his execution. Lord Lovat was executed in 1747. His execution was notable because it was the last by beheading in England. Huge crowds gathered to watch and a temporary grandstand collapsed, killing twenty onlookers. This happened before Lovat had ascended the scaffold and he is said to have found the sight highly amusing.

Westminster Old Palace Yard witnessed the death of Guy Fawkes and two other Gunpowder Plot conspirators and later that of Sir Walter Raleigh. Charles I met his end outside the Banqueting Hall in Whitehall on 30 January 1649. Other sites of execution have also been identified but Tyburn is the one above all that remains synonymous in the popular mind with the pageantry in reverse that was public execution in London.

ELEVEN

The Lore of the Tyburn Crowd

From the very end of the twelfth century until 1783 large numbers of condemned prisoners were dragged or conveyed from Newgate to be put to death at Tyburn. No accurate figure exists for the total number of criminals for whom this was the last journey but estimates put the figure at around 60,000. What would an observer of Tyburn Fair have seen? What ceremonies were enacted? How did the felons comport themselves and how did the crowd react and respond?

An elaborate ritual evolved and was acted out by the authorities before and during the journey to Tyburn. The commonalty responded with rites of its own. By the eighteenth century at least, it had become obvious that those who turned out with such relish to watch the processions to Tyburn, the activities around the scaffold and the death agonies of the felons, had their own individual and collective reasons for being there. These had little to do with any sense that they were being browbeaten by the law and the frightful penalties that it could impose. Much the reverse. Tyburn had become associated with mockery, irreverence and the defiance of authority. The activities there encapsulated rough-and-ready humour, elements of carnival and, on occasion, very public displays of approval or sympathy for the condemned miscreants. For their part, the latter sometimes seem to have relished their brief moment of glory and to have drawn succour from it.

Evidence of the centrality of the spectacle at Tyburn in popular culture is shown by a mass of popular expressions used to refer to the executions carried out there and elsewhere in the London area. A hanging day was a 'hanging match', a 'Paddington Fair' or Tyburn Fair.

To hang was 'to swing' or 'dance the Paddington frisk'. To travel in the cart from Newgate to Tyburn was 'to go west'. The gallows was the 'three-legged mare' or the 'deadly nevergreen'. There were innumerable euphemisms for death by hanging. These included 'collared', 'frummagemmed', 'scragged', 'tucked up' or 'turned off'. A 'Tyburn check' was a rope and a 'Tyburn tippet' was a halter. The importance in popular culture of the rites surrounding hanging is confirmed by the extensive use of slang words for it. The ordinary people enjoyed the spectacle and gave it a prominent place in their communal culture; it provided a welcome break from everyday drudgery.

Hanging sessions at Tyburn took place after the eight annual sittings at the Old Bailey. Sometimes there was a postponement so that the felons from two sessions could be dealt with on the same occasion. This provided a more salutary spectacle, or so the authorities believed. It also provided more entertainment for the crowd.

A period of several days – typically at least a week – elapsed between the prisoner being sentenced and the execution itself. During this time rumours, sometimes wildly exaggerated ones, would spread around London about the criminal and the nature of his or her crime. The writers and printers would get to work retelling these crimes and where the reality was not considered lurid enough, they made liberal use of their imaginations to sensationalise the stories and therefore, as they hoped, to sell more copies. Some prisoners who enjoyed the good life and had money to spend, passed their last few days sharing their quarters with friends and relations, abandoning themselves to uproarious feasting, drinking and general junketing. Prisoners who were particular celebrities might entertain members of the public. The latter had bribed the turnkeys well so they could boast to their friends that they had made the acquaintance of the prisoner during his last days. Other condemned felons spent their last few days in belated soul-searching and spiritual introspection, attempting to shrive themselves of their sins and preparing for the awful fate ahead of them.

Newgate had little to offer those who wanted to engage in peaceful meditation during their last days. The place was extraordinarily noisy. Inmates moaned, argued, shouted; some screamed dementedly. Warders bellowed orders, chains and manacles clanked, hinges creaked and great wooden doors clanged shut, the reverberations echoing to and fro down cheerless stone passages. Hucksters bawled their wares; prostitutes plied their trade; prisoners with money called out for more beer; others shouted insults at passers-by and sometimes urinated on them. The stench of Newgate was pestiferous. For some condemned prisoners, the prospect of going out into the fresh air, even if only to ride to Tyburn, must have come as something of a relief.

On the last evening the chaplain would offer the prisoner the final sacrament and at midnight a bell was tolled in the tower of St Sepulchre's Church, close by Newgate. This part of the ritual was the result of a bequest whereby St Sepulchre's had been given an annual sum of £50 for the purpose of paying the bellman. The benefactor, whose munificence must have been regarded as something of a mixed blessing by the condemned inmates of Newgate, went by the name of Robert Dow. This practice started in 1604 and involved the handbell being rung loudly within the precincts of the prison itself, accompanied by the following cry:

> All you that in the condemned hole do lie,
> Prepare you, for tomorrow you shall die;
> Watch all and pray; the hour is drawing near,
> That you before the Almighty must appear.
> Examine well yourselves; in time repent,
> That you may not to eternal Flames be sent.
> And when St Sepulchre's Bell in the morning tolls,
> The Lord above have mercy on your souls.

As day dawned, the prisoner, most likely quaking with abject terror, possibly suffering from a severe hangover, perhaps prudently already drunk but in a few cases apparently indifferent, would be taken to the Press Room where his irons were struck off. Then he dressed for the occasion. The choice of apparel was the prisoner's. Some went to their deaths wearing finery specially bought for the occasion, although many chose to don a funerary shroud which symbolised contrition. Some, the more hard-nosed, wore a simple garment such as a cheap nightshirt, seeking to thwart or at least frustrate the hangman, one of whose perks it was to sell the clothing the condemned prisoner had worn on his last public appearance. A cord was then bound round the arms, the elbows being pinned in such a way that the arms and hands had some freedom of movement. Handcuffs were left on those prisoners thought to be particularly slippery. A halter was placed around the neck by an official quaintly known as the 'Knight of the Halter'. The Under Sheriff would make a ceremonial demand for the condemned prisoner to be given into his custody and, when he was handed over, issued a formal receipt for the body as if it was already dead.

From the seventeenth century, most of the condemned felons rode in a horse-drawn cart to Tyburn while a well-to-do prisoner, if in possession of an extrovert personality, might ride in his own carriage or hire a grand conveyance for the occasion. Where two or more prisoners were to be hanged on the same day, the rich prisoner might graciously offer his fellows a ride in the coach. For many this might be the first time they had ever climbed into such a conveyance – except for the purposes of robbery, perhaps. The cart was sometimes draped in black. The ride to Tyburn provided a spectacle and, to emphasise the supposedly salutary lessons to be drawn from the sight, there was a rule of precedence. When multiple executions took place at Tyburn, the felons who sat in the front seats of the first wagon were those convicted for the most serious crimes. Significantly these were major offences against property and therefore highwaymen and those who had robbed the mail often rode in the front rank. Although the purpose of the authorities was to impress the watching multitude with the punishment meted out for such serious offences, the effect was the very opposite. The treatment accorded by the crowd to those who rode in the front ranks encouraged them to see themselves as popular and glamorous heroes which, in most cases, they were. Far from being shamed by their valedictory public appearance through the streets to Tyburn, it is clear that some felons took considerable succour from their brief time in the limelight. Those who were especially popular with the crowd would be besieged with requests to provide a lock of hair or any other souvenir of the occasion.

Robert Dow's bequest also allowed for the tolling of the great bell in the tower of St Sepulchre as the procession formed up outside Newgate Prison. The procession always set off with an escort. It was led by the City Marshal and an Under Marshal who commanded a force of constables and soldiers armed with pole weapons, often described as 'javelins'. Sometimes the procession had literally to force and fight its way through drunken, jeering or hostile crowds. The result might be broken heads and noses streaming blood. On other occasions the crowd might be so incensed by the sight of a prisoner whose crime was considered particularly heinous that they would rush the procession and try to seize him with a view to a lynching. A guard of as many as 200 soldiers might therefore be needed in anticipation of trouble. The hangman would ride in a cart in advance of the main procession because he had various preparatory arrangements to make. The chaplain also rode in one of the carts along with the condemned prisoners. He was there in an often futile attempt to persuade the prisoner to atone for his sins and thereby prepare himself for the afterlife. The Ordinary's job was understandably greatly sought-after because his purpose was frequently other than purely spiritual. He had probably spent the previous weeks gathering material for the broadsheet he wrote purporting to contain the last confession of the condemned prisoner. These sometimes appeared on the streets several days before the execution! In the case of notorious prisoners, they sold extremely well and brought the Ordinary a very handsome profit.

From the official point of view, the presence of the Ordinary was not just symbolic. It indicated the involvement of the Church in the punishment of sin and recognised that although the prisoner's physical life was about to be terminated, his soul could still be saved even at this late hour. Prisoners with influence could have a priest of their own choice with them on their last journey. The coffin allocated to each prisoner was carefully placed in the cart in which he was to make his last journey. On occasions, family and friends of the condemned felons also rode in the procession but this usually only occurred where the prisoner had influence.

All along the route, large numbers would turn out eating, drinking and making merry as well as shouting, jostling for a good view, quarrelling and sometimes fighting among themselves. Hawkers would be out in large numbers along the way and at Tyburn, selling everything from pies, baked potatoes and sweetmeats to the broadsheets containing the supposed valedictory confessions of the condemned prisoner or prisoners. There was also a trade in human flesh because prostitutes would be touting their wares among the carefree revellers. Pickpockets and cutpurses were everywhere, pickings being rich in the densely packed crowds. Youthful pickpockets were known as 'Tyburn blossoms'.

The mood of the gathering partly depended on the nature of the crimes which the condemned prisoners had committed, as did the number of spectators who were attracted. All, however, hoped for good entertainment. A prisoner considered a hero would bask in the adulation and good wishes of the crowds, admired perhaps because he had done those things which they themselves were afraid to do. However, a felon whose crimes aroused the crowd's ire might be assailed by a rain of stones, rotting fruit and vegetables and excrement. So the people stood and watched, most at street level, others on rooftops or poking their heads out of upstairs windows and they cheered or jeered as they considered appropriate.

The behaviour of the watching crowds along the route was not always predictable. A fifteen-year-old youth called Joseph Harris who was condemned to death for stealing two half-sovereigns and some silver was so terrified that he had to be lifted into the cart at Newgate. The authorities allowed his father to travel with him. He did so, cradling his son's head in his lap. The crowd watched in silence, all sense of derision and mockery replaced by simple compassion, as the cart passed containing the pitiful youth and his weeping grey-haired father. Although the common impression is of crowds flocking to gloat at the pain and misery of the condemned felons, there were some, admittedly a small minority, who went in order to pray for the souls of those being executed. The crowds were not totally callous. There is a story of an orange-seller in the crowd at Tyburn who was knocked down and robbed by footpads. He was carried off to a nearby alehouse to have his injuries attended to and remained there for a few days being visited by literally hundreds of people solicitous for his welfare. This contrasts very sharply with the changing mood which coursed through the crowd when a procession to Tyburn was brought to a sudden unexpected halt because the hangman, William Marvell, was arrested for debt. Against a background of derisive and scoffing comments from the crowd, Marvell was hustled away. The procession continued, albeit no longer with Marvell at its head, until it reached Tyburn. There a bricklayer in the crowd volunteered to carry out the executioner's duty but he was seized and beaten up severely. As something of an anti-climax for the expectant crowd, the prisoners were taken back to Newgate and their sentences commuted to transportation.

Jonathan Wild, when he was at the height of his power, loved to regale and possibly terrify the people watching a procession to Tyburn with tales of how one or more of the prisoners passing by were there because of his relentless thief-taking efforts. This is probably one of the reasons why the crowds gave him such a torrid time when he made the same journey some time later.

The journey was one of about three miles but no sooner had a start been made than the entourage would halt outside St Sepulchre's, where the bellman would ring his handbell sonorously. He would then intone the following speech:

All good people, pray heartily unto God for these poor sinners, who are going to their death, for whom this great bell doth toll. You that are condemned to die, repent with lamentable tears; ask mercy of the Lord for the salvation of your souls through the merits, death, and passion of Jesus Christ, who now sits on the right hand of God, to make intercession for as many of you as penitently return unto him. Lord have mercy upon you! Christ have mercy upon you!

The bellman would conclude by exhorting the crowd to pray for the souls of those soon to die after which he presented colourful nosegays to the condemned prisoners. Something likely to assist the chance of escaping would probably have been better appreciated.

The procession would then resume its slow journey, stopping at one or more inns and taverns along the route to allow the condemned prisoners to take some refreshment. Another regular place for a halt was outside the hospital at St Giles-in-the-Fields where ale was available for the main participants in the spectacle. The story is told how on one occasion a solitary prisoner being conveyed from Newgate to Tyburn loftily spurned the offer of wayside drinks. He rather self-righteously informed all and sundry of his utter rejection of strong drink. The procession continued on its way and reached Tyburn where the hanging duly took place. If only the man had taken his drink, he would have lived to tell the story because a reprieve arrived a few minutes after he was hanged! This story may well be apocryphal because it is told about many other places of execution. Tyburn lore assures us that many prisoners took full advantage of the hospitality on offer. They were certainly encouraged to do so by the publicans along the way because where prisoners were allowed to get off the cart and enter their premises, they brought hordes of well-wishers with them and business boomed. The practice of allowing prisoners to drink may also have been for more rough-and-ready humanitarian purposes. The drinks acted as something of an anodyne to the terror that was obviously felt by most prisoners.

Depending on their personality and character, some prisoners seemed to revel in their temporary stardom and waved to friends in the crowd and blew kisses or made lewd suggestions to pretty girls among the bystanders. Others, however, huddled in the bottom of the cart trying to be as inconspicuous as possible, suffused with terror and shaking like aspens. Prisoners of this sort attracted nothing but scorn from the crowd. Some prisoners apparently believed that even at this stage a reprieve might be possible and so they tried to slow the procession down. Even without their efforts, the journey could easily take at least three hours. Occasionally a prisoner would try to escape. If he was popular with the crowd they might do all they could to assist him. If he was disliked, he would find his way barred and would be quickly retaken.

At Tyburn itself, a crowd would be waiting and the food and drink vendors would be doing a roaring trade, as would the thieves and pickpockets. Seats could be hired on viewing platforms known as 'Tyburn pew openers'. Admission prices were carefully adjusted to take account of the fame and notoriety of the felon or felons being dealt with on that occasion. The most famous of these grandstands was known as 'Mother Proctor's Pew' after its original owner and it would fill up very early if the occupants thought they were in for a good show. This structure had proved to be an excellent investment. First used in 1724, in 1760 when Earl Ferrers was executed it had netted its owner an estimated £5,000 or something approaching £450,000 in today's prices. He was a star attraction despite the revulsion evoked by his behaviour. The theme of overcharging for these grandstand seats was a constant one until executions at Tyburn ended but, grumbling or not, patrons continued to pay the prices asked. In 1758 Dr Henesey delivered an apparently endless last speech from the gallows. It drove the spectators to distraction. They wanted to see him swing! A wave of fury coursed through the crowd when a reprieve was announced and a riot broke out in which the viewing stands were demolished. Their owner, protesting at the destruction, narrowly escaped being hanged herself!

The area around the gallows could become unpleasantly crowded as those devotees of a good hanging who had accompanied the procession jockeyed for a good view with those who had the foresight to get to Tyburn early. Tensions would build up in the crowd and a great cry of 'Hats off! Hats off!' went up as the procession made its way to the foot of the gallows platform. This was not intended to be a mark of respect for the condemned prisoner but rather a demand that those near the front should take their hats off so that those at the back could get a better view. Excitement and anticipation led to further roars as the hangman stepped forward and the condemned prisoners ascended the gallows. A few minutes might then pass while the hangman and his assistants placed nooses around the prisoners' necks and, as became the practice, put hoods or bags over their heads. Large numbers of people could be milling about on, or close to, the scaffold at this point because friends and relatives wanted to offer the condemned prisoners last-minute moral support. The Ordinary might be fussing about, getting on everybody's nerves, trying to extract juicy tit-bits from eleventh-hour confessions that would see the light of day in further broadsheets to be touted around the streets later. A homing pigeon was released when the entourage reached Tyburn to let those at Newgate know of the procession's safe arrival.

In one sense this was theatre. A convict by the name of Paynes, about to be hanged for murder, was enthusiastically applauded by the crowd when he unceremoniously pushed the Ordinary out of the cart. He then pulled off his own boots, declaring loudly that he was going to honour his mother and to confound the old proverb about not dying with one's boots on! William Borwick, taken to Tyburn because he had murdered his wife, had the crowd in fits of laughter when he looked critically at the rope, felt it and tugged it with some care. He then told the onlookers that he hoped it was strong enough because he hated to think it might break. If it did, he would fall to the ground, fracturing some bones and might be crippled for life! Condemned robber Tom Austin, while waiting on the scaffold, was asked whether he had anything he wanted to say. His reply, which must have surprised those who heard him, was that he could see a woman in the crowd who had some curds and whey. These were one of his favourite comestibles. To a roar of approval from the crowd, he said that he wanted to know if he could buy a penn'orth because he wasn't sure when he was going to have a chance to try them again.

There is no doubt that some of those who died at Tyburn gained considerable spiritual strength from the act of doing so in front of an appreciative and supportive audience. As Henry Fielding, the zealous and perceptive magistrate of Bow Street, wrote in 1751:

The day appointed by Law for the Thief's Shame is a Day of Glory in his Opinion. His procession to Tyburn, and his last moments there, are all triumphant; attended with the compassion of the meek and tender-hearted, and with the Applause, Admiration, and envy of all the bold and hardened . . .

The technology of the hanging process changed over time. In the earliest period, the gallows consisted of two uprights with a cross-beam joining them. The cross-beam could accommodate up to ten victims, although only one could be hanged at a time. The prisoner was forced to mount a ladder placed against the cross-beam in a kind of do-it-yourself form of execution. He already had a noose around his neck which was attached to the cross-beam and he could throw himself off if he chose to do so, death coming by slow strangulation. If he showed understandable signs of reluctance to do this, he was liable to be unceremoniously pushed off as the ladder was twisted and turned. This explains the phrase 'turned off' as gallows humour would have it. Later, although this method hardly involved major technological advance, the prisoner was required to stand on the tail of a cart, probably the one in which he had ridden from Newgate. The horses were then lashed and as they lurched forward, the prisoner was left dangling in mid-air. Several simultaneous executions could be carried out in this way. In 1571 the 'Triple Tree' was brought into use at Tyburn. It was a triangular gallows consisting of three uprights joined to each other by cross-beams and it considerably increased the potential productivity of the hangman. Now twenty-four criminals could be hanged at one go, eight on each beam. The only time this happened was in 1649.

It was not uncommon for a prisoner to give money to the hangman to try to ensure that death was quick. Otherwise he might take twenty agonising minutes to expire. As the prisoner dangled, the hangman might therefore allow his relatives to rush forward and pull on his legs, trying to assist a swift demise. However the hangman had to ensure that they were not rushing forward with the opposite purpose – of lifting him up and preventing strangulation. It was widely believed that if death did not occur on this occasion, the prisoner might be reprieved, a clear case of 'where there's life, there's hope'. Undignified scenes might ensue as fights broke out between the hangman and the guards on the one hand and the relatives and friends of the prisoner on the other. This all helped to provide the spectators with just the kind of knockabout entertainment that many of them had spent good money hoping to see. It was the custom to leave the body hanging for an hour before it was cut down. During that time, women might rush forward to grab the still-twitching hand of the dying convict and press it to their cheeks or bosoms because it was widely regarded as possessing curative powers, especially against skin problems. Additionally, children might be lifted up and made to press any infected limbs in the 'death sweat'. Pieces of dried skin from those who had been hanged fetched high prices as lucky charms. In 1739 John Morris was hanged at Tyburn for highway robbery. When perpetrating an earlier crime, he had had his jawbone shot off. He had carefully saved all the pieces he could find and while he was waiting execution, he distributed them as good-luck charms to his fellow inmates of Newgate.

In the crowd there would be veterans of innumerable public executions who provided a running commentary for the benefit of those around who were less well versed in the nuances of a hanging. Perceptive remarks would be made about the prisoner and his demeanour; most particularly about whether he was displaying any signs of fear. Those who seemed stoical were admired but others who were openly defiant were loudly applauded. Especially savoured were tirades which scorned or lambasted the legal authorities, the whole system of justice and the peculations of the powerful for which they seemed to have almost complete immunity. Some prisoners took the opportunity to make jokes and jests and exchange witticisms with those in the crowd. Such prisoners were greatly appreciated but the onlookers took less pleasure in cringing and self-pitying confessions or last-minute appeals for clemency. The barracking might be so loud that the condemned man had little option but to stop. The onlookers did not want the speeches to go on too long because they delayed the day's main pleasure which was, of course, the one or more hangings. Other perceptive remarks came from experienced spectators who commented on and analysed the skill displayed by the hangman. Although they seem not to have turned a hair as the condemned man twitched and convulsed in his death agonies, they did require the hangman to do all he could to make the execution a quick and clean one. They were swift to spot evidence of nerves or incompetence on the part of the hangman and these would elicit a torrent of jeers and ribald comments. Any hangman making a particularly cack-handed job might have to run from the gallows under a hail of missiles and verbal derision.

Most felons wished to die well. Folklore is full of examples of gallows humour and last-minute defiance but for all those who went down fighting, there were far more who went to their deaths clearly in the uttermost transports of terror. Few managed a swashbuckling swan song. Most died as obscurely and hopelessly as they had lived.

The day's events were not over just because the prisoner was swinging and expiring in mid-air. An undertaker might be on hand to take the corpse away and give it a decent burial but sometimes he had to move very quickly. He might be competing with the relatives of the deceased who believed that the victim might be revived. A surgeon called Chovet had experimented on the windpipes of dogs and supposedly discovered a way of restoring them to life. For these reasons, a pitched battle sometimes took place after the corpse was taken down as the undertaker, if any, or the friends and relatives of the deceased, fought with those who wanted simply to touch the corpse or to remove parts of its anatomy for their allegedly therapeutic properties. Also likely to join in were those who intended to spirit the corpse away and sell it to a school of anatomy where it could serve as an object lesson for those training to be doctors and surgeons. Further chaos might be caused by spectators joining in the fight if they thought that the corpse had been grabbed by the surgeons' men, because their activities excited almost universal revulsion. In the middle of all this confusion, the hangmen might be desperately trying to hold on to the corpse so that he could sell the clothes, the shroud or the rope with which it had been hanged, all of which had considerable commercial value. The more notorious the dead convict, the higher the price these relics would command. As far back as ancient Roman times, it was believed that wrapping a hangman's rope round the temples was a sure way of getting rid of headaches. Possession of a hangman's rope or even one single strand from it was thought to enable a person to fend off all manner of ailments when the relic was worn round the neck. Gamblers also eagerly availed themselves of a piece of the rope believing that it would improve their luck. In the mêlée, some of the crowd would even be trying to prise splinters off the gallows. These were rubbed on the gums as an infallible cure for toothache.

Sometimes it seems that the hangman was regarded more as the villain of the piece than the condemned felons. He was the person everyone loved to hate and would be on the receiving end of a constant stream of unhelpful advice, ribald comments and barbed witticisms. This explains the public display of approval and pleasure which marked the ride to Tyburn of a young Irish woman called Hannah Dagoe. Clearly a woman of some spirit, she spent part of the journey divesting herself of most of her clothes. These she flung at random into a highly appreciative crowd. By the time she reached Tyburn she was very scantily clad. The crowd scoffed at the frustration and mortification evident on the hangman's face. Hannah, evidently determined to thwart the hangman, now proceeded to remove most of that small amount of clothing she still had on. The crowd were then not only treated to the sight of Hannah capering about almost naked on the scaffold but also of the hangman, Thomas Turlis, doing all he could to restrain her and prevent her casting off any remaining precious items of clothing. He tried to pinion her arms and received a hefty kick in the groin for his trouble. This caused him to double up in agony, to the huge delight of the crowd. Somehow or other he managed to drop the noose over Hannah's head. This only incensed her further and, pushing Turlis aside, she then hurled herself out of the cart only to have her fall fatally arrested by the noose. Hannah had not only prevented Turlis getting what he thought of as his rightful perks but had also made him look a complete fool. Here was a story with which to regale the grandchildren in years to come!

The best pictorial depiction of Tyburn is in William Hogarth's ninth illustration, *The Idle 'Prentice*, in the series entitled *Industry and Idleness* published in 1747. This is Hogarth's most ambitious series of engravings and is a moralistic treatise which contrasts the fates of two Spitalfields apprentices going respectively by the suggestive names of Frank Goodchild and Tom Idle. Hogarth has no interest in the significance of genetic or material influences on the formation of character and behaviour. As far as he is concerned, all are born with equal potential to do good and evil but propensities to virtue or to dissipation and wickedness are down to how individuals choose to handle the opportunities that life presents. Thus Frank Goodchild is wholly virtuous and Tom Idle irrevocably wicked.

Both boys are apprenticed as weavers but in the first illustration a neatly dressed Frank is shown working away on his loom while an unkempt Tom dozes at his post. The second picture shows Goodchild dutifully worshipping in church and sharing a hymn-book with his master's daughter while in the third Idle is shown gambling in a churchyard during the time of the service and attempting to cheat the three wastrels who are his companions. In the fourth, the deserving Goodchild has been promoted to work in the office while Idle, having exhausted the patience of his master, is depicted in the next engraving being sent off to sea. Time moves on and Goodchild's diligence and rectitude are rewarded in the sixth illustration which depicts his marriage to his employer's daughter and his acceptance as a partner in his father-in-law's firm. Tom, whose experiences at sea have only served to degrade him further, is depicted in the next plate in the series as destitute in a squalid garret with a harlot who is also a pickpocket. In the next scene Goodchild has become Sheriff of London, a rich man basking in wealth and public esteem while the ninth in the series shows the continuing degradation of Idle. He is being apprehended for robbery and murder in what was known as 'Bloody Bowl Cellar', a notorious 'sanctuary' in London where fugitives from their debtors and all manner of criminals would resort. In the tenth picture Idle appears in court before a magistrate who, predictably, turns out to be Goodchild, depicted by Hogarth as an alderman. Idle owes his conviction to one of his gambling partners in the churchyard all those years ago, now a fellow criminal, who turns King's Evidence.

This pictorial saga seems extremely unctuous by current standards but Hogarth has handed us a uniquely detailed visual presentation of the life of London in his time. The eleventh picture is entitled 'The Idle 'Prentice executed at Tyburn'. This picture of Tyburn Fair contains a wealth of fascinating detail. The prisoner stands in a cart and is being exhorted to confess by the Ordinary while the hangman, drawing on a foul old pipe, is nonchalantly adjusting the rope on one of the beams of the Triple Tree. Close to the gallows are the grandstands which provide the best view of proceedings. Prominent in them is Mother Douglas, a brothel-keeper who owns the grandstand and is shown standing up and drinking gin. Idle's mother can be discerned weeping and bemoaning the fate of her son. A cake-seller by the name of 'Tiddy Doll' is depicted. He is a familiar sight on all these occasions and is shown hawking his wares. A small boy has overturned a barrow full of apples being pushed by a girl who retaliates by hitting him hard in the face. A man brandishes a little dog that he is about to throw at Idle while a kneeling soldier is seen picking a man's pocket. A bevy of men are engaged in fisticuffs over some unknown dispute and a well-built woman has put down her baby while she prepares to deliver the *coup de grâce* to her assailant in some other argument. At the front of the picture, a bedraggled woman is selling 'The Dying Speech and Confession of Tom Idle' which will have been written and printed several days before the execution. Hogarth gives a good idea of the rural nature of Tyburn at the time because in the background can be seen the grassy slopes of Notting Hill.

As the continuously built-up area of London moved westwards, apparently relentlessly, gracious new streets and squares for the wealthy came to characterise the section stretching towards Tyburn. Hangings constituted a threat to law and order, as they drew a ravening mob, and to property. The permanent gallows at Tyburn was removed and on 4 October 1759 the first executions took place on a new gallows that was erected and dismantled for every hanging day. However, pressure developed for the removal of public hangings from Tyburn to a more remote spot and Camden Town was mooted as one possibility.

From this time executions ordered by the City of London and the Middlesex magistrates took place outside Newgate Prison. This must have been a boon for the authorities who would no longer have to put up with the chaos, disruption to business and frequent lawlessness which ensued at every Tyburn Fair. Hangings would still take place in public but would be much more controllable. This change, however, was not popular. People of all classes railed against it. Dr Johnson argued that Tyburn not only emphasised the power of the law by publicly exposing felons to their fate but that it also provided entertainment for the crowds and gave the felons themselves some support in their last hours. These latter arguments cut little ice with the authorities.

The old Triple Tree was sold and legend says that some pieces were bought by a local innkeeper, possibly of the Carpenters Arms, to be used as stands on which to place barrels. The Tyburn Convent, close by in Hyde Park Place, keeps what it claims are other fragments as a reminder of the Catholics who suffered for their beliefs at Tyburn.

From then on a gallows was erected outside Newgate every time executions were to take place. It was portable although heavy enough to need two horses to drag it from its storage place inside the prison. This was a new piece of technology, an advance on the 'drop' scaffold which had been tried at Tyburn in 1760 for the execution of Earl Ferrers. This had had some serious design shortcomings, not the least of which was that the drop was insufficient to achieve the required purpose. Ferrers had only been despatched because the hangman had pulled powerfully on his legs. The new device had two parallel cross-beams and a platform containing a hatch. The hatch was operated by the hangman using a lever and being 10 feet long and 8 feet wide, it could accommodate ten felons at a time. Indeed, ten criminals did act as involuntary guinea-pigs and were executed on 9 December 1783. This new scaffold was not without its teething problems. The two executioners had had little previous chance to test their new plaything and they used ropes that were far too short. The result was that, although the felons dropped through the hatch gratifyingly, they could not fall far enough to fracture their spinal columns and they died instead from slow and extremely painful strangulation.

Few activities seemed to excite more popular disgust in the eighteenth century than the efforts of the medical world to learn more about human anatomy by obtaining cadavers to use as object lessons with which to teach students of anatomy and surgery. To understand why the issue of surgery is so important to the history of Tyburn, we need to consider the manner in which the dead were disposed of.

The lifeless bodies of criminals have always seemed to attract the attentions of practitioners of the occult arts, especially those pursuing necromancy. People unfortunate enough to be crucified in Roman times were sometimes mutilated even before they had been taken down from their crosses. Allusions in Shakespeare's *Macbeth* to 'Nose of Turk' and 'Tartar's Lip' suggest continuing interest in these practices. One accusation frequently made during the witch-hunting craze of the sixteenth and seventeenth centuries was that witches were in the habit of visiting churchyards where they dug up bodies and removed such parts as teeth, nails and hair.

The College of Physicians opened England's first anatomical theatre in Knightrider Street in the City of London in the seventeenth century. At that time surgeons were not held in high esteem and were certainly thought of as inferior to physicians, who were regarded as men of learning. Surgeons by contrast were 'sawbones', rough-and-ready artisans whose skill lay in removing limbs with the greatest possible despatch and who were seen as little different from 'the poor man's doctor', the barber-surgeons. The latter spent much of his time, for example, cutting hair, removing in growing toenails, extracting rotting teeth, treating chilblains and doing what they could for people suffering with piles. The Company of Barber-Surgeons had been founded in the early sixteenth century and in 1540 had obtained parliamentary sanction to dissect the bodies of four executed felons annually. Four specimens were simply insufficient and an increase to six was made in the reign of Charles II. The barbers and the surgeons went their separate ways in 1745 by which time surgeons were getting hold of corpses to use for demonstration purposes. This was unofficial and required back-handers to such people as the Constable of Holborn who on occasion would provide them with the bodies of felons hanged at Tyburn.

Sometime between 1702 and 1714, William Cheselden started giving private anatomy lessons at his house at Cheapside in the City. To provide the necessary teaching aids he bought the bodies of executed felons from the gallows. In doing this he seems to have started the fear in the minds of the public at large that the surgeons would obtain the bodies of those who died on the gallows and anatomise them. The 'specimens' that were used for this purpose might, after all, be their own friends and relatives. When the notorious Jonathan Wild was executed in 1725, rumours circulated that although he was buried, the surgeons had afterwards paid certain unnamed individuals to exhume his body and deliver it to them. There is a skeleton in the Hunterian Museum of the Royal College of Surgeons in Lincoln's Inn Fields which is said by some to be that of the 'Thief-Taker General'. In 1745, Cheselden played a leading role in the negotiations which led to the establishment of a separate Company of Surgeons which had its base in the street known as Old Bailey. This site was extremely convenient for Newgate.

Surgery had a bad name because of its brutal and frequently terminal nature. However, demand for the services of better surgeons was increasing because of a general rise in expectations in the eighteenth century. Cadavers were required by lecturers for use as object-lessons but were in very short supply. In 1752 the Act to Prevent the Horrible Crime of Murder decreed that, at the discretion of the court, the bodies of hanged felons should be given to the surgeons for dissection and exhibition to the public. Additionally, they should not be given Christian burial nor – unlike other convicted felons – should they be allowed to have the funeral service read over them as they travelled to Tyburn. This Act was seen as exceptionally vindictive because it aggravated the punishment of judicial hanging by taking away the felon's hope of salvation. In practical terms it made more cadavers available for the surgeons.

Meanwhile private teachers of surgery continued to obtain unclaimed corpses from workhouses and hospitals. After 1752, however, their agents no longer engaged in undignified brawls around the scaffold with the executioner and relatives of the deceased and freelance opportunists hoping to whisk the corpse away for sale to the professional surgeons.

The Act was not a great success. To start with it provided more, if still insufficient, corpses to meet the needs of the surgeons. It was hated by the members of the criminal fraternity, their relations and friends. This was not just because of the fear, little more than superstition in a criminal world not known for the strength of its religious beliefs and practices, that if they were dismembered they would not be able to rise again at the Day of Judgment. More immediate was the fear that because death by strangulation was usually less than instantaneous, those who were hanged might be taken down while still having some life in them. They then might be whisked away to some medical school only to come round to experience the agony of a surgeon's knife making an incision into their vitals, something which actually happened to a convicted rapist by the name of William Duell.

Possibly the first person to be claimed by the 1752 Act was a one-armed, seventeen-year-old youth by the name of Thomas Wilford. His marriage lasted just three days and ended with him murdering his wife in a fit of jealousy. The *Gentleman's Magazine* records that Wilford was executed at Tyburn on 1 July 1752 and that his body was to be 'dissected and anatomised according to the late Act'. The same periodical was concerned with the same Act some months later when it recorded that on 22 September 1752 'Randolph Branch and William Descent . . . were executed at Tyburn, after which their bodies were delivered to the surgeons, pursuant to the late Act of Parliament'. Despite this legislation, conflicts at the scaffold still occurred from time to time. On 18 December 1758, for example, a riot broke out and several people were injured as the surgeons' men attempted to remove the body of a man executed at Tyburn. On this occasion the crowd won and the body was carried away in triumph.

Surgeons' Hall near Newgate had a lecture theatre and this is depicted by William Hogarth in the fourth and last of the series of engravings he produced in 1751 as *The Four Stages of Cruelty*. As with many other of Hogarth's works there is a heavily didactic and moralistic tone to this saga. It follows the brief and dismal life of Tom Nero, born in the notorious rookery of St Giles where all kinds of repulsive cruelties were perpetrated on animals. When little more than a child, he joins in this sadism while refusing a bribe from a horrified passer-by to desist. He is evidently hardened and brutalised by his upbringing in these surroundings. These factors come together to bring about his inevitable fate when he is found guilty of murdering a servant girl whom he had first made pregnant and then persuaded to rob her mistress on his behalf. In the final scene, Hogarth shows Nero's corpse on the dissecting table at Surgeons' Hall. A hangman's rope still around its neck, the corpse is being worked on by three men with aprons under the close scrutiny of a crowd of students and voyeurs. Presiding over this unedifying spectacle is the lecturer who, as in so many of Hogarth's works, can be recognised as one of his contemporaries. In this case it is the famous surgeon John Freke, who had been a close friend until Hogarth had quarrelled with him some time before. In the niches around the walls can be descried the skeletons of two anatomised criminals. They are James Field, a well-known prize-fighter, and James Maclaine, the notorious highwayman who was hanged at Tyburn in 1750. Tom Nero has truly received the reward for his cruelty.

Criminals appeared on the scene prepared to obtain corpses illicitly to meet the demands of the surgeons. The courts dealt very harshly with those taking bodies from graves but turned a blind eye towards the surgeons and doctors who bought the cadavers. The general public execrated both parties in this trade. There were some, however, who contemptuously dismissed superstitious fears of dissection. It was not unknown for condemned prisoners to sell their bodies to the surgeons for their use after they were executed. They then spent the money buying the best services that could be had in Newgate or a suit of fine clothes for an eye-catching valedictory appearance at Tyburn.

Ruth Richardson states that corpses began to acquire market value and become commodities during the late seventeenth and early eighteenth centuries (Richardson 1989: 52), but limited trading in cadavers had been going on much earlier. Henry Machyn records that in February 1561, eighteen men and two women were executed at Tyburn and the Barber-Surgeons claimed one of the felons. In December 1561 after an execution it was recorded that 'one of the surgeons took [the body] for anatomy into their hall' (Nichols 1848: 273). The month of December is significant because anatomical studies were more a winter than a summer occupation given the lack of an effective preservative agent for dead bodies. Surgeons frequently complained that the effluvia from corpses made the demonstration theatre offensive. Public anatomy sessions took place over three days and the procedure was first for the Clerk of the Barber-Surgeons' Company to be informed that a body would be available after an execution. The Beadle and his assistants then had the unenviable task of facing the hostile crowd and securing possession of the body. Other trades also played their part in the arrangements for disposing of a dead felon from Tyburn. In 1731 a Mr Osmond was paid £6 for doing 'plumbers work on the trough for the dead body' and a Mr Ashfield was paid £1 14s for 'carpenters work for the said trough'. This was payment for a wooden coffin lined with lead in which the subjects were placed on their arrival from Tyburn.

The Company of Barber-Surgeons went to great length and considerable expense to obtain the corpses of the condemned. Gifts were made to the hangmen at Christmas for allowing agents to secure the body from the scaffold (Sawday 1995: 60). In 1743 it was recorded that the hangman signed with an 'X' for receipt of his Christmas box and that the clerk styled him 'John Thrift Esq. Hangman'. The accounts of the Barber-Surgeons from 1717 provide evidence of the growing contention around the scaffold as conflicting claims were made for the bodies of the condemned. The Barbers' Company often prosecuted rioters and was continually compensating the beadles who were injured in the fights around the scaffold at Tyburn and other places of execution in London. The following examples from the Annals of the Barber-Surgeons of London give some idea of the conflicts at Tyburn:

1717 Paid my Lord Chief Justice Parker's Tipstaffe for taking four Dead Bodies from Tyburn this year – expenses £2.8.0.
1719–20 Paid the Beadles for going to Tyburn for a Body for the Muscular lecture when they could not get one by reasons of a Great Mobb of Soldiers and others. £0.13.0.
1720 Paid the hangman for the dead man's clothes which were lost in the scuffle and for his Christmas Box. £0.15.0.
1739 Paid the Beadles for their being beaten and wounded at the late execution. £4.4.0.
1740 Paid for mending the windows broke upon bringing the last body from Tyburn. £0.6.0.

(Young 1890)

There was a great deal of hostility from the gallows crowd to the presence of the men working for the surgeons. For this reason they often found it wise to disguise themselves while they waited around the gallows for the body of the condemned. Bernard de Mandeville writing in 1725 commented on the scene following an execution:

the next entertainment is a squabble between the surgeons and the Mob, about the dead bodies . . . They have suffered the Law (cries the rabble) and shall have no other barbarities put upon them . . . If the others are numerous and resolute enough to persist in this Enterprise, a Fray ensues.

(Sawday 1995: 59)

The scenes around the scaffold and the conflicting, often violent, claims made by various people over the bodies of executed felons greatly worried the state, which was anxious to control this kind of behaviour. Most of the condemned were deeply concerned about their impending agony on the gallows and about what would happen to their bodies after death, a fear that was shared by their friends and relatives. Many families intervened to claim a body. For example, John Casey rode with his brother in the cart from Newgate to Tyburn in 1721 and managed to protect his brother's corpse from the unwelcome attentions of the surgeons' men. Sometimes relations made long journeys for the same purpose as in the case of the wife of William Seston who travelled from Lancashire to safeguard her husband's body at Tyburn in 1721. A few years later, Oliver White's father journeyed from Carlisle to London to keep watch over his son's freshly buried remains, a long, difficult and expensive journey and an indication of the concern he felt that his son should rest in peace.

When hangings at Tyburn ceased in 1783 this ammounted to an informal re-evaluation of the purposes and utility of public hanging. Indeed, a sea change in attitudes is indicated in the writings of Daniel Defoe and Bernard de Mandeville earlier in the century. Defoe advocated solitary confinement and an austere regime for the prisoner in his last few days while de Mandeville suggested a much larger force of guards for the procession and the execution as a way of reducing the disorder and moral laxity he considered the inevitable accompaniment to Tyburn Fair. Henry Fielding's work as a magistrate convinced him that the drunken and unruly crowds attending hangings made a mockery of the law. He expands on the matter:

> The day appointed by law for the thief's shame is the day of glory in his opinion. His procession to Tyburn and his last moments there, are all triumphant; attended with the compassion of the meek and tender-hearted, and with the applause, admiration and envy of all the bold and hardened. . . . The executions of criminals . . . serve, I apprehend, a purpose diametrically opposite to that for which they are designed; and tend rather to inspire the vulgar with a contempt for the gallows rather than a fear of it.

This analysis was supported by a Scottish clergyman who was clearly appalled by a hanging scene he witnessed:

Among the immense multitude of spectators, some at windows, some upon carts, thousands standing and jostling one another in the surrounding fields – my conviction is that, in a moral view, a great number were made worse, instead of better, by the awful spectacle. Of the ragamuffin class a large proportion were gratified by the sight; and within my hearing expressed their admiration of the fortitude, as they termed the harshness and stupidity, of one of the sufferers. 'Well done, little coiner', 'What a brave fellow he is!'.

(Fielding 1751)

Francis Place, the radical, provided the most incisive criticism of the public hanging ritual. He argued that the support which the crowd gave to the criminals, the felon appearing as hero and the general atmosphere of revelry, failed to deter serious crime and indeed undermined the whole process of the law. In what he said there is little sense of humanity or of the needless humiliation inflicted on the condemned felon. Instead public hanging is being subjected to cold and critical scrutiny. It led to social disorder; it disrupted everyday life including trade and commerce; it subverted the law and was ineffective.

It could certainly be extremely inefficient. Until the 'drop' form of hanging was introduced which broke the neck, death was from asphyxia. However, this more primitive form of hanging could be influenced by the executioner. He could be bribed to tie the knot in such a fashion that the prisoner would become unconscious for quite some time and might survive being taken down and be revived by friends. This is almost certainly what was intended to happen in the case of Dr Dodd at Tyburn in 1777, although in his case the incompetence of the hangman meant that Dodd was hanged anyway.

Although hangings without extinction of life were never common, they were frequent enough to keep hope of resuscitation by relatives and well-wishers alive and examples have gone on record. In 1709 John Smith was hanged at Tyburn and left for some time before being cut down and taken to a nearby house where he was bled and given other treatment from which he made a complete recovery. For the rest of his life he rejoiced in the nickname 'Half-Hanged Smith'.

In 1736 Thomas Reynolds was hanged at Tyburn and on being cut down and placed in his coffin, pushed back the lid and made an effort to get out. The hangman then descended on his victim with the intention of stringing him up once more but the onlookers intervened and carried him off. Although they made attempts to save his life, he died shortly afterwards.

There were many who even in the earlier part of the eighteenth century denounced Tyburn Fair as an unedifying spectacle and one such was Bernard de Mandeville writing in 1725. In *An Enquiry into the Causes of the Frequent Executions at Tyburn*, he fulminates against the whole ritual:

> All the way, from Newgate to Tyburn, is one continual Fair, for Whores and Rogues of the meaner Sort. Here the most abandoned Rakehells . . . here trollops . . . And there are none so less lewd, so vile or so indigent, of either sex but . . . may find a Paramour . . . . No modern Rabble can long subsist without their darling Cordial, the grand Preservative of Sloth, Jeneva, that infallible Antidote against care and frugal Reflexion . . .

Hangings on the gallows at Tyburn and elsewhere were more than simply a public display of the carrying out of justice. They were events that were deeply etched into the collective consciousness and the culture of the urban masses throughout the assize towns in the provinces but most of all in London. In spite of the utterances of isolated individuals like de Mandeville in 1725 and a growing undercurrent of criticism through the eighteenth and into the nineteenth centuries, hanging remained central to the popular culture. The progress of some felons to Tyburn acquired the attributes of burlesque, a ridiculing of the law which cemented popular derision for authority. In this way, the procession to Tyburn came to have the opposite effect to that intended by the authorities. As Frank McLynn said, 'There can be little question but that Tyburn hangings had become, not an awestruck acceptance of the remorseless majesty of the law, but a ritual of defiance of that very law.' (McLynn 1991: 276).

Tyburn Fair played a central role in the popular culture of London, especially in the seventeenth and eighteenth centuries. This culture was largely enacted on the streets; it was voyeuristic, vulgar and vicarious. It was escapist. Its attractions were built up through the idea of celebrity. Even before developing technology and increasing literacy cheapened the price and thereby widened the potential readership of reading material, there were writers whose efforts were aimed at selling copy through the production of celebrities. These were not moralistic or didactic texts drawing their readers' attention to the awful fate of sinners, rather, they were unashamedly picaresque, glorifying and romanticising a carefully chosen gallery of rogues and villains. Certain types of criminal were deliberately excluded but others were presented in an uncritically favourable light. Examples of this genre are *A General History of the Robbers and Murders of the Most Notorious Pirates* published in 1724 and *A General History of the Lives and Adventures of the Most Famous Highwaymen, Murderers, Street Robbers, etc.* which was published in 1734. These works appeared under the name of Captain Charles Johnson which may have been a pseudonym for Daniel Defoe. Similarly, John Gay (1685–1732) popularised criminals and the criminal world in his immensely popular *Beggar's Opera*.

Of the various kinds of felon that were executed at Tyburn, highwaymen enjoyed greater popularity than most with the crowds. It is hard to explain why they came to be surrounded by such an aura of glamour and popular acclamation. Most of them, after all, were prepared to use violence and even murder in the commission of their crimes and in evading capture. Few were handsome and gallant. Maybe the fact that they rode horses gave them style and an air of derring-do. Perhaps the reality that their victims were frequently the well-heeled made them the darlings of the crowds, although few emulated the reputed actions of Robin Hood in disbursing some of the proceeds from their robberies to the poor and needy. The appearance of a notorious highwayman at Tyburn inevitably attracted a capacity audience. They were the elite of the criminal world in the seventeenth and eighteenth centuries. Few, however, lived long enough to regale their grandchildren with tales of the old days.

TWELVE

Newgate to Tyburn Today

It is still possible to follow the historic route between Newgate and Tyburn, said to be approximately three miles. Some of the buildings to be seen and a selection of the historical associations with which the route is so richly endowed will be described. What cannot be re-created of course are the sights and sounds of the eighteenth century. However, the historian is engaged in a dialogue between the present and the past and there are places along the route where the atmosphere and a dash of imagination can give us some sense of what our ancestors may have experienced. This walk, which can easily be completed in three to four hours, is best done early on a Sunday morning.

The walk starts outside the Central Criminal Court commonly known as the Old Bailey. This building stands at the junction of Old Bailey, Giltspur Street and Newgate Street. A City of London plaque rather misleadingly states, 'Site of Newgate. Demolished 1777'. In fact this refers to the final pulling down of the last of the jumble of ancient buildings which constituted the old prison before reconstruction work started in 1770. The work had hardly been completed when, during the Gordon Riots of 1780, large parts of Newgate were torn down by ravening, drunken mobs. Very quickly it was completely rebuilt by the architect George Dance the Younger. Despite its grand exterior, the conditions experienced by the prisoners and the general corruption of the regime under which it was run soon meant that the reborn Newgate had an even more fearsome reputation than its predecessor. Its notoriety led to a parliamentary inquiry in 1814 and it was one of the first prisons to which the reformer Elizabeth Fry turned her attention. Improvements were slow in coming. Its overcrowding was partly relieved by the opening of Holloway Prison in 1852. In its last years it was used mainly for prisoners committed to trial at the Old Bailey and for those awaiting execution. It closed as a prison in 1881.

When hangings ceased at Tyburn, they were transferred to a spot close to Newgate in Old Bailey. The first public executions on this new site were on 9 December 1783 when ten felons were hanged. In 1789 a woman was burned, having been strangled first, for the crime of coining. To her fell the dubious honour of being the last person in Britain to die in this horrible fashion. In 1864 Franz Muller was hanged outside Newgate, the occasion attracting a densely packed crowd estimated at more than 50,000. Muller had been found guilty of robbing and murdering a senior bank clerk. This act had taken place on the North London Railway and it attracted huge interest because it was the first murder perpetrated on a railway train. Additionally, Muller was of German extraction and the case unleashed an unpleasant wave of xenophobia. He tried to escape by sailing to the United States but his ship was overtaken by a steamship carrying officers of the Metropolitan Police, who arrested him at New York and brought him back to Britain for trial. Interestingly, one of the exhibits for the prosecution was the hat which had been owned by the murdered man. Muller stole it, cut it down in size and wore it himself. Hats of this truncated sort became popular for some years and were known as 'Muller cut-downs'. Another outcome of the Muller case was the development of the communication cord which allowed a passenger in distress to alert the engine driver to stop the train at the first practical opportunity. The last public execution outside Newgate took place on 26 May 1868 when a young Fenian, Michael Barrett, was hanged by the famous executioner William Calcraft. Barrett had tried to blow up the Middlesex House of Correction in Clerkenwell in which some of his compatriots were imprisoned. He achieved a spectacular explosion, failed to extricate his fellows but managed to demolish a row of houses opposite and kill some of their occupants. Charles Dickens, who mentions Newgate in some of his writings and, despite himself, witnessed at least two executions there, campaigned for the abolition of public hangings.

A near neighbour of the Central Criminal Court is the Magpie and Stump in Old Bailey. This ancient although totally rebuilt hostelry used to rent rooms out expensively to those who wished to enjoy a grandstand view of the hangings outside Newgate. The gentry would lounge in the window seats and nonchalantly play cards, dine and drink until the entertainment started. The price for this self-indulgent voyeurism was as much as £50 in the case of a celebrated criminal but a sumptuous breakfast was included. On Sunday lunchtimes 'execution breakfasts' are still available.

The Central Criminal Court was opened in 1834 and the complex of buildings of which it is composed has been added to constantly since that time. It has witnessed innumerable famous trials, among the most celebrated being those of Oscar Wilde in 1895; Hawley Harvey Crippen (1910); George Joseph Smith, the 'Brides-in-the-Bath' murderer (1915); William Joyce (Lord Haw-Haw) in 1945; John Reginald Christie (1953) and the 'Yorkshire Ripper', Peter Sutcliffe, in 1981. The Old Bailey was severely damaged by German bombs in 1941 and suffered a number of IRA bomb attacks in 1973. One curious tradition still observed on certain occasions at the Old Bailey is that of the judges carrying posies of sweet-smelling flowers. This recalls the use of nosegays in earlier days as a way of warding off what were thought of as the lethal miasmas that prisoners who had been incarcerated in Newgate brought with them into court. Atop the Old Bailey is a massive bronze statue portraying Justice.

At the junction of Newgate Street and Giltspur Street stands the Viaduct Tavern, the name of which refers to Holborn Viaduct, close by. This is typical of the large drinking houses built by the big brewers in London in the nineteenth century which were designed to maximise their trade by having frontages on two streets. The pub has thankfully escaped major revamping in recent years and still possesses high-quality carved wooden screens and other mahogany fittings, fine engraved glass, a Lincrusta ceiling and three painted mirrors depicting Greek myths which can perhaps best be described as Victorian soft porn. In Giltspur Street there is a plaque indicating the site of Giltspur Street Compter built in 1791 and demolished in 1854. The compters were the prisons administered by London's two sheriffs, evidence of the great importance once attached to their office. At the junction of Giltspur Street and Cock Lane stands a decidedly plump gilded cherub known as 'the Golden Boy'. It is said that this spot marks Pie Corner where the Great Fire died out in 1666. For many years there was an alehouse on the site called the Fortunes of War which was much frequented by the 'Resurrectionists', refreshing themselves before and after their nefarious visits to local burial grounds in order to obtain specimens for the teachers of surgery at St Bartholomew's Hospital. At 106 Newgate Street a City of London plaque indicates the site of the former Greyfriars Monastery. Later on, the entrance to Christ's Hospital was on this site. This school was founded in 1553 by Edward VI as a hospital for orphans and was known as the Bluecoat School because of the costumes worn by the pupils. Christ's Hospital School moved to a rural location near Horsham in Sussex in 1902. In April 1578 an earthquake occurred in London and in the prevailing climate of religious hatred, many averred that this was the work of the Pope. Only one fatality occurred. This was the unfortunate Thomas Grey who was killed by masonry dislodged from Christ's Hospital. Roman remains have been unearthed in Newgate Street. One of these relics is a tile on which a workman scratched the peevish graffito: 'Austalis has been going off on his own every day for thirteen days.' This tile is now in the Museum of London.

On the other side of Giltspur Street from the Viaduct Tavern stands St Sepulchre's Church, first mentioned in 1137, which is the church referred to in the nursery rhyme at 'When will you pay me, say the bells of Old Bailey'. Just inside Giltspur Street and tucked away at the east end of St Sepulchre's Church is a curious little watch house dated 1791 which was probably erected to guard recent burials against the activities of the 'Resurrectionists'. Extensive rebuilding of St Sepulchre's was carried out in the middle of the fifteenth century by Sir John Popham who was Treasurer to King Henry VI. Much of the fabric was destroyed in the Great Fire and rebuilt in a somewhat haphazard fashion with various subsequent restorations making up a building of rather eclectic character. Among St Sepulchre's many historical associations is that of one of its sixteenth-century incumbents, John Rogers, who was unlucky enough to be the very first Protestant martyr to be burnt for his beliefs at Smithfield, in 1555. Robert Ascham, who had been personal tutor to the tragic Lady Jane Grey and later to Queen Elizabeth I, was buried in the church in 1568. Sir Henry Wood (1869–1944), the conductor who established the Promenade Concerts in 1895, learned to play the organ here and became assistant organist at the age of just fourteen. His ashes were buried in St Sepulchre's in 1944. There are many other associations with the world of music. Sir Henry is shown in a stained glass window as is Dame Nellie Melba, among others. Buried inside the church is Captain John Smith, notable for being rescued from imminent death at the hands of some Native Americans by the famed Princess Pocahontas. The Royal Fusiliers have their Regimental Chapel in St Sepulchre's and they also have a memorial garden in the churchyard. The church contains visual evidence of the famous ritual involving the ringing of the bell and the solemn exhortations on the eve of an execution in the bricked-up entrance to the tunnel which led from St Sepulchre's under the road and to the condemned cell in Newgate. The bell is displayed in a glass case. At the south-eastern corner of the churchyard can be found the surviving portion of the earliest drinking fountain erected by the Metropolitan Drinking Fountain Association in 1859. This is unusual in retaining its original bronze cup and chain.

One of many fascinating 'might-have-beens' of London's history concerns the constant flow of proposals from the 1830s onwards to build a central railway terminus station in London on which all the major lines from the provinces would converge. Perhaps the earliest of these schemes was thought up by George Remington Junior and it was to be called the London Grand Junction Railway. It would have run from Camden Town where it was intended to link with long-distance lines from the West Country, the West Midlands and the north-west via Clerkenwell to Snow Hill and then to the Thames at Blackfriars. A two-level viaduct was envisaged for road-users and pedestrians above with trains running below. A modified scheme eliminated the two tiers and replaced them with one level for the railway. This line would have followed the valley of the Fleet River to terminate just to the west of St Sepulchre's Church. Despite an announcement in *The Times* of 22 February 1837 that work was about to start, this scheme did not go ahead.

We continue to Holborn Viaduct, once wryly described as 'the world's first flyover'. This was completed in 1869, cost over £2 million and was built to bridge the valley of the Fleet River. It was opened with great pomp by Queen Victoria on the same day as the new Blackfriars Bridge over the Thames. Victoria's eight years as a reclusive widow had seriously damaged her popularity and it was good for her public image that she now began to resume public duties. The building of Holborn Viaduct involved many associated roadworks including Holborn Circus, Charterhouse Street and St Andrew's Street and provided a much better route for the growing amount of commercial and other traffic going to the West End from the City and vice versa. The viaduct crosses Farringdon Street and epitomises Victorian civic pride with its allegorical bronze statues. On the north side the statues represent Commerce and Agriculture while those on the south portray Science and Fine Arts. Curiously, there were four rather Italianate yet semi-Gothic houses erected at the corners of the viaduct. These were also decorated with statues and those that can be viewed today depict Henry Fitzeylwin (d. 1212), the first Mayor of the City, and Sir Thomas Gresham (1519–79), immortalised as the founder of the Royal Exchange and Gresham College. The others are of Sir William Walworth, the perfidious Lord Mayor of London who stabbed Wat Tyler while engaged in negotiations during the Peasants' Revolt of 1389 and Sir Hugh Myddleton, who was responsible for the New River which brought the City an excellent water supply from Hertfordshire in the early seventeenth century. On the first floor of Gresham House next to Holborn Viaduct stands a statue of Sir Thomas Gresham that was put on display in 1868.

On the south side we pass the City Temple. This is the only Nonconformist church in the City and its origins can be traced back to 1640. However, the present building dates only from 1874 and replaced an earlier chapel located in Poultry. It was designed by Messrs Lockwood and Mawson in a vaguely Italianate style and was opened with considerable ceremony. After sustaining bomb damage in the Second World War, it was rebuilt and enlarged in 1955–8.

Close by is the church of St Andrew's, Holborn. This church has pre-Conquest origins, was rebuilt by the Normans and evolved through various medieval architectural fashions. In spite of rich financial support from the neighbouring Inns of Chancery, the fabric was considerably decayed by the time of the Great Fire. St Andrew's avoided being engulfed in the fire thanks to the natural barrier provided by the Fleet Valley but it was already in such a state that it was rebuilt by Wren. The rebuilding was on a generous scale and a very large church resulted. During the Civil War, the incumbent, John Hacket, defiantly continued to use the old prayer book. On one occasion some Parliamentary soldiers burst into the church and held a pistol to his head but with remarkable sangfroid, Hacket is reputed to have said, 'I am doing my duty. Now you do yours'. The soldiers immediately left without demur. Various restorations were made but the church was largely obliterated in the Blitz, only the tower and walls being left standing. Rebuilding and restoration were completed in 1961. Many of St Andrew's furnishings have been brought from elsewhere to replace those lost by enemy action and the result is something of a pastiche but quite an attractive one. The tomb of Thomas Coram (*c.* 1668–1751) can be seen. A shipwright born in Dorset who spent much of his life in the North American colonies promoting the Anglican Church, his fame lies in the fact that he planned and established the Foundling Hospital for abandoned children in 1741. Among those associated with St Andrew's is Henry Sacheverell (*c.* 1674–1724). He was a High Tory, an ordained minister who in 1709 used the pulpit of St Paul's to deliver a vitriolic sermon attacking the Whig minister, Godolphin. His point was that Dissenters were threatening the Church of England and that the Whigs and moderate Tories were reprehensibly failing to defend it. He was impeached by the House of Lords but he had much popular support and riots took place in which the meeting houses of Dissenters were attacked. A wooden tablet commemorates this volatile man who was rector of St Andrew's from 1714 to 1724. Other associations are with Samuel Wesley, the father of the more famous John and Charles Wesley, who was ordained here in 1689 and with Marc Isambard Brunel, the somewhat understated father of the better-known Isambard Kingdom Brunel but a first class engineer and inventive genius in his own right. He married Sophia Kingdom in St Andrew's in 1799. William Hazlitt the essayist and literary critic married here in 1808 and Benjamin Disraeli, the future Prime Minister, was christened here at the age of twelve on 31 July 1817. On the west front of St Andrew's can be seen statues of schoolchildren from the parish school which was in nearby Hatton Garden.

We are now at Holborn Circus. Causing something of an obstacle to the free flow of traffic at this busy intersection is an equestrian statue of Prince Albert in bronze, erected in 1874. This has wittily been described as 'the most polite statue in London' because, rather curiously, it is doffing its hat towards the City of London. Hatton Garden can be seen on the north where at no. 57d there is a GLC plaque to Sir Hiram Stevens Maxim (1840–1916). American-born, he was living in Hatton Garden when, in 1883, he designed the machine gun with which he will always be associated. At 5 Hatton Garden is a privately sponsored plaque to Giuseppe Mazzini (1805–72). He was an Italian nationalist whose love for Britain meant that he spent much time in the country and it was here that he formulated his plans for bringing about unity and democracy in the country of his birth. Hatton Garden has acquired international fame as the headquarters of the London diamond traders and takes its name from Sir Christopher Hatton (*c.* 1540–91) who was a statesman and survivor in the shifting sands that were the politics of Elizabethan England.

Along Holborn on the north side the headquarters of the Prudential Assurance Company come into view. This was built on part of the site of Furnival's Inn, one of the Inns of Chancery, and was originally designed by Alfred Waterhouse in something of a Gothic Revival style. Its use of red brick and red terracotta became a house style for the Prudential. The original building came into use in

1879 but what can be seen today is a reconstruction which has been added to ever since. The Prudential Building displays a City of London plaque mentioning the site of Furnival's Inn. Charles Dickens began writing the *Pickwick Papers* while he lived there between 1834 and 1837 and there is a plaque to that effect in the courtyard. In the middle of the street stands a memorial to those members of the Royal Fusiliers who lost their lives in the two world wars. On the south side of Holborn can be seen the Melton Mowbray pub which looks like a traditional London tavern but which was only opened in recent years.

Brook Street is the last road on the north side of Holborn before Gray's Inn Road. This takes its name from Fulke Greville who became Lord Brooke in 1620 and built a long-since demolished mansion here which he modestly named after himself. A short distance up Brook Street is a blue plaque on no. 39 indicating that Thomas Chatterton (1752–70) died there. He was the tragic young man who, fascinated, even obsessed, by the medieval world, claimed to have discovered a mass of verse produced by a fifteenth-century monk, Thomas Rowley. This poetry, which was not without merit, was written by Chatterton himself. It created something of a sensation and on the strength of this, he moved from his native Bristol to London to try to make a living as a writer. When success did not come as quickly as he had hoped, he grew increasingly depressed and committed suicide by taking arsenic in a garret at no. 39. His short unfulfilled life has caught the imagination ever since and inspired poets such as Wordsworth and Keats to write about him and the PreRaphaelite Henry Wallis to paint the *Death of Chartterton* in 1856. At no. 20, William Friese-Greene (1855–1921) had a photographic laboratory where, in 1889, he gave the first ever demonstration of moving pictures. These were of local street scenes and his audience consisted of one rather bemused policeman whom he dragged off the street to witness this historic occasion.

At the junction of Holborn with Gray's Inn Road the picturesque Staple Inn can be seen on the south side. Although this has been rebuilt on a number of occasions, it provides a very good idea of how many of the timber-framed buildings of Tudor London would have looked.

It was of course one of the Inns of Chancery and not a hostelry catering for travellers and others. In 1886 the government bought part of Staple Inn to provide an extension to the Patent Office. Another part was sold to the Prudential Assurance Company. Alfred Waterhouse did much restoration work on the houses and the hall which was built in 1581. The hall boasts a splendid hammer-beam roof, and fine stained glass. Close by is a charming garden, a real oasis from the hurly-burly of Holborn. There is a quaint notice in the entrance gateway forbidding horses to enter or children to play in the precincts. Staple Inn includes, at no. 337, the former premises of John Brumfit who opened his tobacconist's shop there in 1933. It became immortalised when its image appeared on packets of Old Holborn tobacco.

Gray's Inn Road lies at the eastern boundary of Gray's Inn, which is one of the four great Inns of Court. Its gardens were laid out in the 1580s by Francis Bacon who is commemorated by a statue in the South Square. One of the alumni of Gray's Inn was William Cecil, Lord Burghley (1520–98), the highly able and wily servant who proved so invaluable to Queen Elizabeth. The story is told that Cecil, while a young man resident in Gray's Inn, incurred a huge gambling debt to a fellow student whose bedroom was adjacent to his own. He is reputed to have drilled a hole through the partition between the bedrooms and with a roll of paper acting as a voice tube, whispered in sepulchral tones to his colleague that he risked perdition if he did not abjure gambling. The student is said to have been so shaken by what he took to be the divinely inspired advice that next morning he knocked on Cecil's door and humbly begged him to accept the discharge of the debt.

At 22 High Holborn stands the Cittie of York pub. There has been a drinking house on this site since 1430. A rebuilding in 1695 produced Gray's Inn Coffee Shop but what can be seen today is the result of a further rebuilding in the 1890s. The name recalls a drinking place of the same name which was once part of Staple Inn. For many years it was known as Henekey's Long Bar. The interior is unique. The bar is certainly one of the longest in Britain and on a high gallery can be seen a number of enormous vats which Henekey's used for housing their wines and spirits. There is a high, arched ceiling of almost cathedral-like appearance. Other curiosities of this pub are a number of cubicles with swing doors where lawyers could hold private meetings with clients over a drink or meal. Perhaps strangest of all is a stove dating from 1815 from which the smoke escapes by means of a vent under the floor. Holborn and High Holborn once had a very large number of hostelries, many of them taverns and coaching inns, the latter mostly succumbing to the competition of the railways from the late 1830s. At no. 119, a blue plaque may be seen commemorating the work of the horologist Thomas Earnshaw (1749–1829). For many years he had his workshop on this site. His greatest fame probably lies with the improvements he made to the marine chronometer.

High Holborn is the continuation of Holborn to Shaftesbury Avenue. On the south side at no. 208 stands the Princess Louise. This pub, named after Queen Victoria's fourth daughter, was built in 1872. What distinguishes this magnificent pub are its interior decor and fittings. There is a riot of etched and decorative glass, superb pictorial tiling, polished woodwork and gold embossed mirrors. The stonework in the gentlemens' toilet is so splendid that it is the subject of a preservation order. The Princess Louise is a superb example of Victorian pub design and architecture and should on no account be missed by pub aficionados. At no. 270 formerly stood the George and Blue Boar Inn, a major coaching inn in which Cromwell and Ireton in 1645 managed to intercept correspondence between Charles I to his wife Henrietta Maria. This made it clear that the King was prepared to negotiate with the Parliamentarians, whom he thought of as rebels, while also being engaged in other negotiations which he hoped would bring a French army to support him. This treasonable item had been hidden away in the saddle of one of the King's messengers. The house was one of the watering holes which catered for those going in procession to Tyburn and it is referred to in Jonathan Swift's poem, the best-known part of which runs as follows:

As clever Tom Clinch, when the rabble was bawling,
Rode stately through London to die of his calling,

> He stopped at the George for a bottle of sack
> And promised to pay for it when he came back.

Also on the south side is a newish pub by the name of Pendrell's Oak. This recalls the Pendrell family who owned Boscobel House in Shropshire. They were devoted supporters of the Royalist cause in the Civil War and it was to Boscobel that Charles II fled after the battle of Worcester on 3 September 1651. The Pendrells sheltered the King and helped him to escape and were richly rewarded by the grateful Charles after the Restoration. One branch of the family moved to London and William Pendrell, who died in 1671, is buried in St Giles's churchyard. The pub is close to Pendrell House where the Meteorological Office's London Weather Centre is located. On the left is the alley known as Little Turnstile. This probably recalls the revolving stiles that were placed at the four corners of Lincoln's Inn Fields to prevent cattle grazing there from escaping. The stiles may also have helped to ensure that other animals being driven through the area to Smithfield did not stray into these hallowed grounds. Little Turnstile gives access to Lincoln's Inn Fields where at nos 59–60 an LCC plaque commemorates the fact that Spencer Perceval (1762–1812) lived there. He was Prime Minister when he was assassinated by a bankrupt businessman who blamed him for his financial misfortunes.

At 72 High Holborn stands the Old Red Lion. It is said that in 1661 after the Restoration it housed overnight the bodies of Cromwell, Ireton and Bradshaw which had been exhumed and tried for regicide at Westminster Hall. They were then allegedly hanged, drawn and decapitated and the bodies buried while the heads were exhibited at Westminster. There is confusion here because the place of execution is alternatively cited as Tyburn and what is now Red Lion Square, close to the pub. For many years there was an obelisk in the square said to mark the place where they were buried. The ghosts of the three men are seen from time to time, walking purposefully across the square and apparently engaged in earnest conversation, as well they might after all these years.

On the north side of Lincoln's Inn Fields, which were laid out in the early 1640s, is the somewhat unsung Sir John Soane's Museum. Soane lived from 1753 to 1837 and personified that rare phenomenon, the rise from rags to riches. He was a bricklayer's son who became the architect of the Bank of England. In no. 13 he accumulated an extraordinarily eclectic hoard of artistic and antiquarian items. There are Gothic fantasies, Egyptian sarcophagi plus innumerable other exhibits, many of them extremely odd, and paintings by Canaletto and Watteau. Perhaps most significant for those interested in London life in the eighteenth century, the museum contains Hogarth's original eight engravings making up *The Rake's Progress* dated 1735 and also *The Election*, four scenes completed in 1757.

On the south side of Lincoln's Inn Fields is the Royal College of Surgeons which on its first floor contains the Hunterian Museum. This exhibits some of the enormous collection of anatomical specimens and body parts accumulated by the avid Scottish scientist, surgeon, physiologist and anatomist, John Hunter (1728–93). The most fascinating exhibit is probably the skeleton of the renowned Irish giant, Charles Byrne who was almost 8 feet tall. Hunter employed considerable skulduggery to obtain the skeleton given Byrne's clearly expressed wishes that he should be buried at sea to avoid the attention of the anatomists. Placed next to Byrne's mortal remains are those of a midget named Caroline Crachami, otherwise known as the 'Sicilian Fairy', who was only 23 inches tall when she died at the age of nine.

High Holborn is crossed at right angles by Kingsway and Southampton Row. Kingsway was part of a great Victorian scheme for improving the metropolitan road system. Opened in 1905, its name honoured King Edward VII. A feature seen when crossing Kingsway is the northern end of the tram subway that used to run to the Embankment. This subway, possibly unique in Britain, linked the north and south London tram systems and allowed trams to avoid road congestion by using a specially designed underpass. This subway even possessed its own stations at Aldwych and Holborn which provided easy interchange with the

Underground system. The last tram to use the subway did so on 5 July 1952. As late as 1950 the subterranean Holborn tram station was lit by powerful gas lamps, the loud hissing of which added to its very distinctive atmosphere.

Close by, on the north side of High Holborn, once stood British Museum Underground station on what was originally the Central London Line. It was opened in 1900 and from the start irked passengers who wanted to change to the Northern Line at Holborn station because they had to emerge from the bowels of the earth and walk a short distance in the open. Proposals to improve interchange by closing British Museum and enlarging Holborn station eventually came to fruition and in 1933 the new Holborn station came into use and British Museum was closed. Before it had closed, however, stories circulated that the station was haunted by a spectre in the form of an Egyptian mummy that had escaped from the museum. Many people came forward claiming to have seen one or more ghastly apparitions, frequently mummies, running around the platforms and passages trailing the bandages in which they had been swathed. It was probably the flurry of excitement caused by these events which inspired the makers of the 1935 film *Bulldog Jack* to present much of the film's action on an imaginary Underground station called 'Bloomsbury', which possessed a secret tunnel leading to a sarcophagus in the museum. Nothing can be seen of British Museum station at street level but the now grubby white tiled walls can just be discerned from Central Line trains running between Holborn (Kingsway) and Tottenham Court Road stations.

At 83 Southampton Row, Edgar Allan Poe arrived in 1815 at the age of six. His youthful years were somewhat dissipated and he ran away to join the army from which he was soon dishonourably discharged. This forced him to turn to writing. In 1838 he wrote *The Narrative of Arthur Gordon Pym*. This macabre story tells of three men and a cabin boy cast adrift in an open boat. They only survive by killing and eating the boy whose name was Richard Parker. Poe's fame and literary success brought him neither financial security nor contentment. Many years later a merchant vessel sank in the Atlantic. Four crew members took to an open boat and three were picked up some time later. The other member of the crew was a cabin boy and he had been killed and eaten. His name? Richard Parker.

Shaftesbury Avenue dates from the mid-1880s. It was built as part of the same scheme as Kingsway to improve road communication between the West End and the Tottenham Court Road and Bloomsbury areas. The name 'Shaftesbury' recalls Anthony Ashley Cooper (1801–85). As Earl of Shaftesbury, he was a philanthropist and leading campaigner for factory reform. Another reason for the construction of these roads was to open up and sanitise some of London's worst rookeries or criminal sanctuaries, namely St Giles and Seven Dials. The latter, previously known as 'Cock and Pye Fields' after a local inn, got its strange name from a Doric pillar topped in fact by only six sundials. This stood at the intersection of seven streets and was a noted rendezvous for criminals. It was taken down in 1773 amid great excitement because it was rumoured that its base contained a large amount of money. It did not. The pillar was subsequently re-erected at Weybridge in Surrey. Shaftesbury Avenue lacks architectural distinction but is noted for being the centre of London's theatreland. At the junction of High Holborn and Shaftesbury Avenue, Endell Street can be seen on the left and this contains the Swiss Protestant Church founded in 1762 where Sunday services are conducted in French. Beyond Endell Street is Bow Street. A courthouse was opened here in 1748 where Henry Fielding and his half-brother, Sir John Fielding, were magistrates. They attempted to bring some degree of rationality to the workings of the law and it was here that the Bow Street Runners started their operations. Bow Street Magistrates Court now stands on the site.

We proceed along the old route up St Giles High Street. On the south side is the Angel pub. This is an ancient hostelry although it was rebuilt in 1898 and was previously known as the Bowl. It is said to have been one of the major stopping places for the condemned felons and their hangers-on making their way from Newgate to Tyburn and is reputed to be haunted. Other drinking places nearby also claim this distinction. They include the White Hart, Drury Lane and the Three Tuns, South Portman Mews, although both lie slightly off the direct route. Immediately on the left is the church of St Giles-in-the-Fields topped by a fine steeple 150 feet high. St Giles is close to where the Great Plague of London broke out in 1665; in just one month in that year 1,391 burials were recorded to have taken place in its churchyard. This church has many historical associations of which only a few can be given here. George Chapman was buried there in 1634. It was his translation of Homer which sent John Keats (1795–1821) into such poetic raptures. Five now beatified Jesuits, put to death after the Popish Plot, were buried in the north part of the churchyard in 1678. Lying close by was the canonised Oliver Plunkett, Archbishop of Armagh, who was executed for high treason in 1681. In his tomb was buried a copper plate with this inscription: 'Accused of high treason, through hatred of the faith, by false brethren, and condemned to death, being hanged at Tyburn and his bowels being taken out and cast into the fire, suffered martyrdom with constancy.' He was soon exhumed and it was reported that miraculously his bodily parts became reunited. Much earlier, in 1417, the Lollard Sir John Oldcastle died after being hanged over a hot fire. The prolific if somewhat pedestrian portrait painter, Sir Geoffrey Kneller, was buried in St Giles in 1723. Luke Hansard was interred in 1828. He and his descendants printed parliamentary reports from 1774 to 1889 and his surname has been immortalised as the title of the verbatim reports of Parliament's deliberations. It is possible that Claude Duval, the famous highwayman, is buried within the precincts. As with so many of his kind, he went to meet his Maker while only young. He was hanged at Tyburn in 1670. Others buried here include Arthur William Devis (1762–1822), an artist who mostly painted charming portraits of children but is best remembered for his *The Death of Nelson* and a painting of Dr William Balmain, the co-founder of New South Wales, whose name lives on in a suburb of Sydney. He was buried in St Giles in 1803. On the west front of St Giles the name of its architect, Henry Flitcroft, is displayed prominently on a frieze, and close by is what can best be described as a stone lych gate, erected in 1804. This rather curious structure incorporates a wooden bas-relief of the Resurrection which was carved in 1687 and may be based on Michelangelo's *Last Judgement* in the Sistine Chapel in the Vatican.

The interior of St Giles contains many fine seventeenth- and eighteenth-century furnishings.

From St Giles High Street the route passes Andrew Borde Street where St Giles Hospital stood before it was dissolved. Andrew Borde himself was a noted wit who lived during the reign of Henry VIII. Very briefly we join New Oxford Street. This was completed in 1847 and had been built to reach Holborn more directly than the old route which curved through St Giles High Street. Its construction involved the knocking down of some of London's most festering slums. Now we enter Oxford Street proper which has long been a traditional route out of London to the west. The systematic development of buildings along Oxford Street dates from the late 1730s. By the end of the century, development was complete from the Tottenham Court Road end to Park Lane. At first the buildings lining Oxford Street were largely residential. Slowly one or two places of entertainment were opened such as the Pantheon at no. 173, now occupied by a Marks & Spencer store. The Princess's Theatre was opened in 1840 where the Oxford Walk shopping precinct now stands. At no. 275 stands Regent Hall. This building which at one time contained a skating rink is now occupied by the Salvation Army but remains surprisingly unaltered. After 1850, Oxford Street began to assume its more modern character as a centre of retailing. At first, however, the shops were mostly small private ones largely serving the rich families who lived in the fashionable residential streets and squares on both sides of Oxford Street. Gradually these gave way to department stores of the sort which can now be seen on most of the nation's high streets.

The first road junction along Oxford Street on the north side is that with Hanway Street. This is probably named after Jonas Hanway (1712–86) who was assured immortality as the first Englishman reputed to have ventured out on to the streets of the capital brandishing an umbrella to protect himself from the rain. Hanway was a man of many interests including foreign travel, prison reform, philanthropy and hatred of the tea-drinking habit. He alienated the great Dr Johnson when he attacked tea on the grounds that he believed it led to adultery and other social evils.

Berwick Street joins Oxford Street on its south side. At no. 22 a Westminster City Council plaque is affixed to the house where Jessie Matthews, actress and dancer, was born. The last role for which she is remembered is as 'Mrs Dale' in the 1950–60s radio soap opera *Mrs Dale's Diary*. On the north side of Oxford Street is Berners Street. At no. 13 the Swiss painter Henry Fuseli (1741–1825) lived, in the early nineteenth century. The best known of his works was probably the puzzling, even disturbing, *Nightmare* of 1781. It was perhaps the powerful quality of this work that led an admirer to call on Fuseli and expect to be welcomed by some enormous and sturdy bearded figure resembling a Viking warrior. Imagine the visitor's surprise when he was greeted by a diminutive silver-haired man wearing an old flannel dressing gown and what appeared to be part of his wife's work-basket on his head. In 1809, Berners Street was the scene of a cruel hoax. This was carried out by a young reprobate named Theodore Hook who had been expelled from Harrow, had written thirteen operas while he was still a minor and was under investigation for fraud. For reasons unknown he decided to play a complex practical joke on a Mrs Tottingham who lived at no. 54. He spent six weeks making his preparations and the result of these was that on one memorable day hundreds of tradesmen descended on her house presenting her with a vast quantity of goods varying from coffins to coffee and snuff. As if that was not enough, other callers included a cosmopolitan selection of clergymen to shrive her soul, doctors to cure her body, lawyers to assist her with the writing of her will and even stay-makers to fit her up with corsets.

About one-third of the way along Oxford Street is the junction with Regent Street. This was part of an ambitious scheme by John Nash (1752–1835), the town planner and architect, and others, to connect what came to be called Regent's Park with the official residence of the Regent, Carlton House. In the early part of the nineteenth century property speculators were keen to maximise the value of residential development planned for the Marylebone district by having easier road access from the Charing Cross and Strand areas. This would help to raise land values in run-down areas such as the Haymarket and Pall Mall through which any new road was likely to run. Nash wanted the proposed road to be part of a grandiose programme of improvements that would bring London's architecture up to the standards of other European capital cities. Parliamentary approval was obtained in 1813 and work started quickly. Nash was severely frustrated in his attempt to place his own imprimatur throughout the scheme, individual developers using their own designs where it suited them. However, Nash was very successful in the work he undertook between Piccadilly and Oxford Street in the Quadrant. This part of Regent Street did represent something close to the model he had envisaged. For many years in the nineteenth century, along with Bond Street close by, Regent Street was the shopping resort of the very rich and fashionable but by 1900 they had tended to drift away and Regent Street was beginning to look somewhat down-at-heel. Many of the buildings were showing serious structural faults and it was evident that shortcuts had been taken when this part of Regent Street had originally been put up. Complete redevelopment was considered and the prominent architect Richard Norman Shaw (1831–1912) was asked to come up with suggestions. The shopkeepers, led by the managing director of Swan & Edgar, totally rejected these as too expensive and also because they thought that adding to the height of the buildings would make the street seem cavernous and off-putting. Eventually a new design for the Quadrant was accepted and rebuilding was completed in the 1920s.

Today Regent Street remains one of the leading shopping areas of central London. Visible from Oxford Circus just down the east side of Regent Street is Liberty's. This famous, highly idiosyncratic emporium traces its origins to Arthur Lasenby Liberty who started selling oriental fabrics and other goods in Regent Street in the 1870s. Liberty had an almost devotional enthusiasm for oriental art and design and was also fired by a passionate desire to encourage craftsmanship and to improve public taste. He became a fervent supporter of the Aesthetic Movement, a reaction to what was seen as the brash vulgarity of the standardised, mass-produced articles associated with the Industrial Revolution. Liberty was convinced that the beauties of oriental colour and design could be reproduced using the latest mechanical aids. It did not prove easy but Liberty was possessed of a persuasive missionary zeal. British manufacturers eventually managed to produce fabrics that displayed both original oriental and new designs and which often incorporated ancient dyeing techniques, again using new technology. For those occasions when designs could only be hand-printed, he established a printing works at Merton Abbey. His influence on taste and fashion was enormous and he came to hobnob with some of the leading artists, aesthetes and critics of his time such as William Morris, John Ruskin, Thomas Carlyle, Edward Burne-Jones and Dante Gabriel Rossetti. Such was his success that he eventually occupied all the buildings from 140 to 150 Regent Street. However, redevelopment took place in the 1920s and the buildings we see now are highly eclectic, the result of the conservative agents of the Crown who own the land and the flamboyant Liberty reaching an uneasy compromise. Eastern and British motifs in curious juxtaposition adorn the Regent Street facade while that part of the building fronting on to Great Marlborough Street has a half-timbered Tudor appearance with an interior incorporating oak and teak timber work from three naval men-o'-war. There is high quality stained glass, linenfold panelling and also galleries with hammer-beam roofs.

Just before the intersection of Oxford Street and Regent Street, Argyll Street comes in from the south. Close to Oxford Street are 8 and 10 Argyll Street. These display blue plaques commemorating Washington Irving and William Roy respectively. Washington Irving (1783–1859) was an American who was also something of an Anglophile and is perhaps best known for his American adaptation of German folk tales such as 'Rip van Winkle' and 'The Legend of Sleepy Hollow'. At no. 10, Major General William Roy's residence is remembered. He lived from 1726 to 1790 and was a skilled surveyor and cartographer whose work on mapping Scotland after the defeat of Bonnie Prince Charlie at the battle of Culloden in 1746 provided the model for the development of the Ordnance Survey. Immediately after Argyll Street stands Oxford Circus Underground station. This has largely managed to retain the facade with glazed dark ruby red tiling which was so characteristic of the work of

Leslie W. Green, appointed in 1903 as the architect of the Underground Electric Railways Company of London. Close to Oxford Circus and running between Great Portland Street and Titchfield Street is Market Place, the name of which recalls the Oxford Market which served the affluent residential quarters nearby from around 1720 up to the late nineteenth century.

On the north side of Oxford Street, Hollies Street gives access to Cavendish Square from which Harley Street runs up towards Regent's Park. One interesting resident of 33 Harley Street was Jane Digby, who gained notoriety in the 1820s and 1830s. She came from a very privileged social background and was only seventeen when she married a peer twenty years her senior. Jane was a young woman of great beauty, being tall, well proportioned and having the most winsome eyes. She was also an accomplished linguist and painter. These qualities were combined with a rapacious appetite for amorous adventures. In the first two years of marriage she took a succession of lovers by one of whom – reputedly her cousin – she had a child. At the age of twenty-one she met the love of her life. There was little that was understated about this man, starting with his name. This was Prince Felix Ludwig Johann von Nepomuk Friederich zu Schwarzenburg, an attaché at the Austrian Embassy. Their relationship became the focus of much disapproving gossip but such was the Prince's contempt for the mores of fashionable society that when Jane went to Brighton for a few days, he decided to make a surprise visit to her and did so in a garish yellow coach sporting his family arms. Divorce was inevitable and after the birth of a daughter by the Prince, Jane found a new theatre for her activities in the Mediterranean. Here she took a succession of eminent lovers. These included three kings, some princes and a German baron before she decided to go native. After frolicking with an Albanian brigand, she made for the deserts of Syria and enjoyed a number of Bedouin lovers, one of whom she ended up marrying. She died in 1881 and was buried in a Christian cemetery in Damascus.

Moving westwards along Oxford Street, New Bond Street soon joins from the south. This was developed from the early 1700s and while few buildings of great architectural distinction are still to be seen, there are some fine Victorian shop-fronts because Bond Street became the place where the rich shopped for the expensive fripperies they regarded as essential to their lifestyle. Bond Street was the place to perambulate, to do a spot of window-gazing and shopping while also trying to see and be seen. The street was also a favoured residential area in early times and boasted many famous residents. These include Jonathan Swift (1667–1745), the cleric and satirical writer; Edward Gibbon (1737–94), author of the monumental *The History of the Decline and Fall of the Roman Empire*; William Pitt the Elder (1708–78), the Whig politician; and, by a neat coincidence, Horatio Nelson and Emma Hamilton, although not at the same time. New Bond Street has maintained its position as a location for fashionable and expensive shops.

Duke Street crosses Oxford Street and on the north side leads across Wigmore Street into Manchester Square and then Manchester Street. Here at no. 38 there was a great deal of excitement in 1814. This stemmed from the announcement that a virgin woman of sixty-four had been impregnated by a divine partner and that she was going to give birth to the second Christ, the specific date for this event being 19 October in that year. The woman concerned was Joanna Southcott (1750–1814), a farmer's daughter from Devon. Born into the Anglican Church, she later converted to Methodism which she embraced with great ardour. She began to attract the limelight in 1792 when she declared that she had been divinely appointed to announce to the world the imminent Second Coming of Jesus. In that year she wrote a book of prophecies, the first of a series of writings which began to attract followers. In 1802 she started giving letters promising eternal life to those people she decided had divine favour. These included Mary Bateman who turned out to be a particularly brutal murderess. Joanna attracted a devoted following who showed their support by showering her with gifts in cash and kind. A chapel for her followers was opened in 1802. In 1813 she declared that she was pregnant and that the child, to be called 'Shiloh', would be the second Messiah. The nation was on tenterhooks when Joanna retired to bed to await her confinement. The promised date came and went but no baby arrived. With a great sense of anticlimax Christmas came and a few days later Joanna died. An autopsy showed that chronic flatulence and glandular swelling in the breasts had produced something of the appearance of pregnancy. She left a box of undisclosed 'treasures' which was only to be opened in the presence of twenty-four bishops at a time of national crisis. By the 1920s a number of these boxes had appeared, all vying with each other to be regarded as the genuine article. When one of them was opened in 1927, albeit with only one bishop present, it was found to contain nothing of significance. Some of Southcott's supporters in the Panacea Society still aver that this box was not the real one.

At the junction of Oxford Street and Marylebone Lane, opposite Bond Street underground station, a lamp-post bears a small black plaque which reads, 'Marylebone Lane follows the course of the ancient Tyburn stream now underground'. There is a slight depression in Oxford Street where it crosses the small valley that the Tyburn has made. At the junction of Oxford Street and Edgware Road another lamp-post bears a plaque also erected by Westminster City Council which is inscribed with the legend, 'Site of Tyburn Gallows. For four centuries [sic] Londoners celebrated executions on this spot with public hangings.' Four centuries seems something of an underestimate. In the complex of roads and bedlam of traffic that surround Marble Arch, there is a short slip road, used only by buses, called Tyburn Way while closer to Marble Arch itself is a plaque which reads:

The location is on an axis of two great Roman roads. One linked Colchester to the West Country, the other Watling Street (Edgware Road), linked with St Albans to the North. The Romans are thought to have built both these roads alongside the line of two older tracks which followed the high ground to avoid marshy land. Edgware Road is midway between the Tyburn and the Westbourne streams. For 600 years this crossroads was known as Tyburn. A plaque in the traffic island at the junction of Edgware Road and Bayswater Road marks the site of where the gallows is thought to have stood from 1571 to 1759. The gallows were known as the 'Tyburn Tree' but were replaced by a moveable gallows where a Toll House for the turnpike road was built on its site. In the eighteenth century Oxford Street was called Tyburn Road and Park Lane was called Tyburn Lane . . . the last execution was at Tyburn in 1783.

This plaque can be found adjacent to Exit 3. The Triple Tree is reputed to have had each of its legs standing in adjoining parishes – those of St George, Hanover Square, St Marylebone and Paddington.

Marble Arch itself was designed by John Nash reputedly using as an example the Arch of Constantine in Rome. It was erected in 1827 and placed in front of Buckingham Palace. Originally it was intended to top the arch with a colossal bronze representation of 'Victory' but this was superseded by a decision to erect instead a statue of George IV by the sculptor Francis Chantrey (1781–1841). In the event this was located in Trafalgar Square. Marble Arch was moved to its present site in 1851 and in 1908 marooned on an island in the middle of what even then was a maelstrom of traffic chaos. None but senior members of the royal family and the King's Troop Royal Horse Artillery are allowed to pass through it. The panels of the arch represent the Spirit of England inspiring Youth, Valour and Virtue and Peace and Plenty. A room in the attic of Marble Arch was at one time used by the Metropolitan Police.

To the west of Marble Arch a short way along the north side of Bayswater Road in Hyde Park Place is Tyburn Convent housing the Shrine of the Sacred Heart and the Tyburn Martyrs which contains relics recalling over a hundred Catholic martyrs who died at Tyburn. In the crypt is the Martyrs' Altar over which stands a replica of Tyburn Tree. Stained glass windows commemorate other aspects of the life and works of those Catholics who died for their beliefs. On the external wall of the convent there is an image of the gallows with the inscription: 'Tyburn Tree. The circular stone on the traffic island 300 paces east of this point marks the ancient gallows known as Tyburn Tree demolished in 1759.' Above this stone is a green City of Westminster plaque which reads: '105 Catholic martyrs lost their lives at the Tyburn gallows near this site.' Above this a further stone is inscribed: 'To the glory of God and in honour of the sacred heart of Jesus, this stone was blessed and laid by Cardinal Godfrey, Archbishop of Westminster on 10 Dec 1961 in honour of the glorious martyrs who laid down their lives in defence of the Catholic faith here on Tyburn Hill 1535–1681.' Another plaque reads: 'In 1585 Gregory Gunne predicted that one day a religious house would be founded at Tyburn. His prediction was fulfilled when Tyburn Convent was established in 1903.'

Just north of Marble Arch on the west side of Edgware Road is Connaught Place where a blue plaque at no. 2 commemorates Lord Randolph Churchill (1849–95). A descendant of the Duke of Marlborough, he was the father of Winston Churchill. His apparently precocious political abilities led to the prediction of a great future in the Conservative Party. At the age of thirty-seven, however, he was revealed as totally out of his depth when, as Chancellor of the Exchequer, his first and only budget was received with hostility and total derision. He resigned from political life and died while only in his mid-forties, almost certainly from the physical and mental effects of syphilis.

At the junction of Edgware Road and Seymour Street there is (January 2003) a café-bar appropriately called the Hanging Tree. Further up Edgware Road at no. 195 is a branch of Lloyds Bank where a stone gatepost is on display in the window on which the words 'Tyburn Gate' can just be descried. This is from one of the Tyburn toll gates and there is a commemorative plaque bearing this legend:

This stone . . . originally stood opposite the junction of Star Street and Edgware Road. . . . The stone is half a mile from the south end of Edgware Road where at the junction of that road with Oxford Street and Bayswater Road, Tyburn Turnpike house with three gates stood from about 1760 to 1829. Tyburn permanent triangular gallows stood from 1571 to 1759 in the position afterwards occupied by the Toll House. Tyburn was used as a place of execution from time immemorial until 1783. The first recorded execution took place in 1196.

On the opposite side of Edgware Road a little further to the south is a lamp-post with a City of Westminster plaque which reads: 'Cato Street. In 1820 a conspiracy to overthrow the government was foiled at nearby 6, Cato Street.' The conspirators were hanged at Newgate and then decapitated, the last time this form of execution took place in Britain.

In 1851 the Great Exhibition was held in Hyde Park. It was of course housed in the building that by popular acclaim became known as the Crystal Palace. The exhibition was an enormous success and Londoners took the Crystal Palace to their hearts. One of the conditions under which the exhibition had been staged was that the building had to be dismantled afterwards. This condition was very unpopular and all sorts of suggestions were put forward as to what use could be made of the building if only it was allowed to stay there. Arguably the most bizarre was that which proposed turning the Crystal Palace on its end to create a multi-storey glass tower 1,000 feet high. Had this ever happened, it would have created one of the most eye-catching features of London's townscape and skyline in Victorian times.

At the north-eastern corner of Hyde Park is Cumberland Gate which was erected about 1744 and took its name from the Duke of Cumberland, the same who later inflicted a bloody defeat at Culloden on the Scottish clansmen who had supported Bonnie Prince Charlie. At first it was called Tyburn Gate.

Annually on the last Sunday in April, since 1910, a Roman Catholic bishop leads a silent procession along the route that has been described from Old Bailey to Tyburn in memory of the Catholic martyrs and it concludes with a Benediction close to the supposed location at which they died.

Tyburn and the stories surrounding it have left an indelible mark on the history of London. When they think of London, many people call to mind St Paul's Cathedral, the Tower, Buckingham Palace and perhaps today the Millennium Wheel. These attractions draw tourists in vast numbers. The traffic bedlam of Marble Arch does not encourage visitors to tarry. For all that, it is still a place of brooding memories and deserves to be recognised as such.

Appendix: Tyburn in Literature

Tyburn doth deserve before them all
The Title and addition capital,
Of Arch or great Grand gallows of our Land,
Whilst all the rest like ragged Lackeys stand.

John Taylor (1578–1653)

Tyburn's significance was reflected in a wide range of literature particularly from the sixteenth century. That it left its mark on the popular consciousness is evidenced through the growth in the availability of ballads and cheap prints which refer to its events. Some ballads not only described the life and crimes of the condemned but could be sung because they were accompanied by music. An example was published in 1594 entitled *The lamentable lyfe and death of John Sturman who suffered at Tyburne the 24 of Januarie* (Palmer 1988: 122).

A well-known ballad was that of Jack Hall, executed at Tyburn in December 1707. Hall, a pickpocket and house-breaker, had been arrested and branded on the cheek, before he was sentenced to death for burglary. Jack had been a chimney sweep in his youth and the ballad dwells on this:

O my name it is Jack Hall, chimney sweep, chimney sweep . . .
I have twenty pounds in store, that's no joke, that's no joke . . .
And my neck shall pay for all, when I die, when I die . . .

O I rode up Tyburn Hill in a cart,
O I rode up Tyburn Hill in a cart.
O I rode up Tyburn Hill, and 'twas there I made my will,
Saying, the best of friends must part, so farewell, so farewell.

Up the ladder I did grope, that's no joke . . .
Up the ladder I did grope, and the hangman spread the rope,
O but never a word I said coming down, coming down.

(Palmer 1988: 124)

In 1647 the Charing Cross was destroyed. This was one of several crosses that had been erected by Edward I to mark the overnight resting places of the body of his first wife, Eleanor, as it made its way south from where she had died at Harby in Nottinghamshire in 1290. The Charing Cross marked her last resting place before her burial at Westminster Abbey, but in 1643, Parliament ordered its demolition as well as that of some of the other crosses. The popular ballad, 'The Downfall of Charing Cross', makes reference to Tyburn:

> Methinks the common-council shou'd
> Of it have taken pity,
> 'Cause, good old cross, it always stood
> So firmly in the city.
> Since crosses you so much disdain,
> Faith, if I were as you,
> For fear the King should rule again,
> I'd pull down Tiburn too.
>
> (Palmer 1979: 20)

One of the earliest references to Tyburn in literature appears in the fourteenth-century poem by William Langland, *Piers Plowman*, in the B and C texts. The former dates from about 1377 and contains an allusion to the advantages of learning so as to gain from benefit of clergy:

> Wel may the barne blisse that hym to boke sette:
> That lyuyne after letterure saved him lyf and soule!
> Dominus par hereditatis mee is a meri verset,
> That has taken fro Tyboune twenty stronge theves:
> There lewed theves been lolled up loke how thei be saves!

Tyburn found its way into the writings of a wide range of literary figures such as Shakespeare, Jonson, Dryden, Boswell, Fielding and Pepys. Shakespeare mentions hanging or uses the popular oath 'go hang' in several of his plays. For example, the durability and strength of the scaffold are well depicted in *Hamlet* (Act V, sc. i):

> CLOWN. What is he that builds stronger than either the mason, the
>   shipwright, or the carpenter?
> OTHER. The gallows-maker; for that frame outlives a thousand tenants.

In *Love's Labour's Lost* (Act IV, sc. iii), specific reference is made to Tyburn:

> BIRON. I could put thee in comfort. Not by two that I know:
> Thou makest the triumviry, the corner-cap of society,
> The shape of Love's Tyburn that hangs up simplicity.

Appendix

In *King Henry VI* (Part 2, Act II, sc. iii), Henry reflects on the class distinction of punishment as discussed earlier in the case of Bolingbroke:

> KING HENRY VI. Stand forth, Dame Eleanor Cobham, Gloucester's wife:
> In sight of God and us, your guilt is great:
> Receive the sentence of the law for sins
> Such as by God's book are adjudged to death.
> You four, from hence to prison back again;
> From thence, from thence unto the place of execution:
> The witch in Smithfield shall be strangled on the gallows.
> You, madam, for you are more nobly born,
> Despoiled of your honour in your life,
> Shall, after three days' open penance done,
> Live in your country here in banishment,
> With Sir John Stanley, in the Isle of Man.

In The *Tempest* (Act I, sc. i), the ship is tossed about in a storm and Gonzalo tries to cheer up the other passengers. In doing so, he refers to a proverb, 'He that is born to be hanged is in no danger of drowning.'

Within a year of the emergence of the Triple Tree, the poet John Donne was born. Donne, a metaphysical poet who later became Dean of St Paul's Cathedral, reflected solemnly on life and drew on Tyburn to reinforce his imagery:

> We are all conceived in close prison, in our mothers' womb we are close
> prisoners all . . . our life is but a going out of the place of execution and death.
> Now was there ever man to sleep in the cart, between Newgate and Tyburn?
> Between the prison and the place of execution, does any man sleep?
>
> (Hertz 2001: 29)

John Taylor (1578?–1653), known as 'The Water Poet', was born seven years after the Triple Tree was erected and he makes clear in his poem that Tyburn was not only the unrivalled gallows of London but the 'Grand Gallows of our Land'. Taylor was born of humble parentage in Gloucester and later became a Thames waterman as well as a spokesman for the Company of Watermen. He took to writing popular verse to increase his earnings and this led to an appointment as a royal waterman, and contact with the royal family.

Access to the cell of the condemned prisoners awaiting execution became common and it was by no means unusual for two or three hundred visitors to take advantage of the opportunity to pay their last respects or, in some cases, to gloat. John Taylor described his visit to the prison, paying the fee and interviewing the prisoners. His poem, 'The Description of Tyburn', gives some idea of the importance to contemporaries of the Triple Tree. His opening line tells us of the number of executions each year at Tyburn:

> I have heard sundry men oft times dispute
> Of trees that in one year will twice bear fruit.
> But if a man note Tyburn, 'will appear,
> That that's a tree that bears twelve times a year.

Nicholas Breton makes a similar comment in 'The Mad-cappes Message':

> goe tell the Swaggrers that doe use to sweare,
> Heere, or in hell, their mouths will sure be stopt:
> That Tiborne trees must once a month be topt.

Taylor also comments on the practice of surgeons who waited at the scaffold ready to claim the body, a practice that became more common in the eighteenth century:

> I further note, the fruit which it produces,
> Doth seldom serve for profitable uses:
> Except the skilful Surgeons industry
> Do make Dissection of Anatomy
> . . . I find this tree . . .
> That what it bears, are dead commodities.

In his reference to the famous Triple Tree he talks of those fools who ascend 'To that Celestial joy . . . more fools from thence to heaven do come, / Than from all Churchyards throughout Christendom.' He follows the theme of the graveyard:

> But at this Tree, in twinkling of an eye,
> The soul and body part immediately,
> There death the fatal parting blow doth strike,
> And in Churchyards is seldom seen the like
> . . . Concerning this dead fruit, I noted it,
> Instead of paste it's put into a pit,
> And laid up carefully in any place,
> Yet worm-eaten it grows in little space.

The highest of praise was given when Taylor paid tribute to Tyburn as the principal place of execution in the capital:

> There are inferior Gallows which bear
> (According to the season) twice a year:
> And there's a kind of watrish Tree at Wapping,
> Whereas Sea-thieves or Pirates are catched napping:
> But Tyburn doth deserve before them all

The title and addition capital,
Of Arch or great Grand gallows of our Land,
Whilst all the rest like ragged Lackeys stand.

Taylor's acknowledgement of Tyburn is also reflected in Thomas Middleton's work of 1618, *The Owl's Almanac*, where he states that 'A Faire paire of gallowes is kept at Tiburne . . . '.

Anthony Munday (1553–1633) was considered a lesser Elizabethan dramatist. He wrote ballads as well as having experience of many occupations such as stationer, actor, 'city-poet' and organiser of pageants. In his play, *Sir Thomas More*, which he wrote in the 1590s with several others, a riot has been inspired by fear of foreigners living in London and a new sheriff is given orders to execute the rioters:

MESSENGER. Is execution yet performed?

SHERIFF. Not yet, the carts stand ready at the stairs,
And they shall presently away to Tyburn . . .
Officers, be speedy,
Call for a gibbet, see it be erected;
Others make haste to Newgate, bid them bring
The prisoners hither, for they here must die.
Away I say, and see no time be slacked.

John Dryden (1631–1700), the English poet and playwright, penned a commemoration on Cromwell's death, celebrated Charles II's restoration and converted to Catholicism on the accession of James II. After 1685 he made an appeal for justice in one of his poems:

Oh Tyburn! could'st thou Reason and Dispute;
Could'st thou but Judge as well as execute;
How often would'st thou change the Felon's Doom
And truss some stern Chief-Justice in his room.
(Dryden, *Miscellany Poems*)

In the poem, Tyburn represents the harshness of the law and Dryden asks of the triangular gallows, 'should thy sturdy Posts support the Laws'. Asking for some moderation in legal decisions he pleads, 'In Matters doubtful to decide / A little bearing towards the milder side.'

The awful circumstances surrounding the execution at Tyburn in May 1726 of Catherine Hayes, who was burnt at the stake after the incompetent executioner had failed to strangle her first, was the basis for Thackeray's *Catherine, A Story*.

Daniel Defoe (1660–1731), whose works include *Robinson Crusoe* and *Moll Flanders*, had spent some time in Newgate in 1703. According to one account,

Defoe had connections with John Applebee, the publisher of the *Original Weekly Journal*, founded in 1714 (Lee 1869). Applebee also specialised in publishing the lives of the criminals hanged at Tyburn. These accounts were based on the writings of the prisoners themselves or on those compiled for them by the chaplain or Ordinary of Newgate. Lee suggested that Defoe worked for Applebee and wrote many of the accounts of the condemned at Tyburn for Applebee's journal. One such account was the 'Narrative of all the Robberies, Escapes, etc of Jack Sheppard'. It has even been suggested that Defoe disguised himself as John Applebee and mounted the executioner's cart. The newspaper reports stated that someone had indeed mounted the cart and received a paper from Sheppard (*Mist's Journal*, 21 November 1724). Whether this was Defoe or not it is impossible to establish without more evidence. Lee also puts forward the idea that Defoe's *Moll Flanders* and *Colonel Jack* were written in the hope of converting criminals in the condemned cell at Newgate.

Samuel Johnson came to personify the literary life of London in the forty years after his arrival in 1737. Among his earliest writings, 'London' (1738) is one of several poems he wrote about the capital at that time. He too offers a reference to Tyburn:

> Scarce can our Fields, such Crowds at Tyburn die,
> With hemp the Gallows and the Fleet supply.
> Propose your Schemes, ye Senatorian Band
> Whose Ways and Means support the sinking Land;
> Lest Ropes be wanting in the tempting Spring,
> To rig another Convoy for the K—G.

William Blake (1757–1827), artist, engraver, philosopher, visionary and poet, comments on Tyburn as the 'fatal tree' in one of his best-known poems, 'Jerusalem' in the section 'The Builders of Golgonooza':

> What are those Golden Builders doing? Where was the burying-place
> Of soft Ethinthus? near Tyburn's Fatal Tree? Is that
> Mild Zion's hill's most ancient promontory, near mournful
> Ever weeping Paddington?

To the north of Tyburn lived one of London's most famous fictional characters, Sherlock Holmes. His creator Sir Arthur Conan Doyle at one time had a medical practice near Baker Street. In the short story *The Adventure of the Three Garridebs*, Holmes and his loyal friend Dr Watson walk south from their Baker Street rooms. Watson records that

> It was twilight of a lovely spring evening, and even Little Ryder Street, one of the smaller offshoots from the Edgware Road, within a stone-cast of old Tyburn Tree of evil memory, looked golden and wonderful in the slanting rays of the setting sun.

Bibliography

(Unless otherwise stated, all titles are published in London)

A True and Perfect Account of the Proceedings at the General Sessions for London and Middlesex of the Number of Persons Condemned to Suffer at Tyburn, 1674.

Abbott, G., *Tortures in the Tower of London*, Newton Abbot, David & Charles, 1986

——, *Lords of the Scaffold: A History of Execution*, Robert Hale, 1991

——, *Rack, Rope and Red-hot Pincers, A History of Torture and its Instruments*, Headline, 1993

——, *The Book of Execution: An Encyclopaedia of Methods of Judicial Execution*, Headline, 1994

Aykroyd, P., *Evil London, the Dark Side of a Great City*, Wolfe, 1973

——, *London: The Biography*, Chatto & Windus, 2000

Adburgham, A., *Shopping in Style: London from the Restoration to Edwardian Elegance*, Thames & Hudson, 1979

Allen, W., *A Briefe History of the Glorious Martyrdom of Twelve Revd Priests: Father Edmund Campion and His Companions*, Long Prairie, Neumann Press (reprint of 1588 edn), 2000

Anon., *The Malefactor's Register, or, The Newgate and Tyburn Calendar Containing the Lives, Trials, Accounts of Execution, and Dying Speeches of the Most Notorious . . .* 5 vols, 1780

Archer, I.W., *The Pursuit of Stability and Social Relations in Elizabethan London*, Cambridge University Press, 1991

Armitage, G., *The History of the Bow Street Runners*, Wishart & Co., 1932

Armstrong, D., *Political Anatomy of the Body*, Cambridge University Press, 1983

Ashton, R., 'Popular Entertainment and Social Control in Later Elizabethan and Early Stuart London', *London Journal*, 9, 1983

Babington, A., *A House on Bow Street: Crime and the Magistracy*, Macdonald, 1969

——, *The English Bastille*, Macdonald, 1971

Bailey, B., *Hangmen of England: A History of Execution from Jack Ketch to Albert Pierrepoint*, W.H. Allen, 1989

——, *The Resurrection Men: A History of the Trade in Corpses*, Macdonald, 1991

Baker, T.F.T. (ed.), *The Victoria History of the County of Middlesex*, Vol IX, *Hampstead and Paddington Parishes*, Oxford University Press, 1989

Bakhtin, M., *Rabelais and His World*, Bloomington, Indiana University Press, 1988

Barker, F. and Hyde, R., *London: As it might have been*, John Murray, 1982

Barker, T., *Medieval London*, Castle, 1970.

Barrett, A. and Harrison, C. (eds), *Crime and Punishment: A Sourcebook*, UCL Press, 1999

Bibliography

Barton, N., *The Lost Rivers of London*, revd edn, Historical Publications, 1992

Beattie, J.M., 'The Pattern of Crime in England, 1660–1800', *Past and Present*, 62, 1974

——, *Crime and the Courts in England, 1660–1800*, Oxford University Press, 1986

——, 'The Cabinet and the Management of Death at Tyburn after the Revolution of 1688–9', in L.G. Schworer (ed.), *The Revolution of 1688–9: Changing Perspectives*, Cambridge University Press, 1992

——, *Policing and Punishment in London 1660–1750: Urban Crime and the Limits of Terror*, Oxford University Press, 2001

Bebbington, G., *Street Names of London*, Batsford, 1972

Beddard, R., 'Anti-Popery and the London Mob, 1688', *History Today*, 38, 1988

Beier, A.L. and Findley R. (eds), *London 1500–1700: the Making of the Metropolis*, Harlow, Longman, 1986

Beier, A.L., Cannadine, D. and Rosenheim, J.M. (eds), *The First Modern Society*, Cambridge University Press, 1989

Bellamy, J., *Crime and Public Order in England in the later Middle Ages*, Routledge & Kegan Paul, 1973

Beloff, M., *Public Order and Public Disturbances, 1660–1714*, Oxford University Press, 1938

Blackstone, W., *Commentaries on the Laws of England*, Clarendon Press, 1773

Blatch, M., *A Guide to London's Churches*, Constable, 1978

Bleackley, H., *The Hangmen of England*, Chapman & Hall, 1929

Bolitho, H. and Peel D., *Without the City Wall*, John Murray, 1952

Boswell, J., *London Journal: A Visit to Tyburn and Newgate (1762–3), a true and perfect relation of the Tryall, Condemning of the 24 Prisoners . . . at Tyburn*, Thomasson Collection, British Museum, 1763

Bowler, H., *London Sessions Records 1605–1685*, John Whitehead, 1934

Brandon, D.L., *Stand and Deliver! A History of Highway Robbery*, Stroud, Sutton, 2001

Bray, A., *Homosexuality in Renaissance England*, Gay Men's Press, 1982

Brewer, J. and Styles, J. (eds), *An Ungovernable People? The English and their Law in the Seventeenth and Eighteenth Centuries*, Hutchinson, 1980

Briggs, J., Harrison, C., McInnes, A., Vincent D., *Crime and Punishment in England*, UCL Press, 1996

Bristow, E.J., *Vice and Vigilance: Purity Movements in Britain since 1700*, Dublin, Gill & Macmillan, 1977

Brooks, J.A., *Ghosts of London*, Norwich, Jarrold, 1991

Burford, E.J., *London The Syneful Citie*, Robert Hale, 1990

Burford, E.J. and Wooton, J., *Private Vices – Public Virtues*, Robert Hale, 1995

Burke, P., 'Popular Culture in Seventeenth-century London', *London Journal*, iii, 1977

Burke, T., *The Streets of London through the Centuries*, Batsford, 1949

Bushaway, B., *By Rite: Custom, Ceremony and Community in England 1770–1880*, Junction Books, 1982

Bushell, P., *London Secret History*, Constable, 1983

Bibliography

Butler, I., *Murderers' London*, Robert Hale, 1971

Byrne, R., *Prisons and Punishments of London*, Grafton, 1992

——, *The London Dungeon Book of Crime and Punishment*, Little, Brown, 1993

Camden Society, 1876

Cameron, D., *London's Pleasures: From Restoration to Regency*, Stroud, Sutton, 2001

Cannadine, D., *The Pleasures of the Past*, Collins, 1989

Cannon, J. (ed.), *The Oxford Companion to British History*, Oxford University Press, 1997

Cartwright, F.F., *A Social History of Medicine*, Harlow, Longman, 1977

Clark, J.C.D., *Revolution and Rebellion: State and Society in England in the Seventeenth and Eighteenth Centuries*, Cambridge University Press, 1986

Clark, P., 'The Mother Gin Controversy in early eighteenth-century England,' *Transactions of the Royal Historical Society*, 38, 1988

Clinch, G., *Marylebone and St Pancras*, Trueshore & Shirley, 1980

Clout, H. (ed.), *The Times London History Atlas*, 2nd edn, Times Books, 1977

Cobbett, W. (ed.), *Cobbett's Complete Collection of State Trials,* vols ii, iii, vi, London, 1809

Cockburn, J.S. (ed.), *Crime in England, 1550–1800,* Methuen, 1977

Cole, G.D.H. and Postgate, R., *The Common People, 1746–1938,* Methuen, 1946

Cole, H., *Things for the Surgeon: a History of the Body Snatchers,* Heinemann, 1964

Collins, P., *Dickens and Crime,* 2nd edn, Macmillan, 1965

Cooper, D., *The Lessons of the Scaffold,* Allen Lane, 1974

Cordingly, D., *Life among the Pirates,* Little Brown, 1995

Corfield, P.J., *The Impact of English Towns 1700–1800,* Oxford University Press, 1982

Critchley, T.A., *A History of Police in England and Wales 900–1966,* 2nd edn, Constable, 1978

Cross, W.L., *The History of Henry Fielding,* New Haven, Yale University Press, 1918

Cruikshanks, E. (ed.), *Hogarth's England,* Folio Society, 1957

Darvall, F.O., *Popular Disturbances and Public Order in Regency England*, 2nd edn, Oxford University Press, 1969

Davidson, L, Hitchcock, T. and Keirn, T., *Stilling the Grumbling Hive: The Response to Social and Economic Problems in England, 1689–1750*, Stroud, Sutton, 1992

Davidson, R.N., *Crime and the Environment*, Croom Helm, 1981

Deehiseekayess, J., *Tyburn Tree*, 1849

Defoe, D., *Minor Single Works, A Hymn to Tyburn, Being a Sequel to the Hymn of the Pillory*, 1703

——, *The History of the Press Yard*, T. Moor, 1717

Denford, S. and Hellings, D., *Streets of Old Holborn*, Camden History Society, 1999

De Sola Pinto, V. and Rodway, A.E., *The Common Muse*, Harmondsworth, Penguin, 1965

Dillon, P., *The Much-lamented Death of Madam Geneva: The Eighteenth-century Gin Craze*, Review, 2002

Dobb, C., 'Henry Goodcole, Visitor of Newgate, 1620–41', *Guildhall Miscellany No. 4, 1955*

Dowdell, E.G., *A Hundred Years of Quarter Sessions, The Government of Middlesex from 1660 to 1760*, Cambridge University Press, 1932

Dudden, F.H., *Henry Fielding, His Life, Works and Times*, Clarendon, 1952

Earle, P., *Monmouth's Rebels*, Weidenfeld & Nicolson, 1963

——, *The World of Defoe*, Weidenfeld & Nicolson, 1976

Ekirch, A.R., *Bound for America: The Transportation of British Convicts to the Colonies, 1718–1775*, Oxford University Press, 1987

Emsley, C., Policing and its Context 1750–1870, Macmillan, 1983

——, *Crime and Society in England 1750–1900*, Harlow, Longman, 1996a

——, *The English Police: A Political and Social History*, 2nd edn, Harlow, Longman, 1996b

Emsley, C. and Walvin, J. (eds), *Artisans, Peasants and Proletarians 1760–1860*, Croom Helm, 1985

Emerson, G., *Sin City: London in Pursuit of Pleasure*, Granada, 2002

Engel, H., *Lord High Executioner: An Unashamed Look at Hangmen, Headsmen, and Their Kind*, Robson, 1997

Ewan, C.L., *Witch Hunting and Witch Trials*, Kegan Paul, 1929

Fido, M., *Murder Guide to London*, Weidenfeld & Nicolson, 1986

——, *Bodysnatchers: A History of the Resurrectionists*, Weidenfeld & Nicolson, 1988

Fielding, H., *An Enquiry into the Causes of the Late Increases of Robbers and with Some Proposals for Remedying this Growing Evil, 1751*

Fletcher, A.J. and Stevenson, J., (eds), *Order and Disorder in Early Modern England*, Cambridge University Press, 1985

Foucault, M., *Discipline and Punish: The Birth of the Prison*, Penguin, 1991

Fox, G., *The Journal of George Fox*, revd edn N. Penney, J.M. Dent, 1924

Gaskill, M., *Crime and Mentalities in Early Modern England*, Cambridge University Press, 2000

Garell, V.A., *The Hanging Tree. Execution and the English People*, Oxford University Press, 1994

George, M.D., *London Life in the Eighteenth Century*, Harmondsworth, Peregrine, 1967

——, *Hogarth to Cruikshank: Social Change in Graphic Satire*, Viking, 1967

Gilmour, I., *Riot, Risings and Revolution*, Hutchinson, 1992

Glanville, P., *London in Maps*, The Connoisseur, 1972

Golby, J.M. and Purdue, A.W., *The Civilisation of the Crowd*, Batsford, 1984

Gomme, G.L., *Tyburn Gallows*, London County Council, 1909

Gordon, C., *The Old Bailey and Newgate*, T. Fisher Unwin, 1902

Gray, R., *A History of London*, revd edn, Hutchinson, 1987

Griffiths, A., *Chronicles of Newgate*, new edn, Bracken Books [1884], 1987

Griffiths, P. and Jenner, M.S.R. (eds), *Londinopolis*, Manchester University Press, 2000

Gurr, T.R., *Rogues, Rebels and Reformers: The Politics of Crime and Conflict*, Sage, 1976

Guy, J., *Tudor England*, Oxford University Press, 1988

Hackman, H., *Wates's Book of London Churchyards*, Collins, 1981

Halle, E., *Hall's Chronicle*, London, 1809

Hamilton, D., *Foul Bills and Dagger Money*, Cassell, 1979

Harben, H.A., *A Dictionary of London*, Jenkins, 1918

Harding, A., *A Social History of English Law*, Harmondsworth, Penguin, 1966

Harding, C. and Hines B., Ireland, R. and Rawlings P., *Imprisonment in England and Wales*, Croom Helm, 1985

Harleian Miscellany, viii, *A Declaration of the Lyfe and Death of John Story, late a Romish Canonicall Doctor, by Professyon. 1571*, John White, 1809

Harrison, J.F.C., *The Second Coming: Popular Millenarianism 1780–1850*, Routledge & Kegan Paul, 1978

Harrison, M., *London Beneath the Pavement*, Peter Davies, 1961

Harrison, W., *Description of England*, 2nd edn, 1587

Hay, D., Linebaugh, P., Rule, J.G., Thompson, E.P. and Winslow, C., *Albion's Fatal Tree*, Harmondsworth, Penguin, 1977

Hay, D. and Snyder, F. (eds), *Policing and Prosecution in Britain, 1750–1850*, Oxford, Clarendon, 1989

Haynes, A., *The Elizabethan Secret Service*, Stroud, Sutton, 1992

Hayter, T., *The Army and the Crowd in Mid-Georgian England*, Macmillan, 1978

Hertz, J.S., 'Under the Sign of Donne', *Criticism*, 43 (2), 2001

Hibbert, C., *The Road to Tyburn: The Story of Jack Sheppard and the Eighteenth-century Underworld*, Longman, 1957

——, *The Roots of Evil: A Social History of Crime and Punishment*, Weidenfeld & Nicolson, 1963

——, *London: The Biography of a City*, Harmondsworth, Penguin, 1980

Hill, C., *The Experience of Defeat*, Faber & Faber, 1984

——, *Liberty Against the Law*, Harmondsworth, Allan Lane, 1996

Hindley, C., *Tavern Anecdotes and Sayings*, 1875

Hobhouse, H., *A History of Regent Street*, Macdonalds & Jane's, 1975

Hobsbawm, E.J. and Ranger, T., *The Invention of Tradition*, Cambridge University Press, 1983

Holston, J., *Ehud's Dagger: Class Struggle in the English Revolution*, Verso, 2000

Home, G., *Medieval London*, Bracken, 1994

Hooper, W. Eden, *History of Newgate and the Old Bailey*, Underwood, 1935

Hopkins, R.T., *This London, its Taverns, Haunts and Memories*, Cecil Parker, 1927

Howson, G., *Thief-taker General*, Hutchinson, 1970

——, *The Macaroni Parson*, Hutchinson, 1973

Hughes, R., *The Fatal Shore*, Pan, 1988

Hyamson, A.M., *A History of the Jews in England*, Chatto & Windus, 1908

Hyde, R., Fisher, J. and Cline, R., *The A–Z of Restoration London*, London Topographical Society, 1992

Ignatieff, M., *A Just Measure of Pain: the Penitentiary in the Industrial Revolution 1750–1850*, Macmillan, 1978

Innes, J. and Styles, J., 'The Crime Wave: Recent writing on Crime and Criminal Justice in eighteenth-century England', *Journal of British Studies*, 25, 1986

Inwood, S., *A History of London*, Macmillan, 1998

Isaac, D.G., 'A Study of Popular Disturbances in Britain, 1714–54', Unpublished Ph.D. Thesis, University of Edinburgh, 1953

James, M.E., 'Ritual, Drama and Social Body in the Late Medieval English Town', *Past and Present*, 98, 1983

Jarrett, D., *England in the Age of Hogarth*, Granada, 1974

——, *The Ingenious Mr Hogarth*, Michael Joseph, 1976

Judges, A.V., *The Elizabethan Underworld*, Routledge & Kegan Paul, 1965

Jupp, P.C. and Gittings, C.(eds), *Death in England*, Manchester University Press, 1999

Kent, W. (ed.), *An Encyclopaedia of London*, J.M. Dent, 1937

——, *London Mystery and Mythology*, Staples, 1952

——, *The Lost Treasures of London*, Phoenix House, 1947

Kenyon, J.P., *The Popish Plot*, Harmondsworth, Penguin, 1974

King, P., 'Decision-makers and decision-making in the English criminal law 1750–1800', *Historical Journal*, 27, 1984

Kingsford, C.C., *Chronicles of London*, Oxford, Clarendon Press, 1905

Klingender, F.D. (ed.), *Hogarth and English Caricature*, Transatlantic Arts, 1983

Lake, P. and Questier, M., 'Agency, appropriation and rhetoric under the gallows: Puritans, Romanists and the state in early modern England', *Past and Present*, 153 (44), 1996

Langbein, J., 'Albion's Fatal Flaws', *Past and Present*, 98, 1983

Langford, P., *A Polite and Commercial People: England 1727–1783*, Oxford University Press, 1992

Laqueur, T.W., 'Crowds, Carnival and the State in English Executions, 1604–1868', in A.L. Beier, D. Cannadine and J.M. Rosenheim (eds), *The First Modern Society*, Cambridge University Press, 1989

Laurence, J.A., *History of Capital Punishment*, Samson Lowe, Marston & Co., 1932

Laxton, P. and Wisdom, J., *The A–Z of Regency London*, London Topographical Society, 1985

Lee, W., *Daniel Defoe: His Life and Recently Discovered Writings*, 1869

Linebaugh, P., 'Eighteenth-Century Crime', *Bulletin of the Society for the Study of Labour History*, 25, 1972

——, 'Eighteenth-century Disorders', *Bulletin of the Society for the Study of Labour History*, 28, 1974

——, 'Tyburn: a study of crime and the labouring poor in London during the first half of the eighteenth century', Ph.D. thesis, University of Warwick, 1975

——, 'The Tyburn Riot against the Surgeons', in D. Hay, P. Linebaugh, *et al.*, *Albion's Fatal Tree*, Harmondsworth, Penguin, 1977a

——, 'The Ordinary of Newgate and His Account', in J.S. Cockburn (ed.), *Crime in England 1550–1800*, Methuen, 1977

——, *The London Hanged: Crime and Civil Society in the Eighteenth Century*, Harmondsworth, Penguin, 1993

Litten, J., *The English Way of Death*, Robert Hale, 1991

Low, D.A., *Thieves' Kitchen: The Regency Underworld*, J.M. Dent, 1982

Luard, H.R. *Flores Historarium*, 3 vols, HMSO, 1890

Lyons, F.J., *Jonathan Wild: Prince of Robbers*, Michael Joseph, 1936

McCall, A., *The Medieval Underworld*, Hamish Hamilton, 1979

Mackenzie, G., *Great City North of Oxford Street*, Macmillan, 1972

MacMans, H.F., *The Death of Oliver Cromwell*, Kentucky, University Press of Kentucky, 1999

McLynn, F., *Crime and Punishment in Eighteenth-century England*, Oxford University Press, 1991

McMullen, J.L., *The Canting Crew: London's Criminal Underworld 1550–1700*, New Jersey, Rutgers University Press, 1984

Malcolmson, R.W., *Popular Recreations in English Society 1700–1850*, Cambridge University Press, 1973

Manchester, A.H., *A Modern Legal History of England and Wales 1750–1950*, Butterworth, 1973

Mandeville, Bernard de, *An Enquiry into the Causes of the Frequent Executions at Tyburn*, Augustan Reprint Society Publications No. 105 (1964[1725])

Manning, B., *The English People and the English Revolution*, Harmondsworth, Penguin, 1978

Manning, R., *Village Revolts: Social Protest and Popular Disturbances in England 1509–1640*, Oxford, Clarendon Press, 1988

Marks, A., *Tyburn Tree: Its History and Annals*, Brown, Langham, 1908

Marshall, P., 'Fear, Purgatory and Polemic in Reformation England', in W.G. Naphy and P. Roberts (eds), *Fear in Modern Society*, Manchester University Press, 1997

Mayhew, H., *London Labour and the London Poor*, Charles Griffin, 1861

Mayhew, H. and Binney, J., *The Criminal Prisons of London*, Griffin, Bohn & Co., 1862; rep. Frank Cass, 1971

Mingay, G.E., *Georgian Delights*, Batsford, 1975

Mitchell, R.J. and Leys M.D., *A History of London Life*, Harmondsworth, Penguin, 1963

Montrose, L.A., 'Idols of the Queen: Policy, Gender and the Picturing of Elizabeth', *Representations*, Fall (1999), v. 68

Moore, L., *The Thieves' Opera*, Viking, 1997

——, *Conmen and Cutpurses. Scenes from the Hogarthian Underworld*, Allen Lane, 2001

Morris, N. and Rothman, J. (eds), *The Oxford History of the Prison*, Oxford University, Press, 1995

Newgate Calendar (various editions)

Newton, D., *Catholic London*, Robert Hale, 1930

——, *London: West of the Bars*, Robert Hale, 1951

Nichols, J.G. (ed.), *The Diary of Henry Machyn: Citizen and Merchant-Taylor of London, 1550–1563*, Camden Society, 1848

Palmer, R. (ed.), *A Touch on the Times: Songs of Social Change*, Harmondsworth, Penguin, 1974

——, *A Ballad History of England: From 1588 to the Present Day*, Batsford, 1979

——, *The Sound of History: Songs and Social Comment*, Oxford University Press, 1988

Parry, L.A., *History of Torture in England*, Sampson Lowe, 1933

Partridge, E., *A Dictionary of Historical Slang*, Harmondsworth, Penguin, 1972

Paulson, R., *Hogarth: His Life, Art and Times*, New Haven, Yale University Press, 1971

——, *The Art of Hogarth*, Phaidon, 1975

Pearson, K. and Morant, G.M., *The Portraiture of Oliver Cromwell with Special Reference to the Wilkinson Head*, University College London, Biometrica Office, 1935

Pendrill, C., *London Life in the Fourteenth Century*, George Allen & Unwin, 1925

Peters, E., *Torture*, Oxford, Blackwell, 1985

Philips, D., *Crime and Authority in Victorian England*, Croom Helm, 1977

Phillips, H., *Mid-Georgian London*, Collins, 1964

Picard, L., *Restoration London*, Weidenfeld & Nicolson, 1997

——, *Dr Johnson's London: Life in London 1740–70*, Weidenfeld & Nicolson, 2000

Pierce, P., *Old London Bridge, The Story of the Longest Inhabited Bridge in Europe*, Headline, 2001

Plumb, J.H., *Georgian Delights*, Weidenfeld & Nicolson, 1980

Pollen, J.H., *The English Catholics in the Reign of Queen Elizabeth*, Longman, 1920

Porter, R., *English Society in the Eighteenth Century*, Harmondsworth, Penguin, 1986

——, *London: A Social History*, Harmondsworth, Penguin, 1996

——, *The Greatest Benefit to Mankind*, HarperCollins, 1997

Postgate, R., *That Devil Wilkes*, 2nd edn, Constable, 1956

Potter, H., *Hanging in Judgement: Religion and the Death Penalty in England from the Bloody Code to Abolition*, New York, Continuum, 1993

Potter, J.D., *The Fatal Gallows Tree*, Elek, 1965

Pringle, P., *Hue and Cry: The Birth of the British Police*, Museum Press, 1955

——, *The Thief-Takers*, Museum Press, 1958

Prokter, A. and Taylor, R., *The A–Z of Elizabethan London*, London Topographical Society, 1979

Pugh, R.J., *Imprisonment in Medieval England*, Cambridge University Press, 1968

Purkiss, D., *The Witch in History*, Routledge, 1996

Bibliography

Purney, C., *The Behaviour, Last Dying Speeches and Confessions of the Four Malefactors who were executed, Tyburn on the 24 of May, 1725*, 1725

Quennell, P., *Hogarth's Progress*, Collins, 1955

Quinault, R. and Stevenson, J. (eds), *Popular Protest and Public Order*, George Allen & Unwin, 1974

Radzinowicz, L., *A History of English Criminal Law*, vols 1–4, Stevens, 1948–68

Reay, B. (ed.), *Popular Culture in Seventeenth-century England*, Routledge, 1988

Redwood, J., *Reason, Ridicule and Religion: the Age of Enlightenment in England, 1660–1750*, Thames & Hudson, 1976

Richards, M., *The Public Notice: An Illustrated History*, Newton Abbot, David & Charles, 1973

Richardson, J., *The Annals of London*, Cassell, 2000

Richardson, R., *Death, Dissection and the Destitute*, Harmondsworth, Pelican, 1989

Ridley, J., *Bloody Mary's Martyrs: The Story of England's Terror*, Constable, 2001

Riley, H.T., *Memorials of London and London Life 1276–1419*, Longman Green, 1908

Rude, G., *Wilkes and Liberty*, Oxford University Press, 1962

——, *Hanoverian London 1714–1808*, Sutton, 2003

——, *Ideology and Popular Protest*, Lawrence & Wishart, 1980

——, *The Crowd in History 1730–1848*, Lawrence & Wishart, 1981

Rule, J., *The Experience of Labour in Eighteenth-century Industry*, Croom Helm, 1981

——, *The Labouring Classes in Early Industrial England*, Harlow, Longman, 1986

——, *Albion's People: English Society 1714–1815*, Harlow, Longman, 1992

Rumbelow, D., *I Spy Blue*, Macmillan, 1971

——, *The Triple Tree: Newgate, Tyburn and Old Bailey*, Harrap, 1982

Salgado, G. (ed.), *Cony-Catchers and Bawdy-Baskets*, Harmondsworth, Penguin, 1972

——, *The Elizabethan Underworld*, J.M. Dent, 1977

Sawday, J., *The Body Emblazoned*, Routledge, 1995

Schworer, L.G. (ed.), *The Revolution of 1688–9: Changing Perspectives*, Cambridge University Press, 1992

Scott, H. (ed.), *The Concise Encyclopædia of Crime and Criminals*, André Deutsch, 1961

Sharpe, J.A., *Crime in Early Modern England 1550–1750*, Longman, 1984

——, 'Last Dying Speeches: Religion, Ideology and Public Execution in Seventeenth-century England', *Past and Present*, 107 (1985a)

——, 'The History of Violence in England: some observations', *Past and Present*, 108 (1985b)

——, *Crime and the Law in English Satirical Prints 1600–1832*, Cambridge University Press, 1986

——, *Early Modern England: A Social History 1550–1760*, Edward Arnold, 1988

——, *Judicial Punishment in England*, Faber & Faber, 1990

Shelley, H.C., *Inns and Taverns of Old London*, Isaac Pitman & Sons, 1909

Shepard, L., *The History of Street Literature*, Newton Abbot, David & Charles, 1973

Bibliography

Sheppard, F., *London: A History*, Oxford University Press, 1998

Sheppard, F.H.W., *Local Government in St Marylebone*, Athlone Press, 1958

Shoemaker, R.B., 'The London "mob" in the early eighteenth century', *Journal of British Studies*, 26 (1987)

——, *Prosecution and Punishment: Petty Crime and the Law in London and Middlesex 1660–1725*, Cambridge University Press, 1991

Simpson, R., *Edmund Campion: A Biography*, Williams & Norgate, 1867

Smith, A.T.H., 'Stealing the Body and its Parts', *Criminal Law Review*, 10 (1976)

Smith, T., *A Topographical Account of the Parish of St Marylebone*, 1833

Snowden, W., *London Two Hundred Years Ago*, Daily Mail Publications, 1948

Spencer, J.N., 'The Tyburn Route', *Justice of the Peace*, May–June 1933

Spierenburg, P., *The Spectacle of Suffering: Executions and the Evolution of Repression, from a Pre-industrial Metropolis to the European Experience*, Cambridge University Press, 1984

Stallybrass, P. and White, A., *The Politics and Poetics of Transgression*, New York, Cornell University Press, 1986

Stevenson, J., *Popular Disturbances in England, 1700–1870*, 2nd edn, Harlow, Longman, 1992

Stow, J., *The Annales of London*, 1605

——, *A Survey of London Written in the Year 1598*, Stroud, Sutton, 1999

Styles, J. et al., 'Crime, Violence and Social Protest', *Social History Newsletter*, 2 (1977)

The Confession and Execution of the Eight Prisoners Suffering at Tyburn on Wednesday 30 August 1676.

The Confession and Execution of the five prisoners that suffered on the new gallows at Tyburn, 1678

Thomas, K., 'Work and Leisure in Pre-Industrial Society', *Past and Present*, 29 (1964)

——, *Religion and the Decline of Magic*, Harmondsworth, Penguin, 1971

Thompson, E.P., 'The Moral Economy of the English Crowd in the Eighteenth Century', *Past and Present*, 50 (1971)

——, 'Patrician Society, Plebeian Culture', *Journal of Social History*, 7 (1974)

——, *Whigs and Hunters: the Origin of the Black Act*, Allen Lane, 1975

——, 'Eighteenth-century English Society: Class Struggle without Class?', *Social History*, 3 (ii) (1978)

——, *The Making of the English Working Class*, Victor Gollancz, 1980

——, *Customs in Common*, Harmondsworth, Penguin, 1993

Thurston, H., *Royal Parks for the People*, Newton Abbot, David & Charles, 1974

Tobias, J.J., *Crime and Police in England 1700–1900*, Dublin, Gill & Macmillan, 1979

Trench, R. and Hillman, E., *London under London: A Subterranean Guide*, John Murray, 1983

Turner, E.S., *May it Please your Lordship*, Michael Joseph, 1971

Tyburn Nuns, *They Died at Tyburn*, Tyburn Convent, 1961

Underdown, D., *Revel, Riot and Rebellion: Popular Politics and Culture in England, 1603–60*, Oxford University Press, 1985

Bibliography

Underwood, P., *Haunted London*, Harrap, 1973

Vilette, J., *The Annals of Newgate*, 1776

Wagner, L., *London Inns and Taverns*, George Allen & Unwin, 1924

——, *More London Inns and Taverns*, George Allen & Unwin, 1925

Wakefield, E.G., *Facts relating to the punishment of death in the metropolis*, 1832

Walford, E., *Old London: Hyde Park to Bloomsbury*, Alderman Press, 1989

Waller, M., *1700: Scenes from London Life*, Hodder & Stoughton, 2000

Wardroper, J., *Kings, Lords and Wicked Libellers: Satire and Protest 1760–1837*, John Murray, 1973

Watney, J., *Mother's Ruin: A History of Gin*, Peter Owen, 1976

Weinreb, B. and Hibbert, C. (eds), *The London Encyclopædia*, Macmillan, 1983

Weitzman, A.J., 'Eighteenth-century London: urban paradise or fallen city?' *Journal of the History of Ideas* (1975)

Willey, B., *The Eighteenth-century Background*, Harmondsworth, Penguin, 1960

Wilson, D., *The Tower 1078–1978*, Hamish Hamilton, 1978

Wright, W.J.P., 'Humanitarian London from 1688–1750', *Edinburgh Review*, CCXIVI, 1927

Wrightson, K., *English Society 1580–1680*, Hutchinson, 1982

Young, E. and Young, W., *London's Churches*, Grafton, 1986

Young, S., *The Annals of the Barber-Surgeons of London*, 1890

Newspapers and Journals

Gentleman's Magazine, 1731–1907

London Chronicle

London Evening Post, 1727–1808

London Journal

London Magazine

London News

London Spy, 1698–1700

Mist's Weekly Journal

Parkers London News

Public Advertiser

Survey of London

Weekly Journal or *British Gazetteer*

Weekly Journal or *Saturday's Post*

The records of the Middlesex Justices

Middlesex County Records

Index